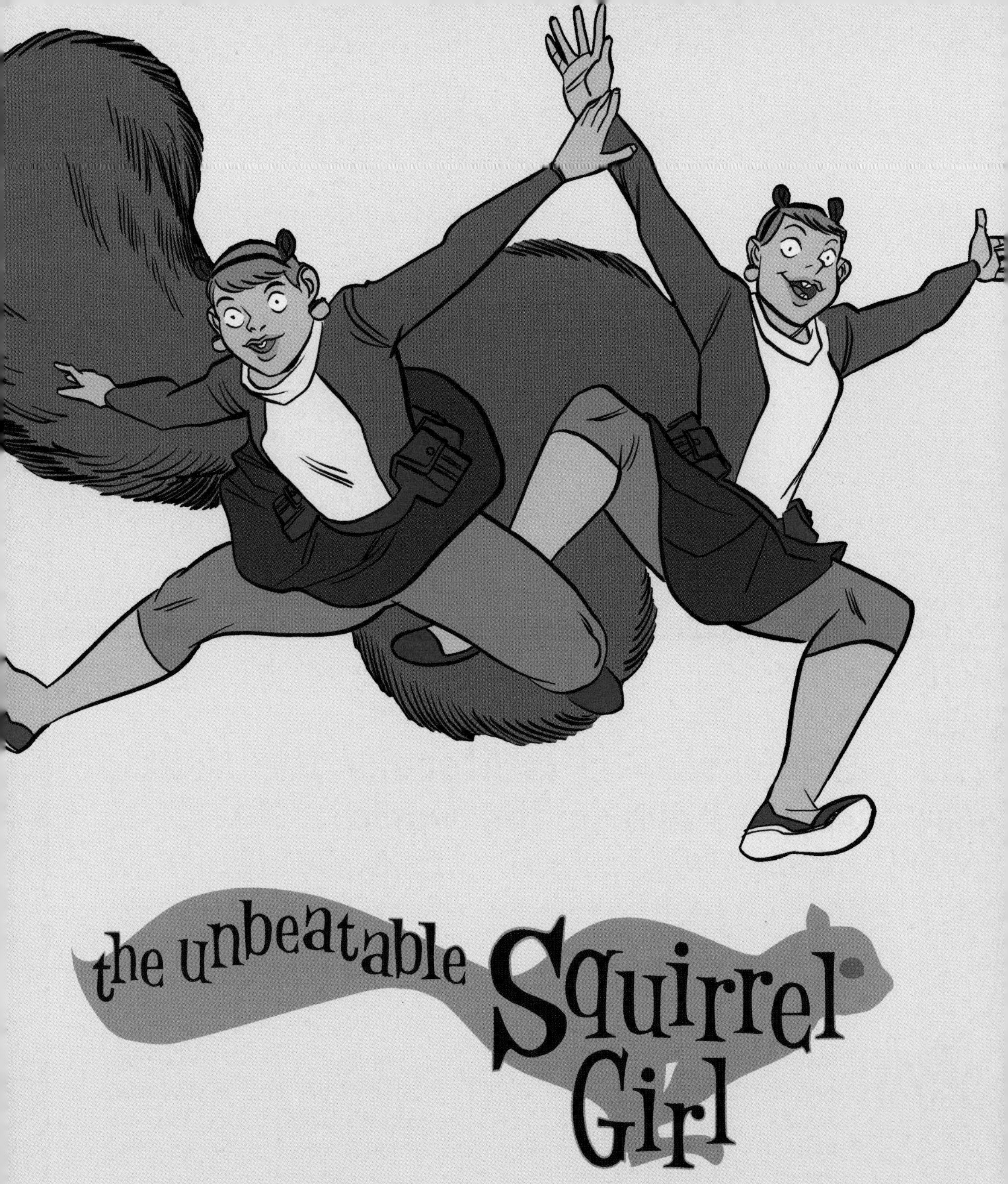

the unbeatable Squirrel Girl

INTRODUCTION!

Squirrel Girl is literally the best super hero in the world.

Evidence: She talks to squirrels. She has a squirrel tail. Her front teeth have super-gnawing power.

Further evidence: She is *unbeatable*. Doctor Doom? Dominated him. Thanos? Him too. Galactus, Devourer of Worlds? Check and mate.

Further *further* evidence: THIS VERY BOOK YOU ARE HOLDING IN YOUR HANDS, which details her best-ness and super hero-ness as well as her best super hero-ness.

Oh, and by the way, in case we forgot to mention, Squirrel Girl also happens to possess the proportional strength, speed and agility of a squirrel. Who else can claim that? Nobody, that's who.

Except...her clone??? Guess where you can get details on some juicy clone drama? Only in THIS VERY BOOK YOU ARE HOLDING IN YOUR HANDS, written by one Ryan North and illustrated by one Erica Henderson.

We've been fans of Ryan and Erica's *The Unbeatable Squirrel Girl* comics from issue #1 (the first one!), because we are sane human beings. They are funny, they are fresh, they are exciting and just a straight-up riot. So when we heard that Ryan and Erica were creating a standalone graphic novel for Squirrel Girl, our house was filled with shouts such as "YASSSS" and "WOOOOOP" and also a fair amount of "SQUEEEEE!"

We are thrilled to report, dear reader, that the final product, THIS VERY BOOK YOU ARE HOLDING IN YOUR HANDS, definitely lives up to those YASSSS-WOOOOOP-SQEEEEEs.

Now, while it's true that Squirrel Girl is fun, it's also true that she *matters*. She matters not only because she has the powers of squirrel, but *because she has the powers of girl*. We love heroes who can *thwack* and *klock* their way out of any battle — big muscly men with hammers and shields and *body armor* who can destroy spaceships and stop alien invasions. But it's also so awesome to get to see this girl — a short-haired, thick-thighed, computer science major with no va-va-voom about her — just step up and kick butt. When she's not simply talking the criminals out of committing their crimes in the first place, of course.

"But how could Squirrel Girl defeat the entire Marvel Universe?" some might say. "That's absurd!" We choose our unbelievables. Would it be more believable if it was Squirrel Woman? How about Squirrel Man? Or Iron Man? They're all unbelievable, if

we're talking about reality. A girl with a squirrel tail is just as silly as a man who develops an infinitely renewable energy source to save his life and power a flying metal suit.

People have a tendency to value tragedy over comedy, the big dramatic heartbreaking stories over hilarious and delightful romps. Many of us might disregard the silly, dismiss the childish, as if they're not worth our time. But Squirrel Girl won't let us. She says, yeah, those serious stories are good too, but get a load of me!

Thank the comic universe for Squirrel Girl.

—Shannon Hale & Dean Hale

SHANNON HALE & DEAN HALE ARE THE *NEW YORK TIMES*-BESTSELLING AUTHORS OF THE UPCOMING *THE UNBEATABLE SQUIRREL GIRL: SQUIRREL MEETS WORLD* YOUNG-ADULT NOVEL.

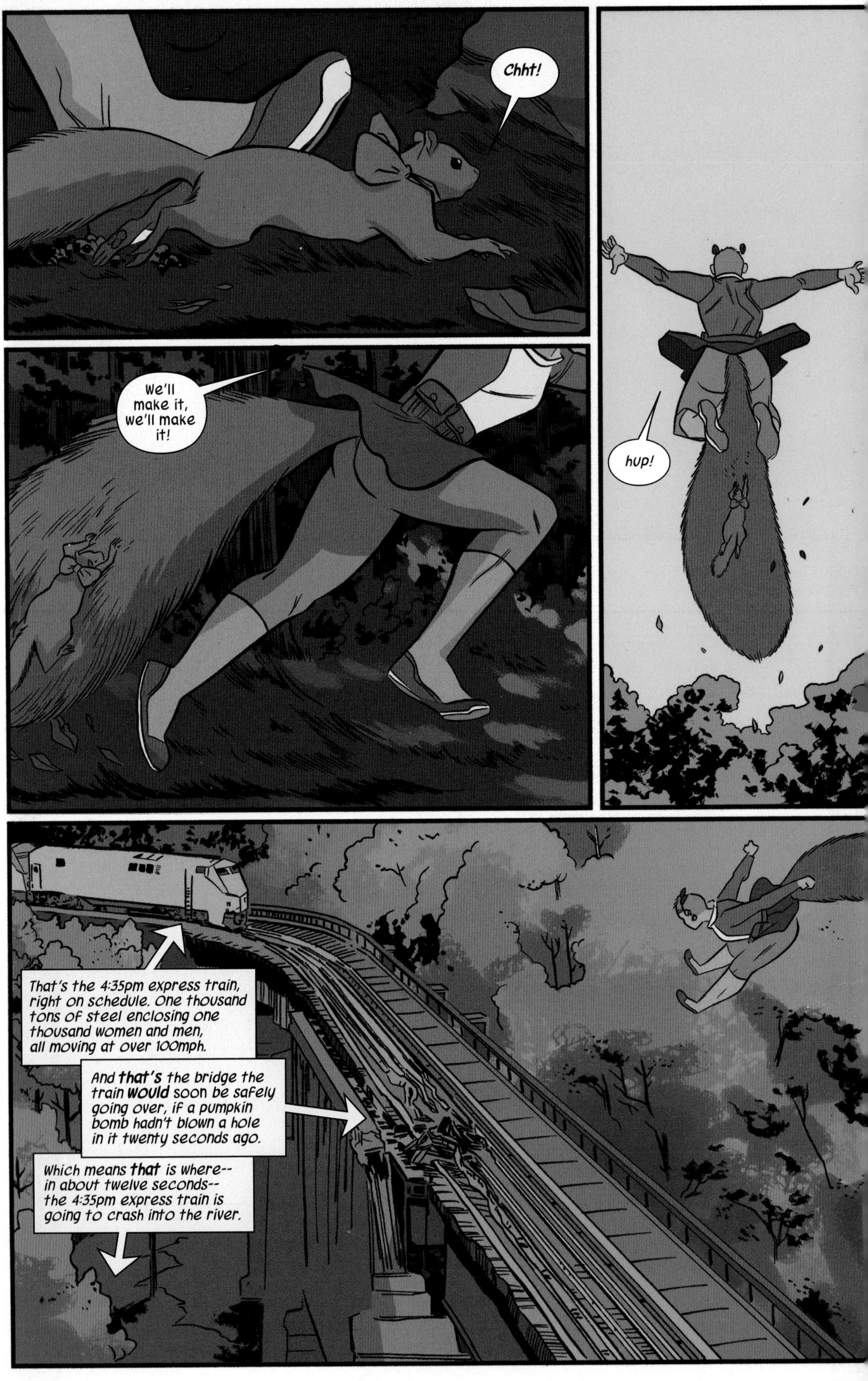

Chht!
We'll make it, we'll make it!
hup!
That's the 4:35pm express train, right on schedule. One thousand tons of steel enclosing one thousand women and men, all moving at over 100mph.
And that's the bridge the train would soon be safely going over, if a pumpkin bomb hadn't blown a hole in it twenty seconds ago.
Which means that is where-- in about twelve seconds-- the 4:35pm express train is going to crash into the river.

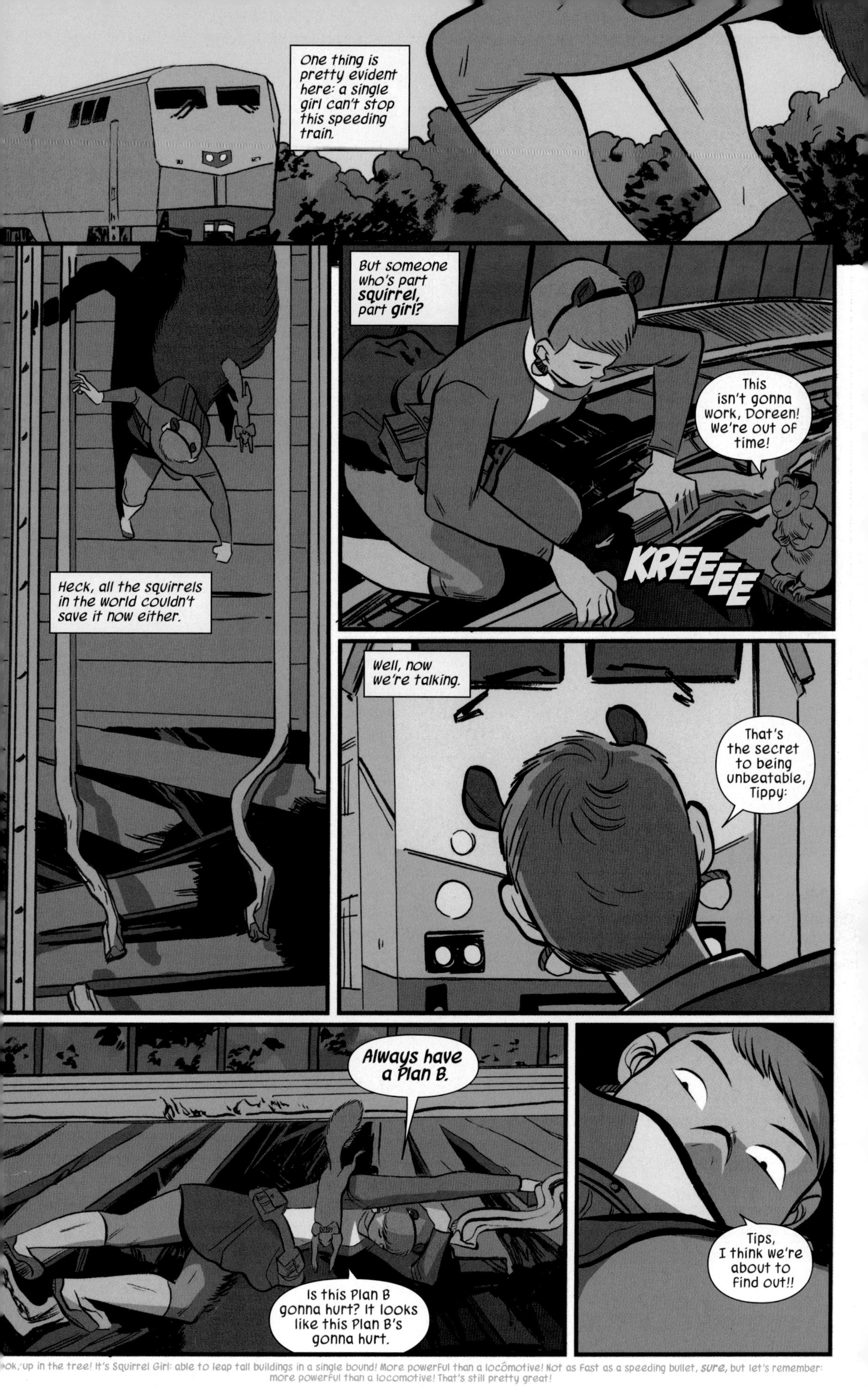
One thing is pretty evident here: a single girl can't stop this speeding train.
Heck, all the squirrels in the world couldn't save it now either.
But someone who's part **squirrel,** part **girl?**
This isn't gonna work, Doreen! We're out of time!
KREEEEE
Well, now we're talking.
That's the secret to being unbeatable, Tippy:
Always have a Plan B.
Is this Plan B gonna hurt? It looks like this Plan B's gonna hurt.
Tips, I think we're about to find out!!

ok, up in the tree! It's Squirrel Girl: able to leap tall buildings in a single bound! More powerful than a locomotive! Not as fast as a speeding bullet, *sure,* but let's remember: more powerful than a locomotive! That's still pretty great!

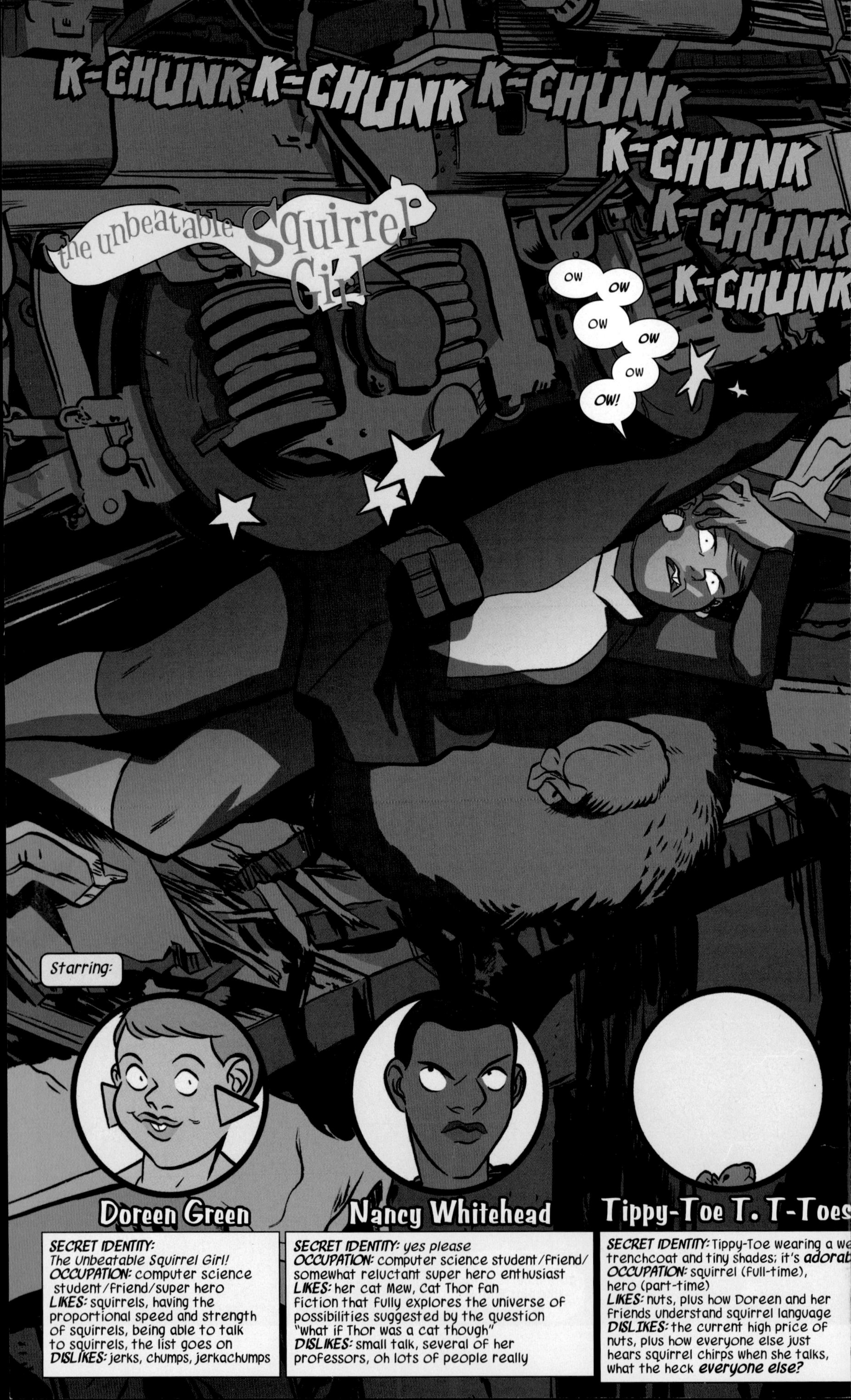

K-CHUNK K-CHUNK K-CHUNK
K-CHUNK
K-CHUNK
K-CHUNK
the unbeatable Squirrel Girl
OW
OW
OW
OW
OW
OW!
Starring:
Doreen Green
Nancy Whitehead
Tippy-Toe T. T-Toes
SECRET IDENTITY: The Unbeatable Squirrel Girl! OCCUPATION: computer science student/friend/super hero LIKES: squirrels, having the proportional speed and strength of squirrels, being able to talk to squirrels, the list goes on DISLIKES: jerks, chumps, jerkachumps
SECRET IDENTITY: yes please OCCUPATION: computer science student/friend/ somewhat reluctant super hero enthusiast LIKES: her cat Mew, Cat Thor fan fiction that fully explores the universe of possibilities suggested by the question "what if Thor was a cat though" DISLIKES: small talk, several of her professors, oh lots of people really
SECRET IDENTITY: Tippy-Toe wearing a we trenchcoat and tiny shades; it's adorab OCCUPATION: squirrel (full-time), hero (part-time) LIKES: nuts, plus how Doreen and her friends understand squirrel language DISLIKES: the current high price of nuts, plus how everyone else just hears squirrel chirps when she talks, what the heck everyone else?

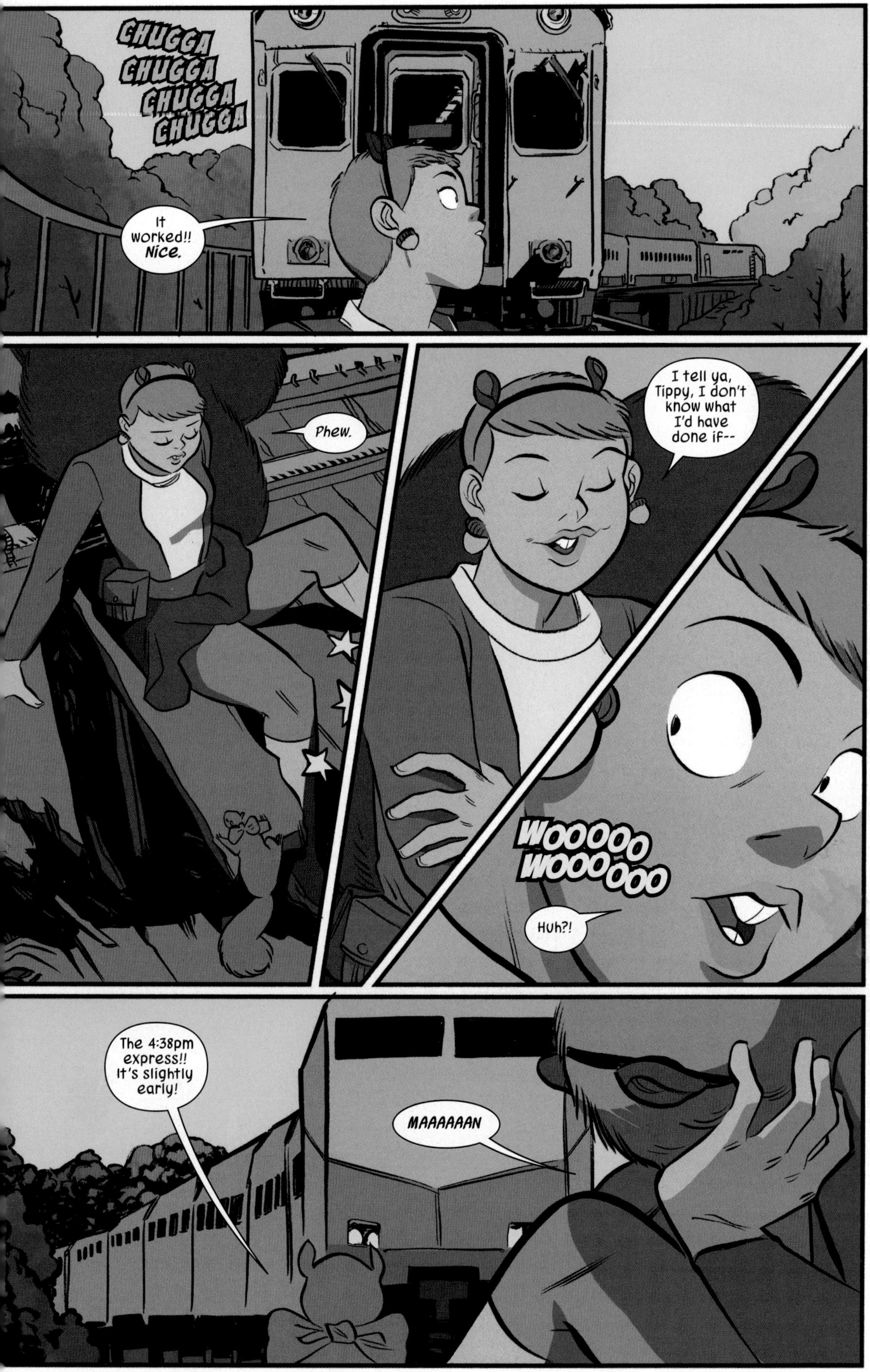
CHUGGA CHUGGA CHUGGA CHUGGA
It worked!! Nice.
Phew.
I tell ya, Tippy, I don't know what I'd have done if--
WOOOOO WOOOOOO
Huh?!
The 4:38pm express!! It's slightly early!
MAAAAAAN

Haha, the train conductor isn't even trying to brake!! Clearly she's got a *lot* of confidence in Squirrel Girl. I admire your boldness, train conductor!!

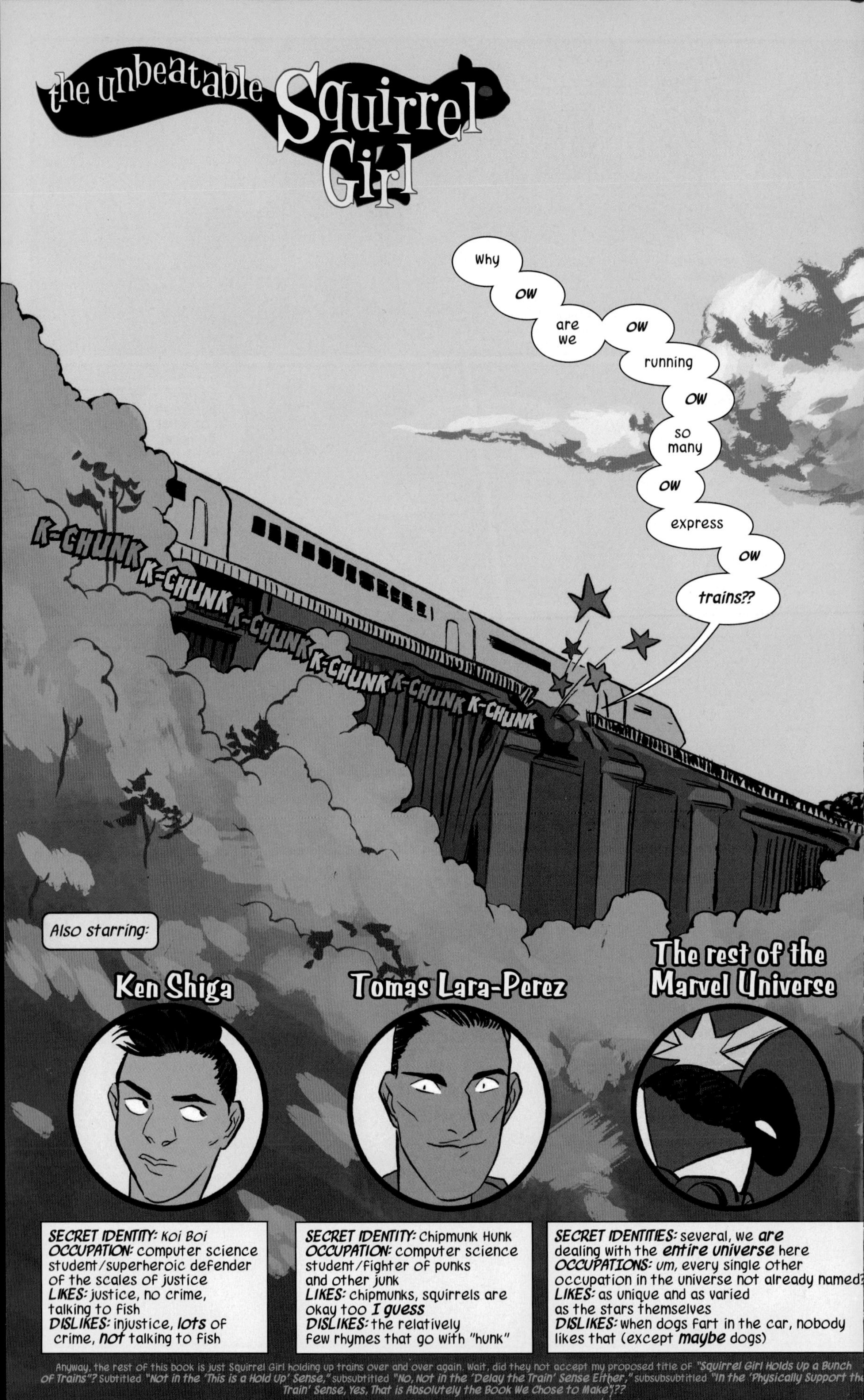
the unbeatable Squirrel Girl
Why ow are we ow running ow so many ow express ow trains??
K-CHUNK K-CHUNK K-CHUNK K-CHUNK K-CHUNK K-CHUNK
Also starring:
Ken Shiga
Tomas Lara-Perez
The rest of the Marvel Universe
SECRET IDENTITY: Koi Boi
OCCUPATION: computer science student/superheroic defender of the scales of justice
LIKES: justice, no crime, talking to fish
DISLIKES: injustice, lots of crime, not talking to fish
SECRET IDENTITY: Chipmunk Hunk
OCCUPATION: computer science student/fighter of punks and other junk
LIKES: chipmunks, squirrels are okay too I guess
DISLIKES: the relatively few rhymes that go with "hunk"
SECRET IDENTITIES: several, we are dealing with the entire universe here
OCCUPATIONS: um, every single other occupation in the universe not already named?
LIKES: as unique and as varied as the stars themselves
DISLIKES: when dogs fart in the car, nobody likes that (except maybe dogs)
Anyway, the rest of this book is just Squirrel Girl holding up trains over and over again. Wait, did they not accept my proposed title of "Squirrel Girl Holds Up a Bunch of Trains"? Subtitled "Not in the 'This is a Hold Up' Sense," subsubtitled "No, Not in the 'Delay the Train' Sense Either," subsubsubtitled "In the 'Physically Support the Train' Sense, Yes, That is Absolutely the Book We Chose to Make"??

the unbeatable Squirrel Girl

BEATS UP THE MARVEL UNIVERSE!

WRITTEN BY RYAN NORTH

DRAWN & COLORED BY ERICA HENDERSON

WITH AN INK ASSIST FROM TOM FOWLER   LETTERED BY TRAVIS LANHAM

DEADPOOL TRADING CARD ART BY RICO RENZI   ACTIVITY PAGES BY RYAN & ERICA

SPECIAL THANKS TO JUAN CASTRO, BECKA KINZIE, DEE CUNNIFFE AND JORDAN GIBSON

COVER BY ERICA HENDERSON   BOOK DESIGN BY JAY BOWEN

ASSISTANT EDITOR: CHARLES BEACHAM   EDITOR: WIL MOSS

COLLECTION EDITOR: JENNIFER GRÜNWALD
ASSOCIATE EDITOR: SARAH BRUNSTAD
EDITOR, SPECIAL PROJECTS: MARK D. BEAZLEY
VP, PRODUCTION & SPECIAL PROJECTS: JEFF YOUNGQUIST
SVP PRINT, SALES & MARKETING: DAVID GABRIEL

EXECUTIVE EDITOR: TOM BREVOORT
EDITOR IN CHIEF: AXEL ALONSO
CHIEF CREATIVE OFFICER: JOE QUESADA
PUBLISHER: DAN BUCKLEY
EXECUTIVE PRODUCER: ALAN FINE

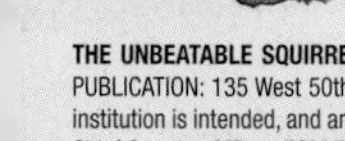

THE UNBEATABLE SQUIRREL GIRL BEATS UP THE MARVEL UNIVERSE. First printing 2016. ISBN# 978-1-302-90303-9. Published by MARVEL WORLDWIDE, INC., a subsidiary of MARVEL ENTERTAINMENT, LLC. OFFICE OF PUBLICATION: 135 West 50th Street, New York, NY 10020. Copyright © 2016 MARVEL No similarity between any of the names, characters, persons, and/or institutions in this magazine with those of any living or dead person or institution is intended, and any such similarity which may exist is purely coincidental. **Printed in the U.S.A.** ALAN FINE, President, Marvel Entertainment; DAN BUCKLEY, President, TV, Publishing & Brand Management; JOE QUESADA, Chief Creative Officer; TOM BREVOORT, SVP of Publishing; DAVID BOGART, SVP of Business Affairs & Operations, Publishing & Partnership; C.B. CEBULSKI, VP of Brand Management & Development, Asia; DAVID GABRIEL, SVP of Sales & Marketing, Publishing; JEFF YOUNGQUIST, VP of Production & Special Projects; DAN CARR, Executive Director of Publishing Technology; ALEX MORALES, Director of Publishing Operations; SUSAN CRESPI, Production Manager; STAN LEE, Chairman Emeritus. For information regarding advertising in Marvel Comics or on Marvel.com, please contact Vit DeBellis, Integrated Sales Manager, at vdebellis@marvel.com. For Marvel subscription inquiries, please call 888-511-5480. **Manufactured between 7/29/2016 and 9/5/2016 by WORZALLA PUBLISHING CO., STEVENS POINT, WI, USA.**

10 9 8 7 6 5 4 3 2 1

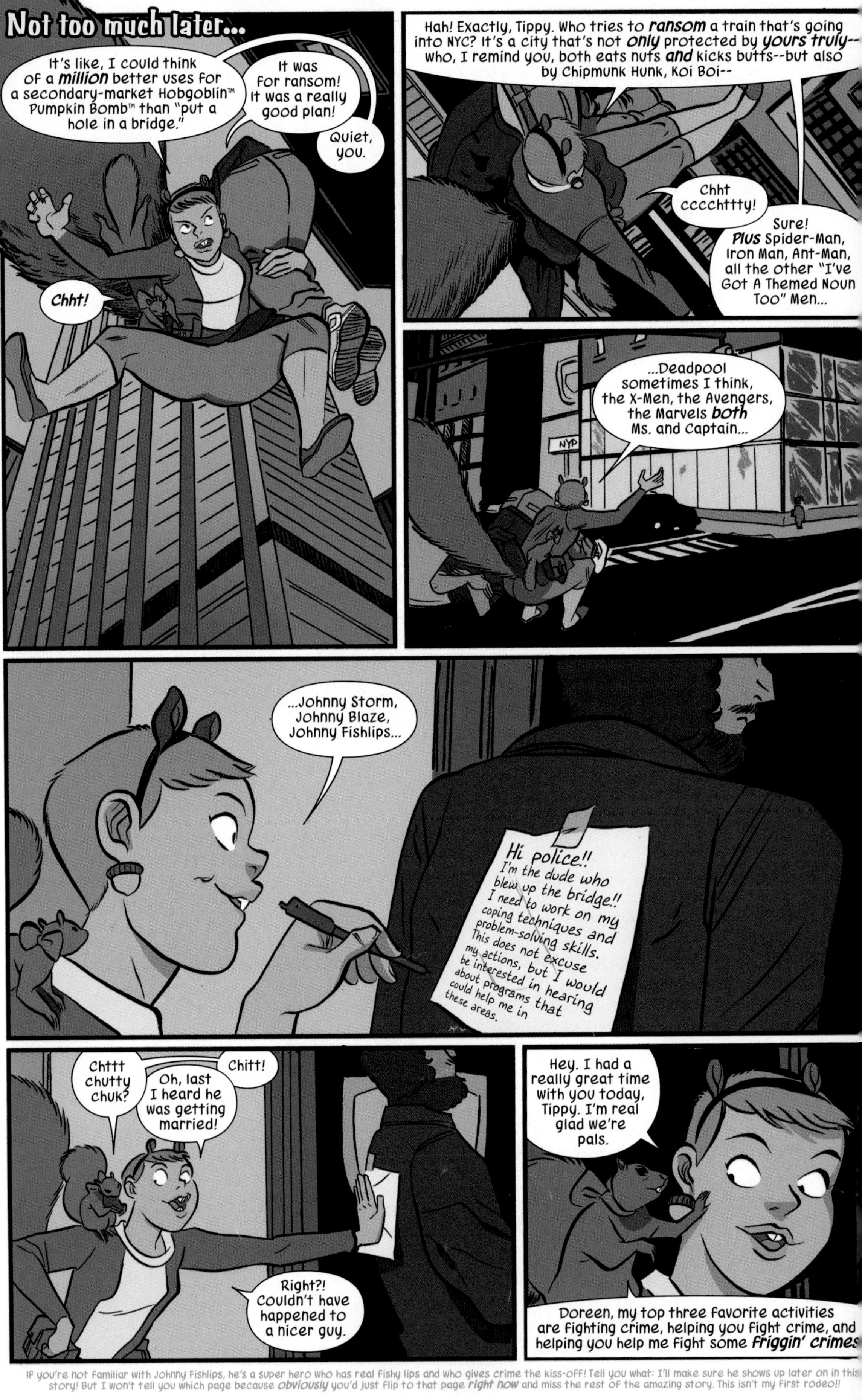
Not too much later...
It's like, I could think of a million better uses for a secondary-market Hobgoblin™ Pumpkin Bomb™ than "put a hole in a bridge."
It was for ransom! It was a really good plan!
Quiet, you.
Chht!
Hah! Exactly, Tippy. Who tries to ransom a train that's going into NYC? It's a city that's not only protected by yours truly--who, I remind you, both eats nuts and kicks butts--but also by Chipmunk Hunk, Koi Boi--
Chht ccccchttty!
Sure! Plus Spider-Man, Iron Man, Ant-Man, all the other "I've Got A Themed Noun Too" Men...
...Deadpool sometimes I think, the X-Men, the Avengers, the Marvels both Ms. and Captain...
NYP
...Johnny Storm, Johnny Blaze, Johnny Fishlips...
Hi police!! I'm the dude who blew up the bridge!! I need to work on my coping techniques and problem-solving skills. This does not excuse my actions, but I would be interested in hearing about programs that could help me in these areas.
Chttt chutty chuk?
Chitt!
Oh, last I heard he was getting married!
Right?! Couldn't have happened to a nicer guy.
Hey. I had a really great time with you today, Tippy. I'm real glad we're pals.
Doreen, my top three favorite activities are fighting crime, helping you fight crime, and helping you help me fight some friggin' crimes

If you're not familiar with Johnny Fishlips, he's a super hero who has real fishy lips and who gives crime the kiss-off! Tell you what: I'll make sure he shows up later on in this story! But I won't tell you which page because *obviously* you'd just flip to that page *right now* and miss the rest of the amazing story. This isn't my first rodeo!!

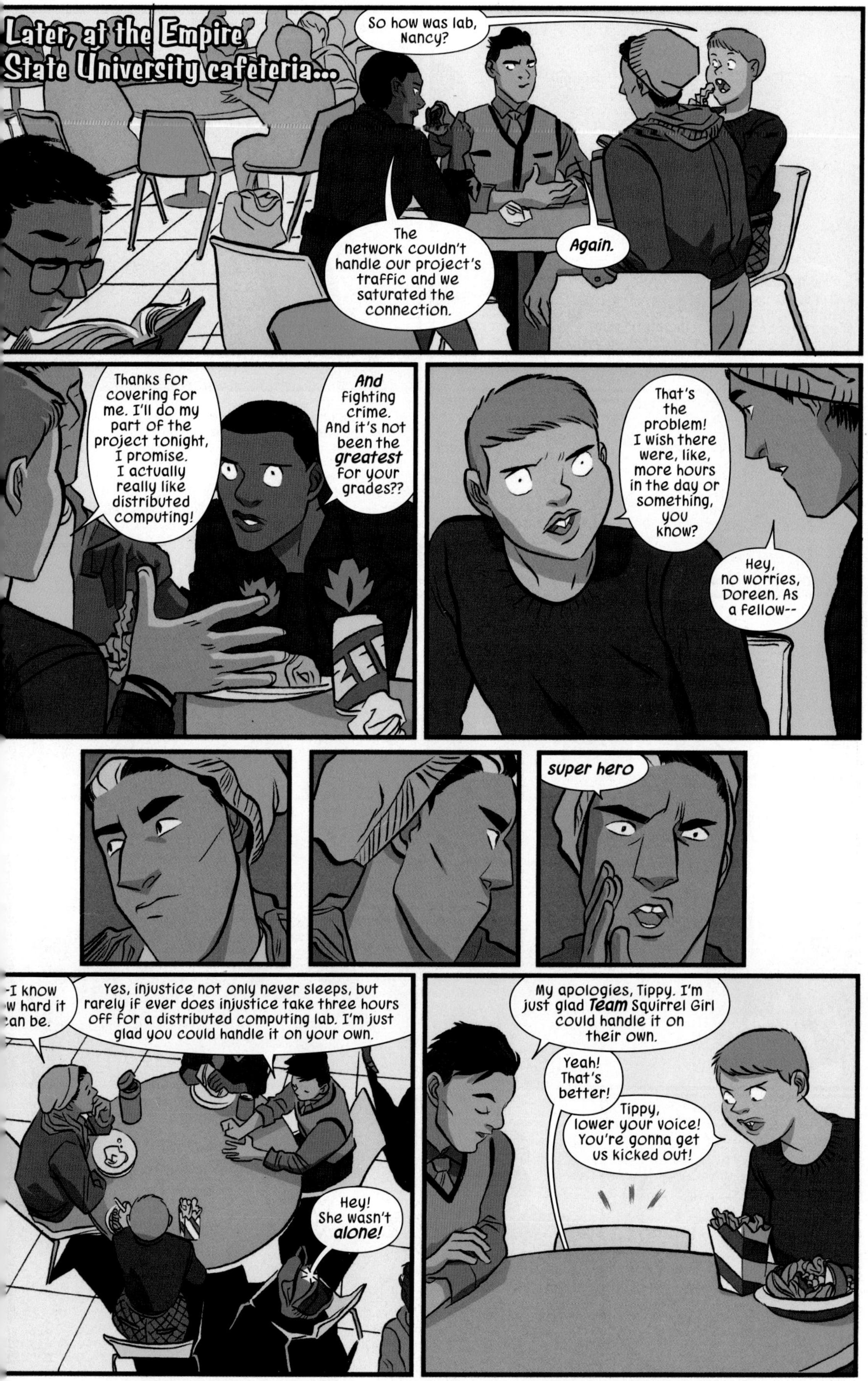
Later, at the Empire State University cafeteria...
So how was lab, Nancy?
The network couldn't handle our project's traffic and we saturated the connection.
Again.
Thanks for covering for me. I'll do my part of the project tonight, I promise. I actually really like distributed computing!
And fighting crime. And it's not been the greatest for your grades??
That's the problem! I wish there were, like, more hours in the day or something, you know?
Hey, no worries, Doreen. As a fellow--
super hero
-I know w hard it can be.
Yes, injustice not only never sleeps, but rarely if ever does injustice take three hours off for a distributed computing lab. I'm just glad you could handle it on your own.
Hey! She wasn't alone!
My apologies, Tippy. I'm just glad Team Squirrel Girl could handle it on their own.
Yeah! That's better!
Tippy, lower your voice! You're gonna get us kicked out!

The school cafeteria doesn't like it when people's purses make squirrel noises, *especially* mine! I'm on like strike fifteen here!!

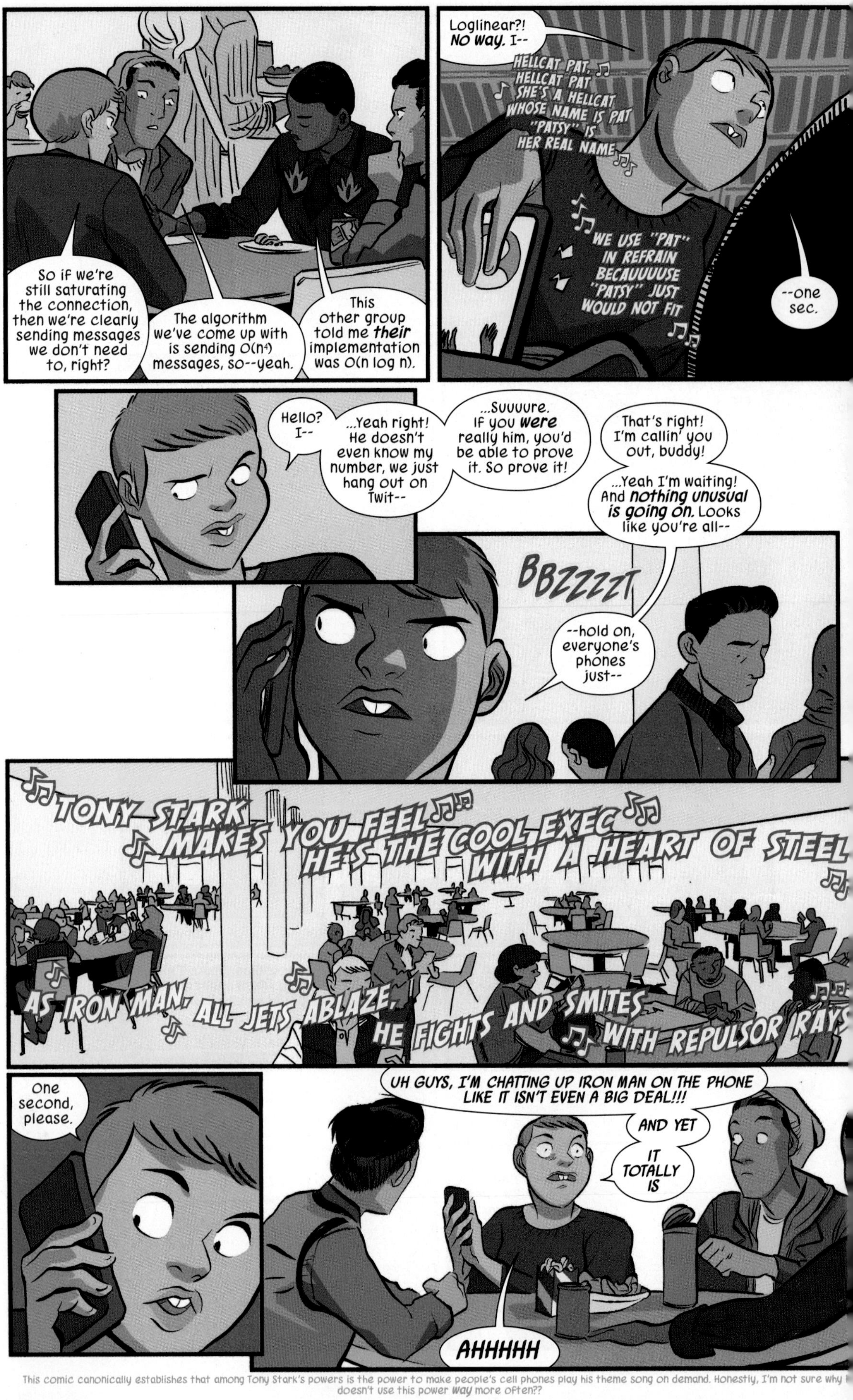
So if we're still saturating the connection, then we're clearly sending messages we don't need to, right?
The algorithm we've come up with is sending O(n4) messages, so--yeah.
This other group told me their implementation was O(n log n).
Loglinear?! No way. I--
HELLCAT PAT, HELLCAT PAT SHE'S A HELLCAT WHOSE NAME IS PAT "PATSY" IS HER REAL NAME
WE USE "PAT" IN REFRAIN BECAUUUUSE "PATSY" JUST WOULD NOT FIT
--one sec.
Hello? I--
...Yeah right! He doesn't even know my number, we just hang out on Twit--
...Suuuure. If you were really him, you'd be able to prove it. So prove it!
That's right! I'm callin' you out, buddy!
...Yeah I'm waiting! And nothing unusual is going on. Looks like you're all--
BBZZZZT
--hold on, everyone's phones just--
TONY STARK MAKES YOU FEEL HE'S THE COOL EXEC WITH A HEART OF STEEL
AS IRON MAN, ALL JETS ABLAZE, HE FIGHTS AND SMITES WITH REPULSOR RAYS
One second, please.
UH GUYS, I'M CHATTING UP IRON MAN ON THE PHONE LIKE IT ISN'T EVEN A BIG DEAL!!!
AND YET
IT TOTALLY IS
AHHHHH

This comic canonically establishes that among Tony Stark's powers is the power to make people's cell phones play his theme song on demand. Honestly, I'm not sure why he doesn't use this power *way* more often??

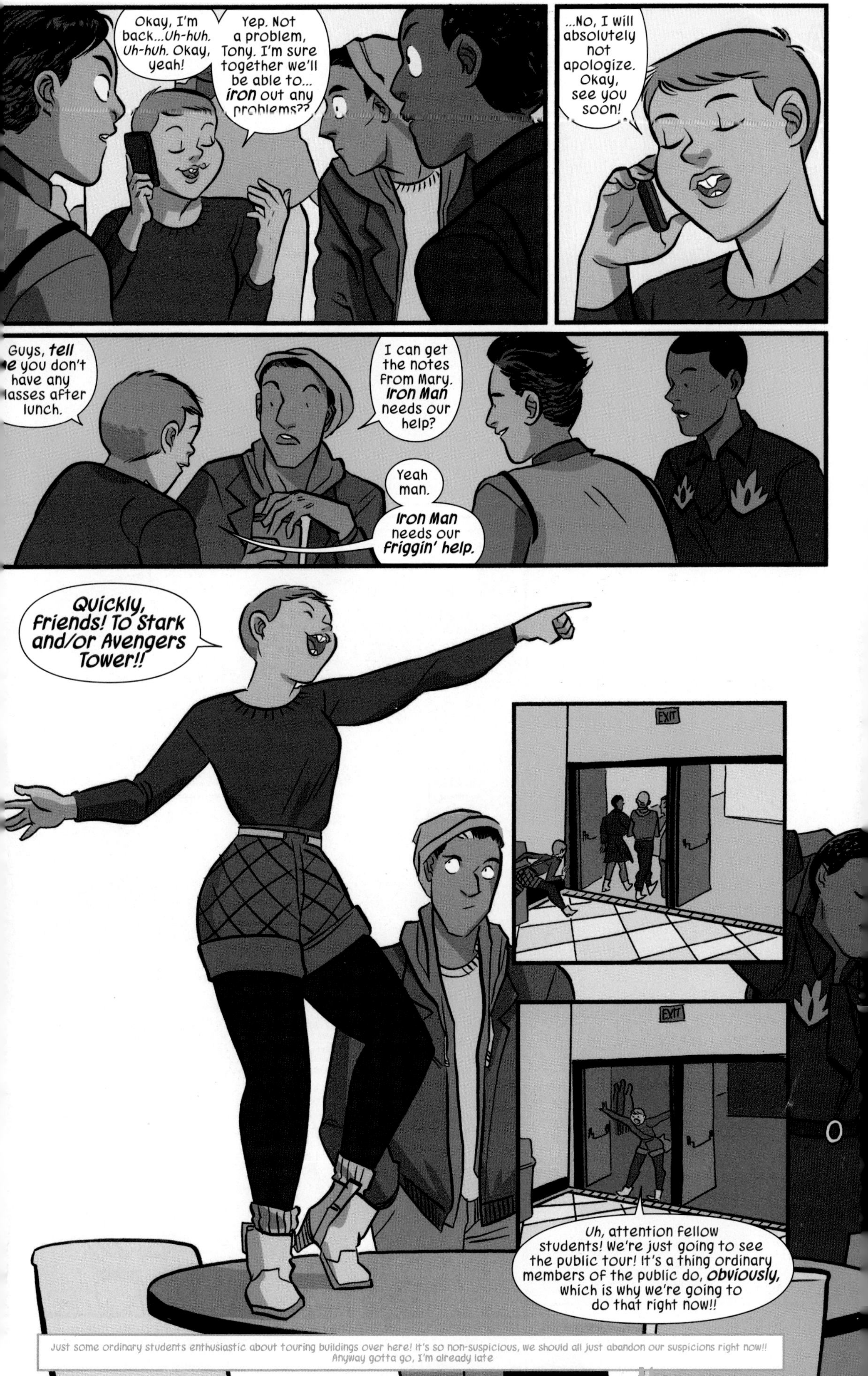

Okay, I'm back...Uh-huh. Uh-huh. Okay, yeah!
Yep. Not a problem, Tony. I'm sure together we'll be able to... *iron* out any problems??
...No, I will absolutely not apologize. Okay, see you soon!
Guys, *tell* e you don't have any lasses after lunch.
I can get the notes from Mary. *Iron Man* needs our help?
Yeah man.
Iron Man needs our *friggin' help.*
Quickly, friends! To Stark and/or Avengers Tower!!
EXIT
EXIT
Uh, attention fellow students! We're just going to see the public tour! It's a thing ordinary members of the public do, *obviously,* which is why we're going to do that right now!!
Just some ordinary students enthusiastic about touring buildings over here! It's so non-suspicious, we should all just abandon our suspicions right now!! Anyway gotta go, I'm already late

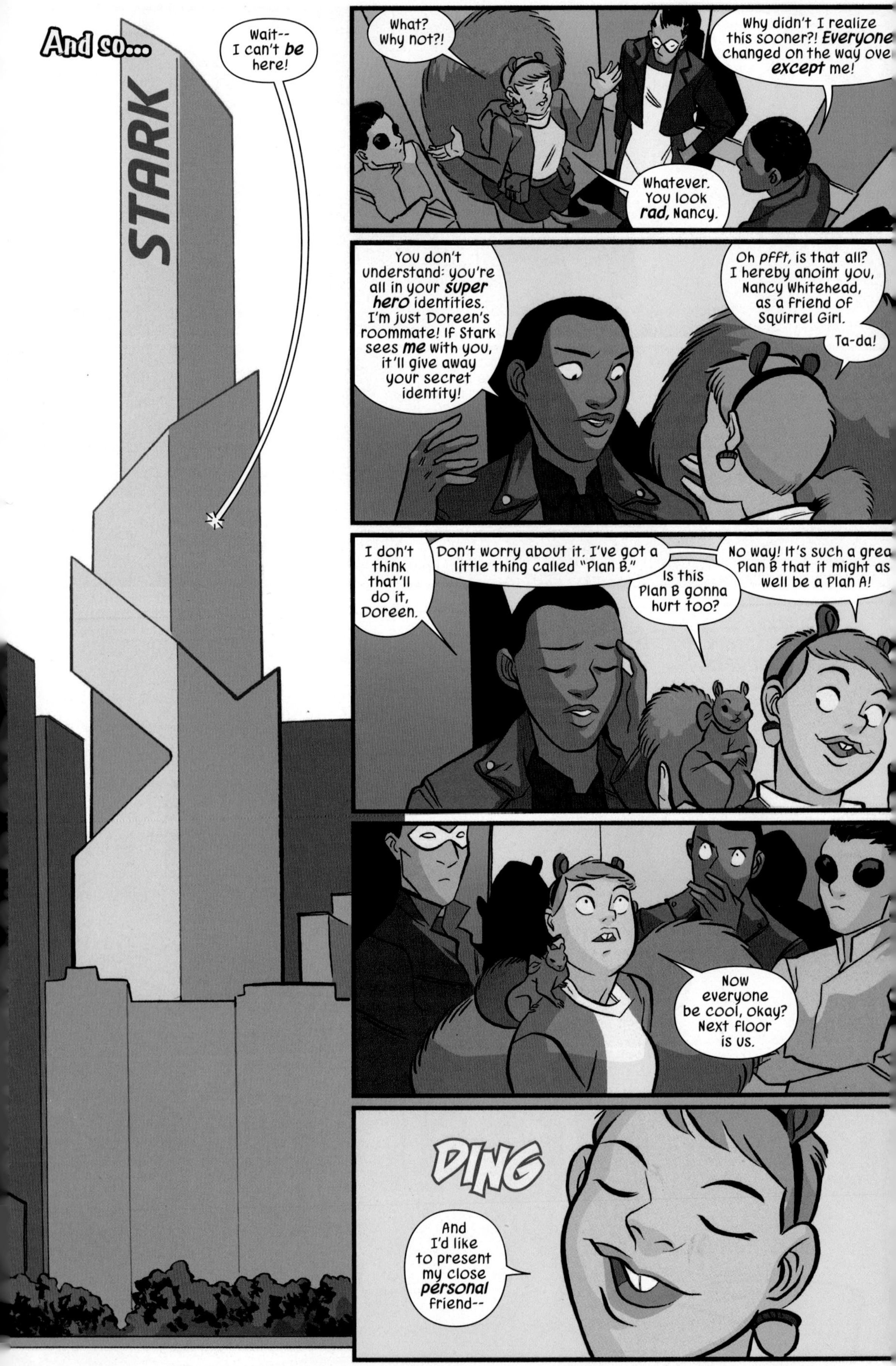
And so...
Wait-- I can't *be* here!
STARK
What? Why not?!
Why didn't I realize this sooner?! *Everyone* changed on the way ove *except* me!
Whatever. You look *rad*, Nancy.
You don't understand: you're all in your *super hero* identities. I'm just Doreen's roommate! If Stark sees *me* with you, it'll give away your secret identity!
Oh *pfft*, is that all? I hereby anoint you, Nancy Whitehead, as a friend of Squirrel Girl.
Ta-da!
I don't think that'll do it, Doreen.
Don't worry about it. I've got a little thing called "Plan B."
Is this Plan B gonna hurt too?
No way! It's such a grea Plan B that it might as well be a Plan A!
Now everyone be cool, okay? Next floor is us.
DING
And I'd like to present my close *personal* friend--

Tony Stark lives on the top floor of his company's building, because this way when he wakes up in the morning, he's *already* at work! *Free career advice:* if you just involuntarily whispered "oh no" when you read that, *do not go become the CEO of a multinational corporation: people expect this sort of thing; it's the worst*

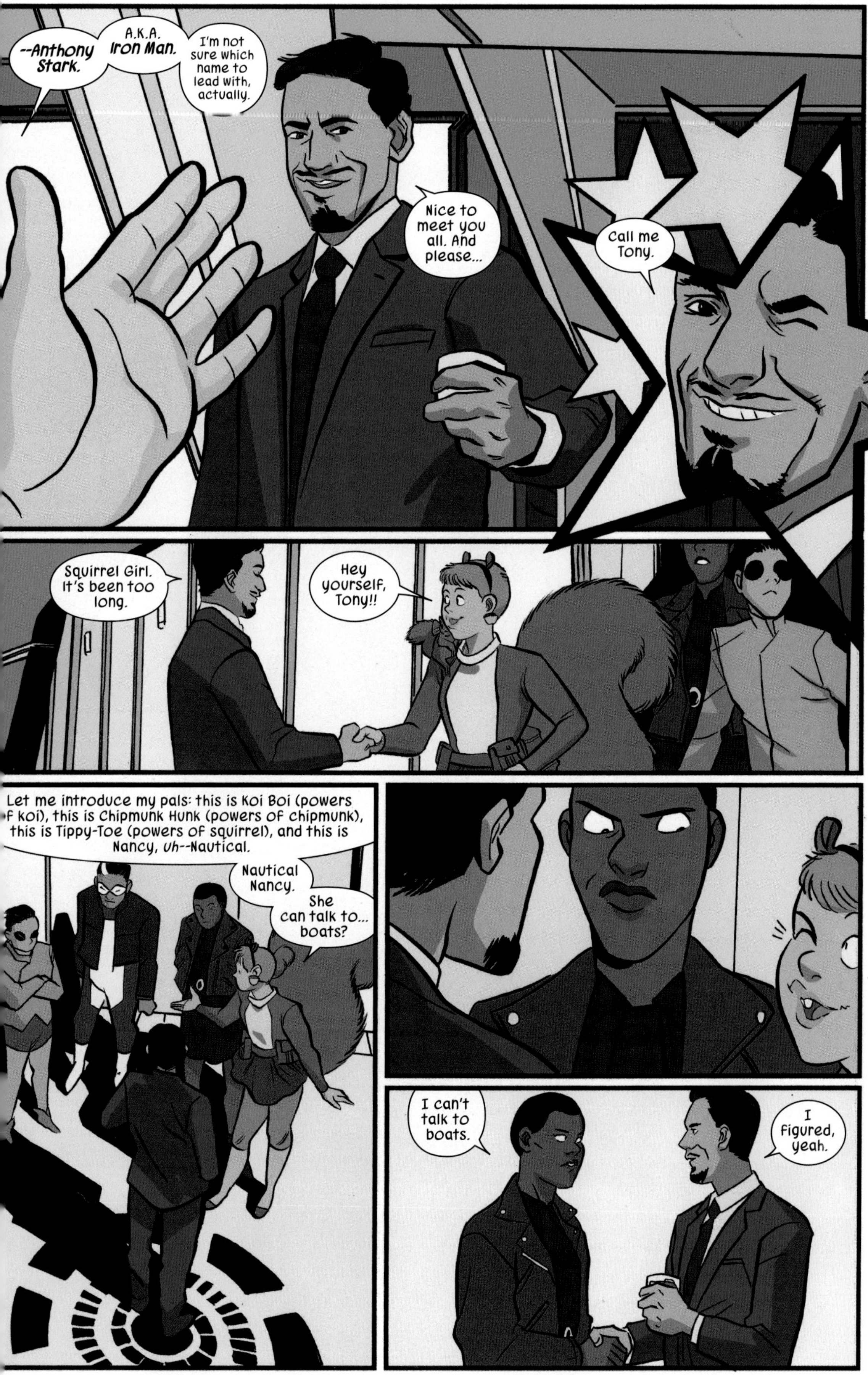
--Anthony Stark.
A.K.A. Iron Man.
I'm not sure which name to lead with, actually.
Nice to meet you all. And please...
Call me Tony.
Squirrel Girl. It's been too long.
Hey yourself, Tony!!
Let me introduce my pals: this is Koi Boi (powers f koi), this is Chipmunk Hunk (powers of chipmunk), this is Tippy-Toe (powers of squirrel), and this is Nancy, uh--Nautical.
Nautical Nancy.
She can talk to... boats?
I can't talk to boats.
I figured, yeah.

Squirrel Girl's Plan C was to refer to her as "The Ultimate Nancifier." She might still do it, honestly.

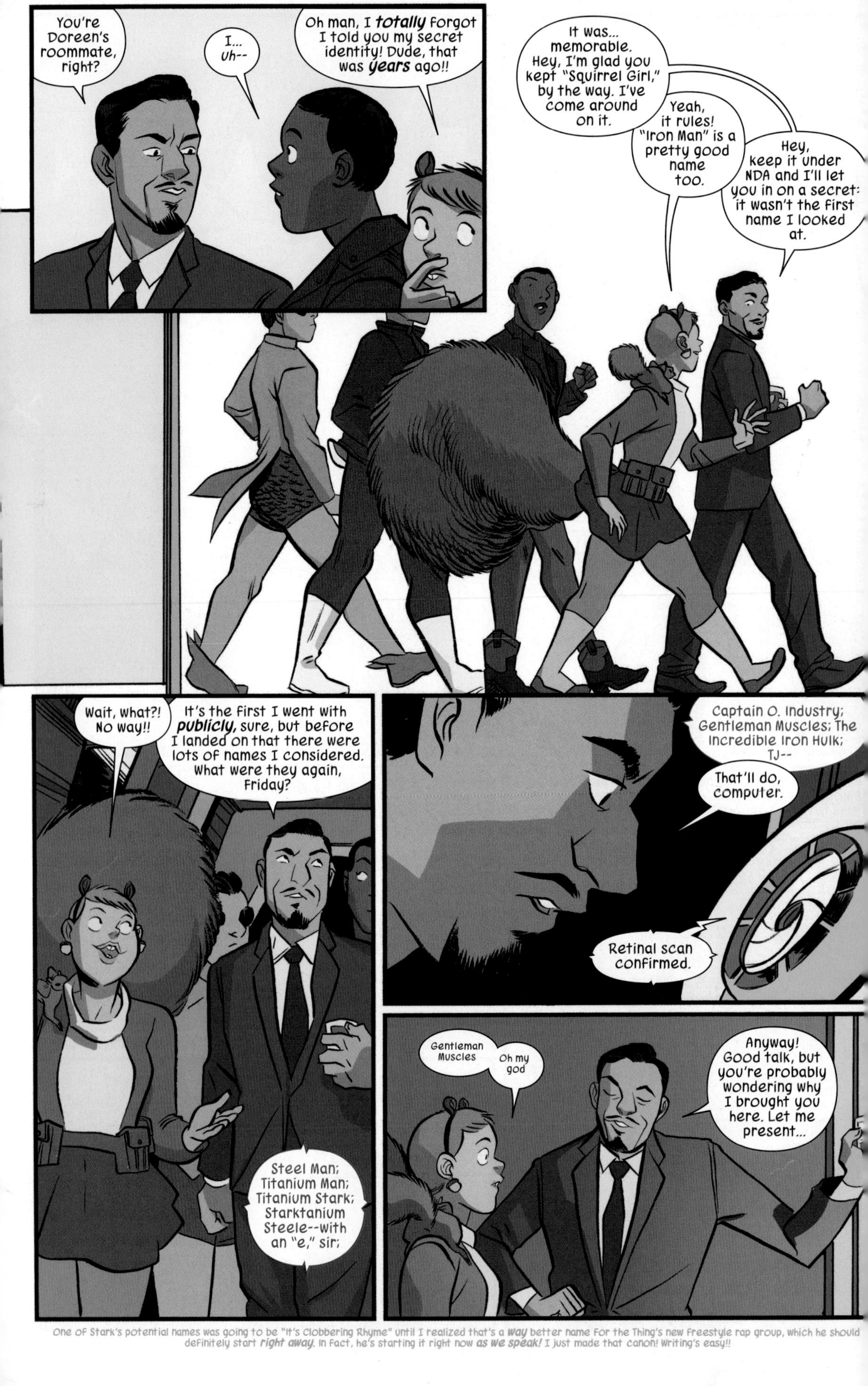
You're Doreen's roommate, right?
I... Uh--
Oh man, I *totally* forgot I told you my secret identity! Dude, that was *years* ago!!
It was... memorable. Hey, I'm glad you kept "Squirrel Girl," by the way. I've come around on it.
Yeah, it rules! "Iron Man" is a pretty good name too.
Hey, keep it under NDA and I'll let you in on a secret: it wasn't the first name I looked at.
Wait, what?! No way!!
It's the first I went with *publicly,* sure, but before I landed on that there were lots of names I considered. What were they again, Friday?
Steel Man; Titanium Man; Titanium Stark; Starktanium Steele--with an "e," sir;
Captain O. Industry; Gentleman Muscles; The Incredible Iron Hulk; TJ--
That'll do, computer.
Retinal scan confirmed.
Gentleman Muscles
Oh my god
Anyway! Good talk, but you're probably wondering why I brought you here. Let me present...

One of Stark's potential names was going to be "It's Clobbering Rhyme" until I realized that's a *way* better name for the Thing's new freestyle rap group, which he should definitely start *right away.* In fact, he's starting it right now *as we speak!* I just made that canon! Writing's easy!!

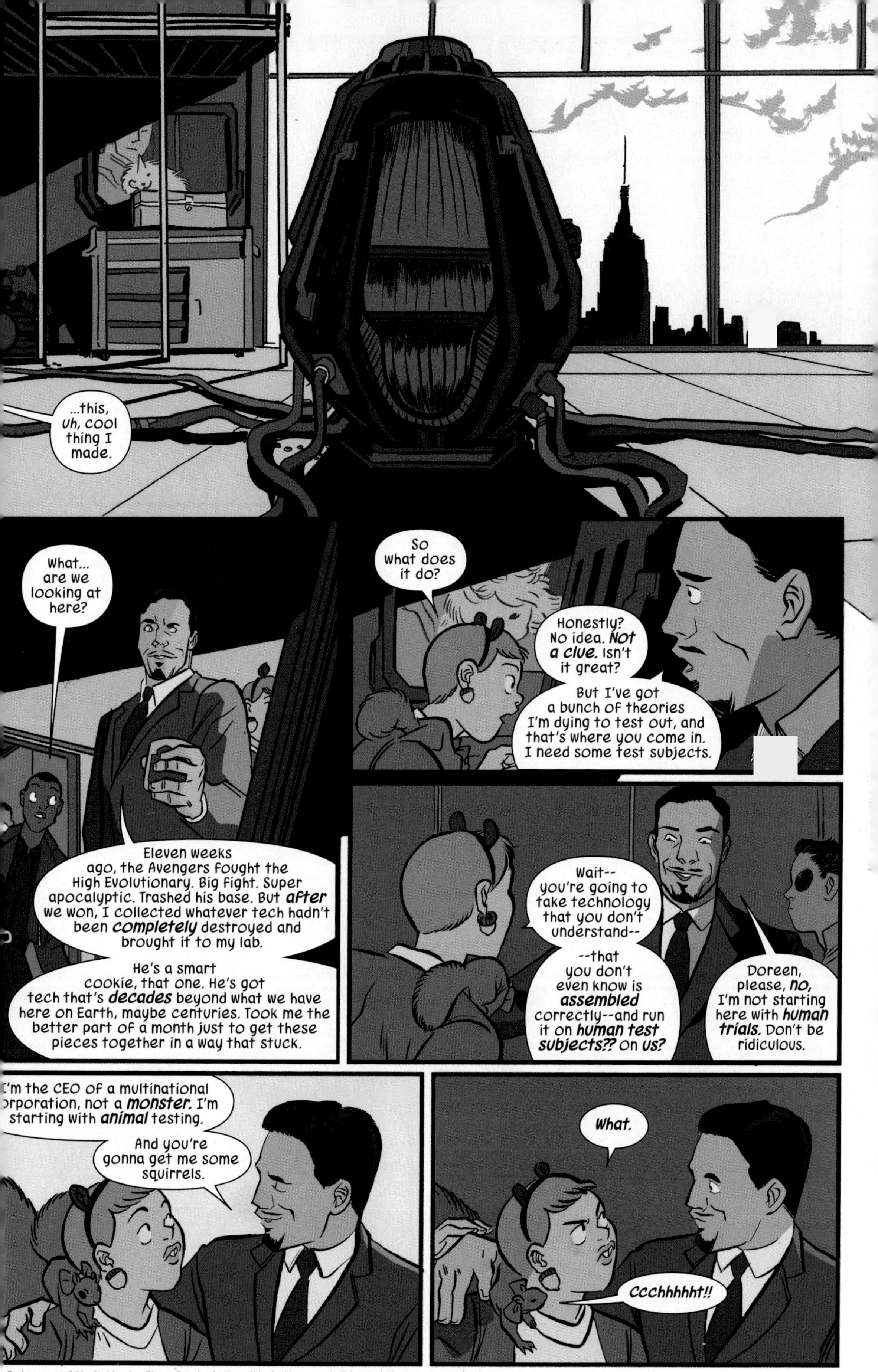

...this, uh, cool thing I made.
What... are we looking at here?
So what does it do?
Honestly? No idea. *Not a clue.* Isn't it great?
But I've got a bunch of theories I'm dying to test out, and that's where you come in. I need some test subjects.
Eleven weeks ago, the Avengers fought the High Evolutionary. Big fight. Super apocalyptic. Trashed his base. But *after* we won, I collected whatever tech hadn't been *completely* destroyed and brought it to my lab.
He's a smart cookie, that one. He's got tech that's *decades* beyond what we have here on Earth, maybe centuries. Took me the better part of a month just to get these pieces together in a way that stuck.
Wait-- you're going to take technology that you don't understand--
--that you don't even know is *assembled* correctly--and run it on *human test subjects??* On *us?*
Doreen, please, *no,* I'm not starting here with *human trials.* Don't be ridiculous.
I'm the CEO of a multinational orporation, not a *monster.* I'm starting with *animal* testing.
And you're gonna get me some squirrels.
What.
Ccchhhhht!!

Bad news on "It's Clobbering Rhyme": nobody likes Thing's "My name is Thing and I'm here to say/I like rapping in a major way" raps and it looks like creative differences might cause the group to break up!!

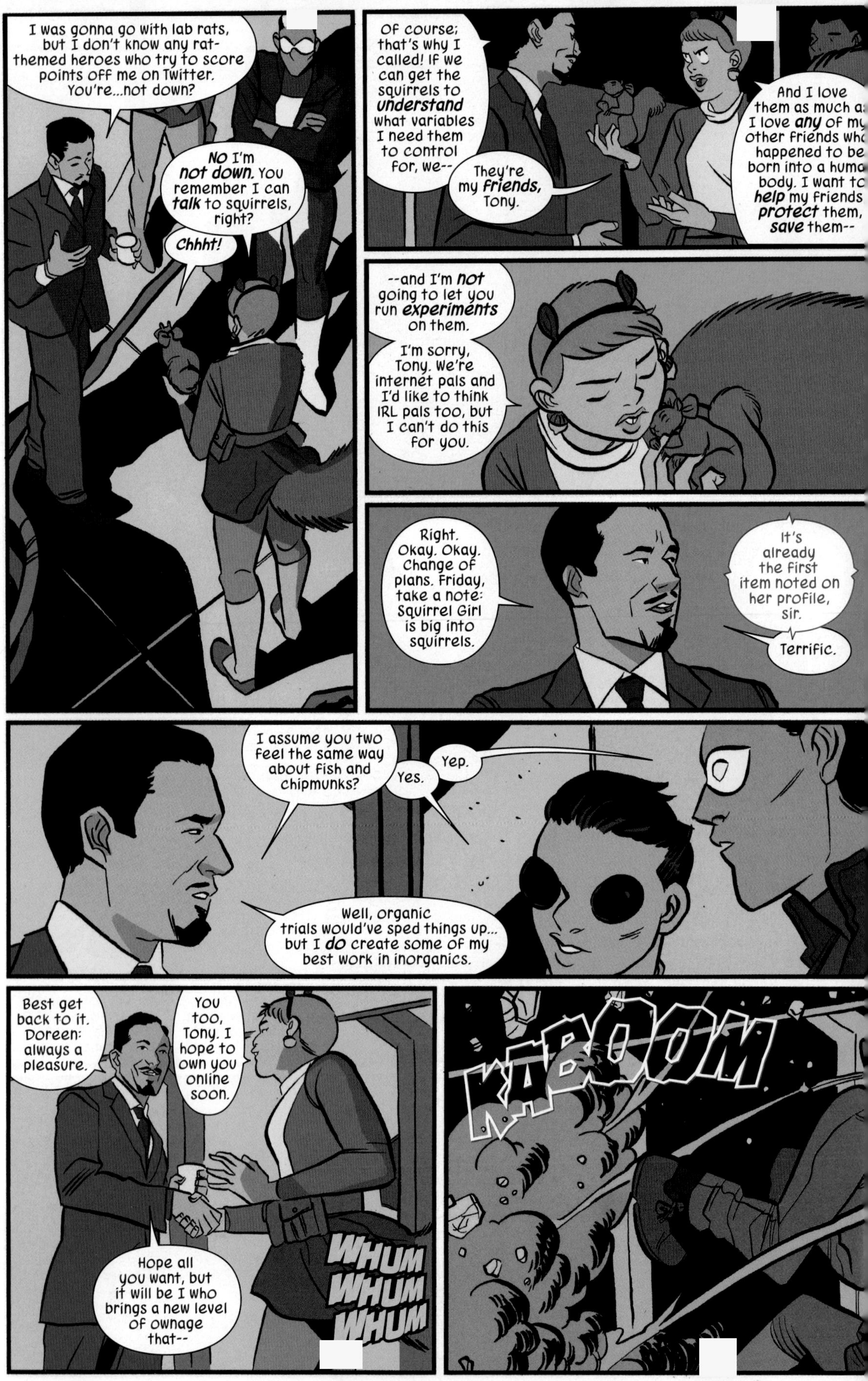
I was gonna go with lab rats, but I don't know any rat-themed heroes who try to score points off me on Twitter. You're...not down?
NO I'm not down. You remember I can talk to squirrels, right?
Chhht!
Of course; that's why I called! If we can get the squirrels to understand what variables I need them to control for, we--
They're my friends, Tony.
And I love them as much a
I love any of my
other friends who
happened to be
born into a huma
body. I want to
help my friends
protect them,
save them--
--and I'm not going to let you run experiments on them.
I'm sorry, Tony. We're internet pals and I'd like to think IRL pals too, but I can't do this for you.
Right. Okay. Okay. Change of plans. Friday, take a note: Squirrel Girl is big into squirrels.
It's already the first item noted on her profile, sir.
Terrific.
I assume you two feel the same way about fish and chipmunks?
Yes.
Yep.
Well, organic trials would've sped things up... but I do create some of my best work in inorganics.
Best get back to it. Doreen: always a pleasure.
You too, Tony. I hope to own you online soon.
Hope all you want, but it will be I who brings a new level of ownage that--
WHUM WHUM WHUM
KABOOM

Tony, Doreen, *please.* Let's just agree that you can both own each other online at your merest whim, and focus on the *real* issue: who among you posts only the freshest of memes.

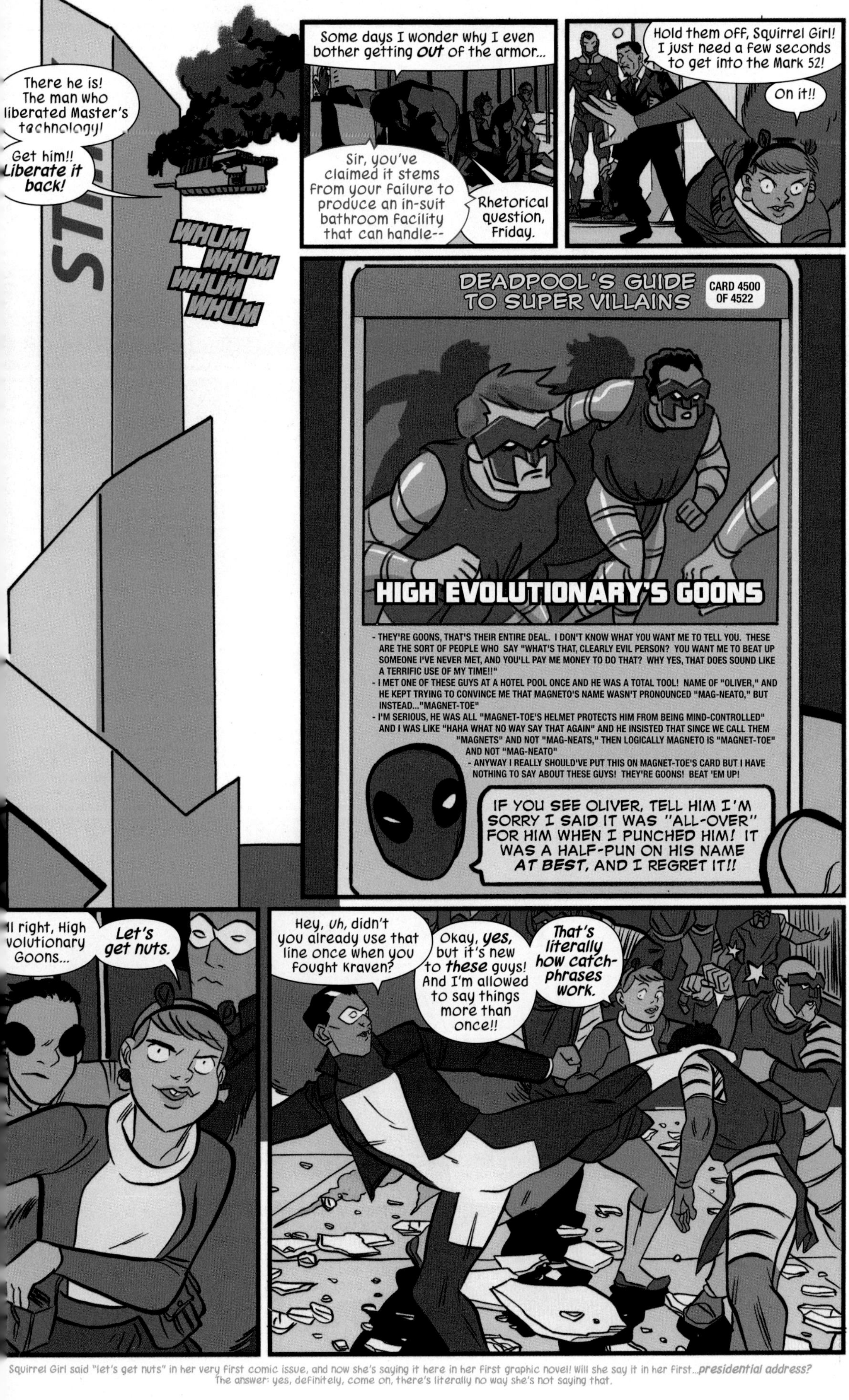
There he is! The man who liberated Master's technology!
Get him!! Liberate it back!
STI
WHUM WHUM WHUM WHUM
Some days I wonder why I even bother getting out of the armor...
Sir, you've claimed it stems from your failure to produce an in-suit bathroom facility that can handle--
Rhetorical question, Friday.
Hold them off, Squirrel Girl! I just need a few seconds to get into the Mark 52!
On it!!
DEADPOOL'S GUIDE TO SUPER VILLAINS
CARD 4500 OF 4522
HIGH EVOLUTIONARY'S GOONS
- THEY'RE GOONS, THAT'S THEIR ENTIRE DEAL. I DON'T KNOW WHAT YOU WANT ME TO TELL YOU. THESE ARE THE SORT OF PEOPLE WHO SAY "WHAT'S THAT, CLEARLY EVIL PERSON? YOU WANT ME TO BEAT UP SOMEONE I'VE NEVER MET, AND YOU'LL PAY ME MONEY TO DO THAT? WHY YES, THAT DOES SOUND LIKE A TERRIFIC USE OF MY TIME!!"
- I MET ONE OF THESE GUYS AT A HOTEL POOL ONCE AND HE WAS A TOTAL TOOL! NAME OF "OLIVER," AND HE KEPT TRYING TO CONVINCE ME THAT MAGNETO'S NAME WASN'T PRONOUNCED "MAG-NEATO," BUT INSTEAD..."MAGNET-TOE"
- I'M SERIOUS, HE WAS ALL "MAGNET-TOE'S HELMET PROTECTS HIM FROM BEING MIND-CONTROLLED" AND I WAS LIKE "HAHA WHAT NO WAY SAY THAT AGAIN" AND HE INSISTED THAT SINCE WE CALL THEM "MAGNETS" AND NOT "MAG-NEATS," THEN LOGICALLY MAGNETO IS "MAGNET-TOE" AND NOT "MAG-NEATO"
- ANYWAY I REALLY SHOULD'VE PUT THIS ON MAGNET-TOE'S CARD BUT I HAVE NOTHING TO SAY ABOUT THESE GUYS! THEY'RE GOONS! BEAT 'EM UP!
IF YOU SEE OLIVER, TELL HIM I'M SORRY I SAID IT WAS "ALL-OVER" FOR HIM WHEN I PUNCHED HIM! IT WAS A HALF-PUN ON HIS NAME AT BEST, AND I REGRET IT!!
ll right, High volutionary Goons...
Let's get nuts.
Hey, uh, didn't you already use that line once when you fought Kraven?
Okay, yes, but it's new to these guys! And I'm allowed to say things more than once!!
That's literally how catch-phrases work.

Squirrel Girl said "let's get nuts" in her very first comic issue, and now she's saying it here in her first graphic novel! Will she say it in her first...*presidential address?* The answer: yes, definitely, come on, there's literally no way she's not saying that.

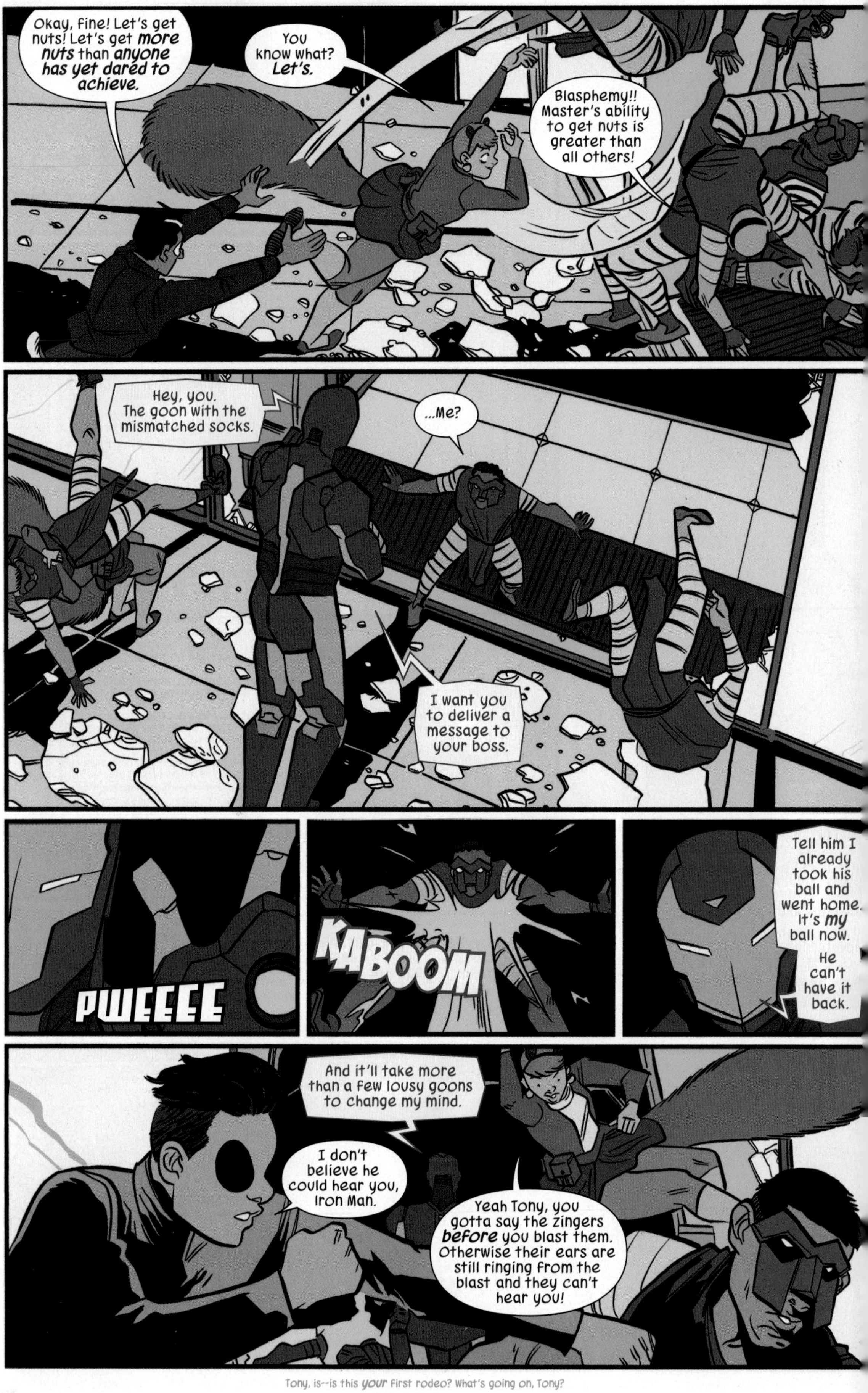

Okay, fine! Let's get nuts! Let's get more nuts than anyone has yet dared to achieve.
You know what? Let's.
Blasphemy!! Master's ability to get nuts is greater than all others!
Hey, you. The goon with the mismatched socks.
...Me?
I want you to deliver a message to your boss.
PWEEEE
KABOOM
Tell him I already took his ball and went home. It's my ball now.
He can't have it back.
And it'll take more than a few lousy goons to change my mind.
I don't believe he could hear you, Iron Man.
Yeah Tony, you gotta say the zingers before you blast them. Otherwise their ears are still ringing from the blast and they can't hear you!

Tony, is--is this *your* first rodeo? What's going on, Tony?

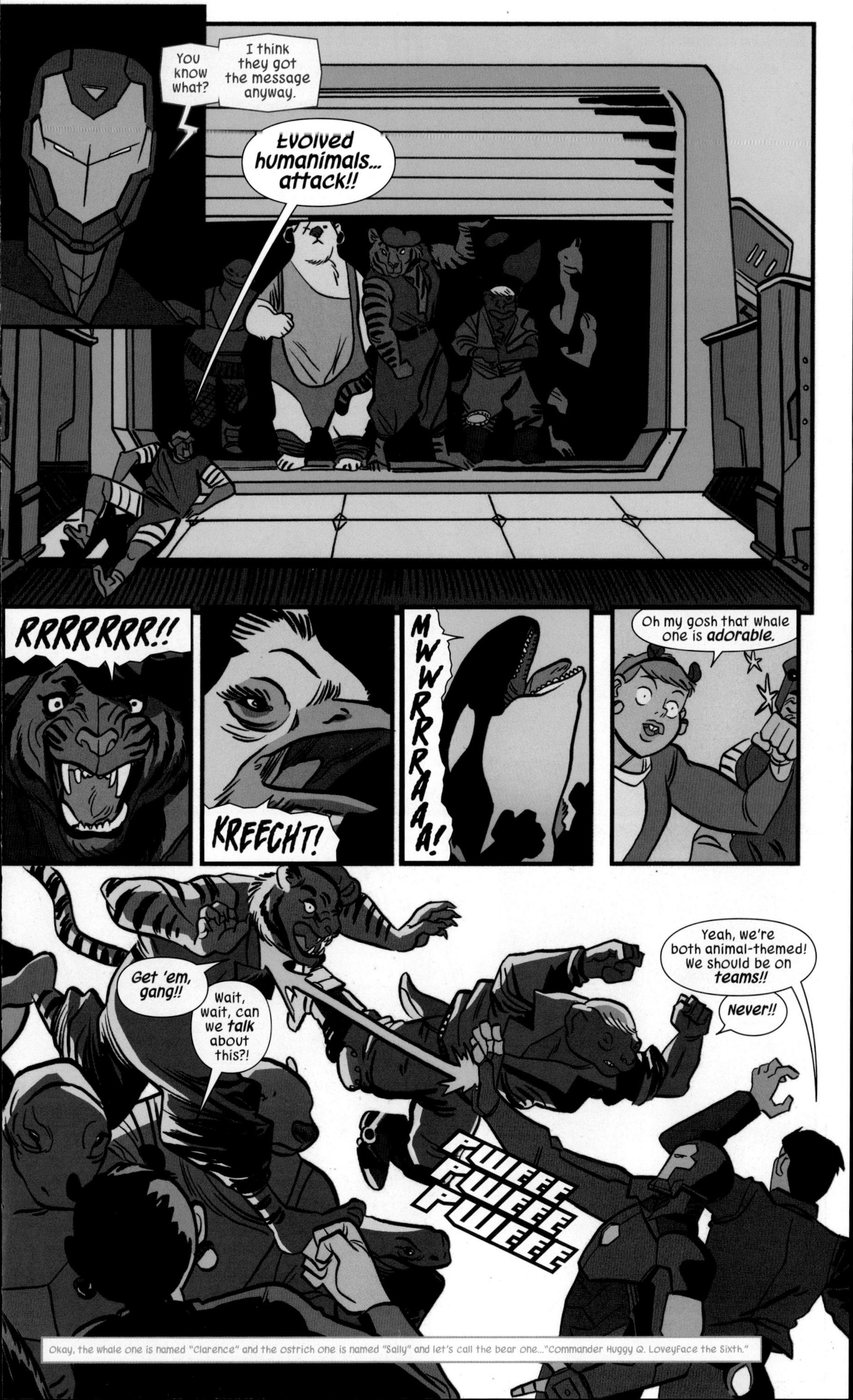
You know what?
I think they got the message anyway.
Evolved humanimals... attack!!
RRRRRRR!!
KREECHT!
MWWRRRAAAA!
Oh my gosh that whale one is *adorable.*
Get 'em, gang!!
Wait, wait, can we *talk* about this?!
Yeah, we're both animal-themed! We should be on *teams!!*
Never!!
PWEEEE PWEEEE PWEEEE
Okay, the whale one is named "Clarence" and the ostrich one is named "Sally" and let's call the bear one..."Commander Huggy Q. LoveyFace the Sixth."

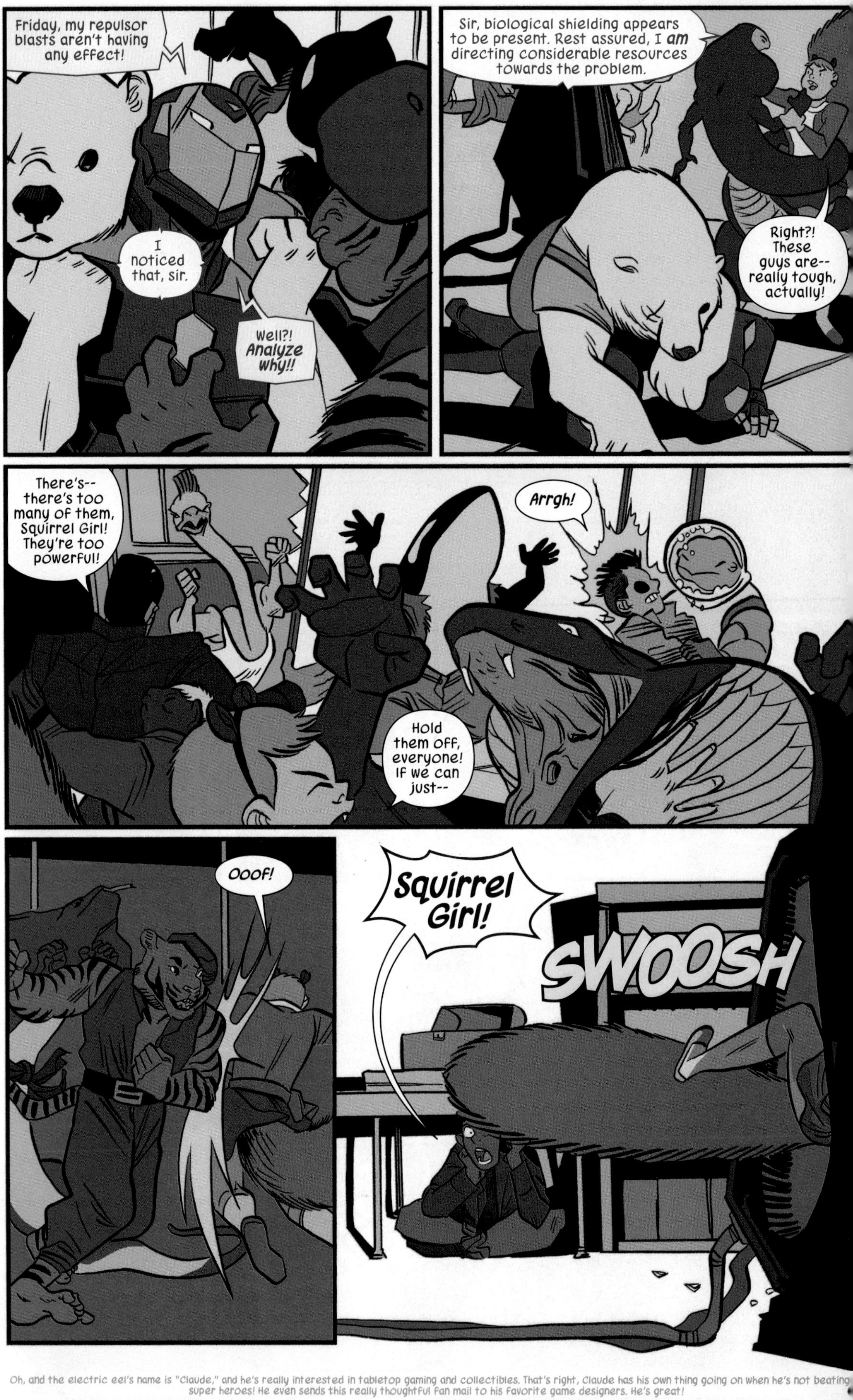
Friday, my repulsor blasts aren't having any effect!
I noticed that, sir.
Well?! Analyze why!!
Sir, biological shielding appears to be present. Rest assured, I *am* directing considerable resources towards the problem.
Right?! These guys are-- really tough, actually!
There's-- there's too many of them, Squirrel Girl! They're too powerful!
Arrgh!
Hold them off, everyone! If we can just--
OOOF!
Squirrel Girl!
SWOOSH

Oh, and the electric eel's name is "Claude," and he's really interested in tabletop gaming and collectibles. That's right, Claude has his own thing going on when he's not beating super heroes! He even sends this really thoughtful fan mail to his favorite game designers. He's great!

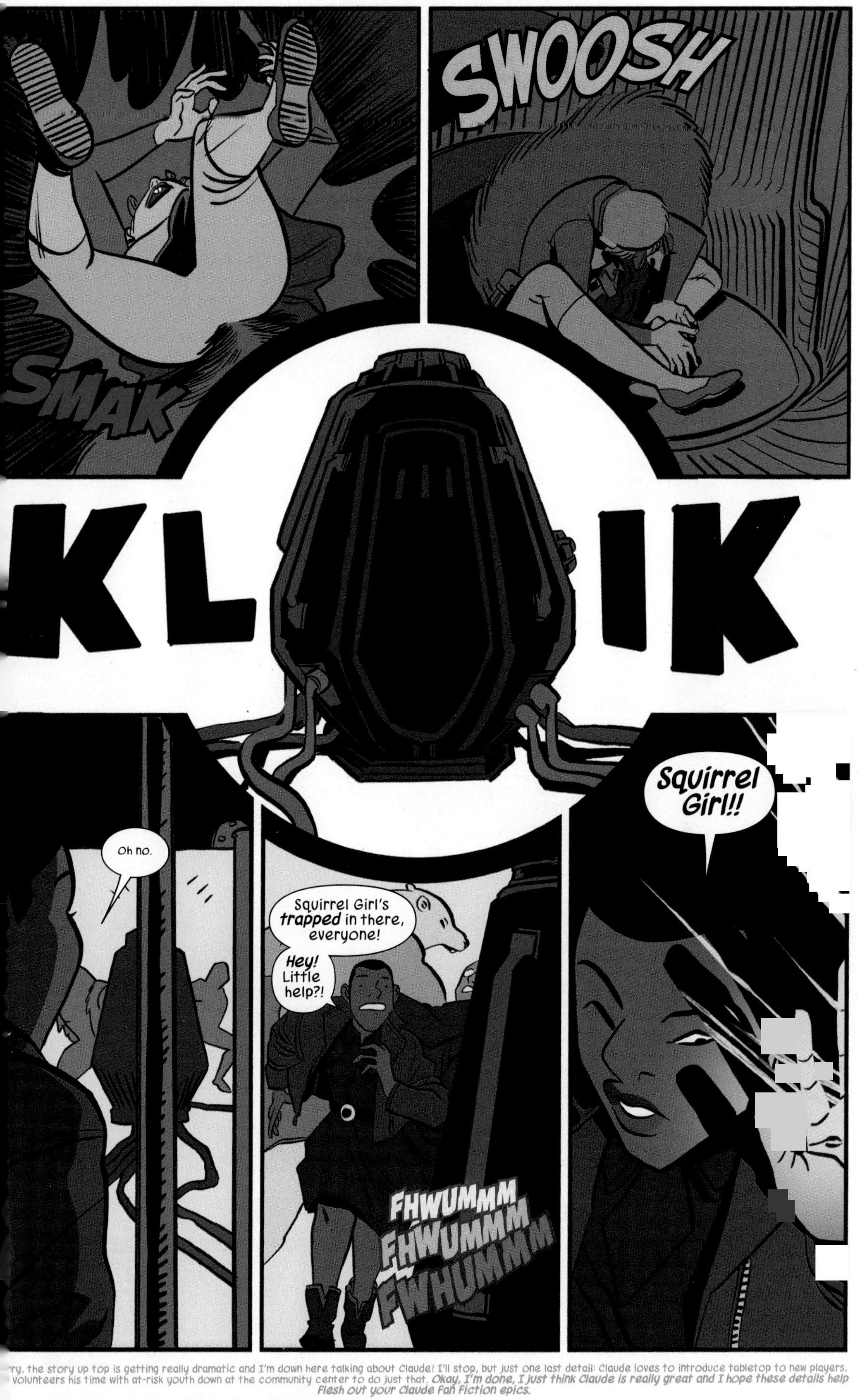
SWOOSH
SMAK
KL
IK
Oh no.
Squirrel Girl's trapped in there, everyone!
Hey! Little help?!
FHWUMMM
FHWUMMM
FWHUMMM
Squirrel Girl!!

ry, the story up top is getting really dramatic and I'm down here talking about Claude! I'll stop, but just one last detail: Claude loves to introduce tabletop to new players, volunteers his time with at-risk youth down at the community center to do just that. *Okay, I'm done, I just think Claude is really great and I hope these details help flesh out your Claude fan fiction epics.*

Special interactive fight scene interlude:

HOW TO DRAW SQUIRREL GIRL!

1 So I guess--start with a circle? For her head?

2 Oh wait, ***you're*** supposed to draw it. Okay, draw the circle here.

3 Draw it again here, but now with some cylinders and stuff. For her body and legs and arms, you know?

I'm pretty sure this is how drawing works. Almost certain.

4 Okay, now draw her again--practice makes perfect! But this time draw her face and tail and boots and stuff.

Ooh, and her headband too, with those little squirrel ears! Adorable.

5 I guess just...keep drawing until whatever comes out looks like Squirrel Girl, and then...stop? Wait, better idea: just copy this into the next panel!! Only make it, you know, better.

6 So did you copy it? Great job! Check it out, I'll add some praise too, so people who look at your drawing know how super great it is.

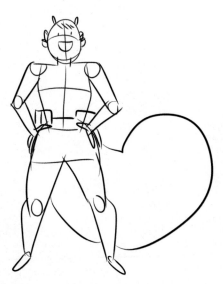

WOW! Another excellent Squirrel Girl drawing by

______________________!!

(your name here)

They are super talented and I love them.

You know what? This isn't working, and drawing Squirrel Girl is **way** harder to explain than I thought. I've got a much better idea instead! ➡️

CONNECT THE DOTS SQUIRREL GIRL!

500% easier than drawing, MINIMUM.

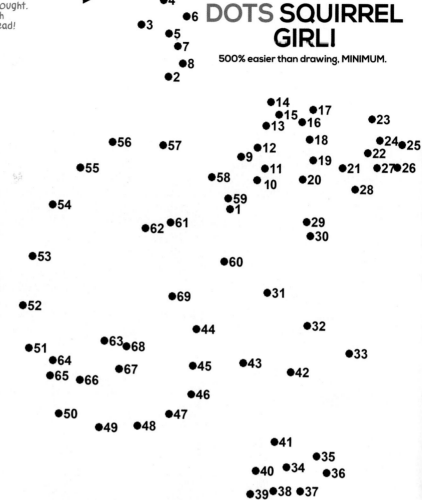

SQUIRREL GIRL'S TRIVIA CORNER

1. Think you know Squirrel Girl? Pop quiz, hotshot: on a scale of 1 to 10, Squirrel Girl thinks squirrels are:
a) 1-4
b) 5-9
c) 10
d) 1,000,000,000,000+

2. Squirrel Girl likes to:
a) study computer science
b) hang out with squirrels
c) all of the above... AT THE SAME TIME

3. Having your own prehensile squirrel tail is:
a) great
b) good for an impromptu chair
c) very cool and good
d) something everyone wishes they had once they think about it, even Spider-Man, and he's already got an animal thing going

ANSWERS: 1) d, 2) c, 3) all are correct, circle them all

WORD SEARCH WITH SQUIRREL GIRL

```
S  Q  U  I  R  R  E  L  S
Q  Q  U  L  E  S  Q  L  Q
U  I  U  S  Q  R  E  S  U
I  Q  R  I  E  R  Q  U  I
R  S  Q  U  R  E  R  L  R
R  E  S  I  S  R  R  L  R
E  Q  U  S  Q  R  E  Q  E
L  Q  S  E  Q  R  L  L  L
S  Q  U  I  R  R  E  L  S
```

Can YOU find the word "SQUIRRELS" six times? Probably, but nobody will believe you until you prove it.

SQUIRREL GIRL'S MATCHING GAME

Draw a line connecting each item and what Squirrel Girl thinks of it! We've started off the puzzle for you.

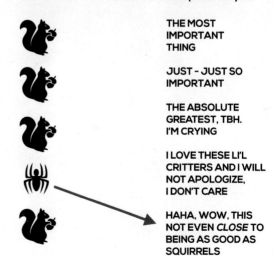

THE MOST IMPORTANT THING

JUST - JUST SO IMPORTANT

THE ABSOLUTE GREATEST, TBH. I'M CRYING

I LOVE THESE LI'L CRITTERS AND I WILL NOT APOLOGIZE, I DON'T CARE

HAHA, WOW, THIS NOT EVEN *CLOSE* TO BEING AS GOOD AS SQUIRRELS

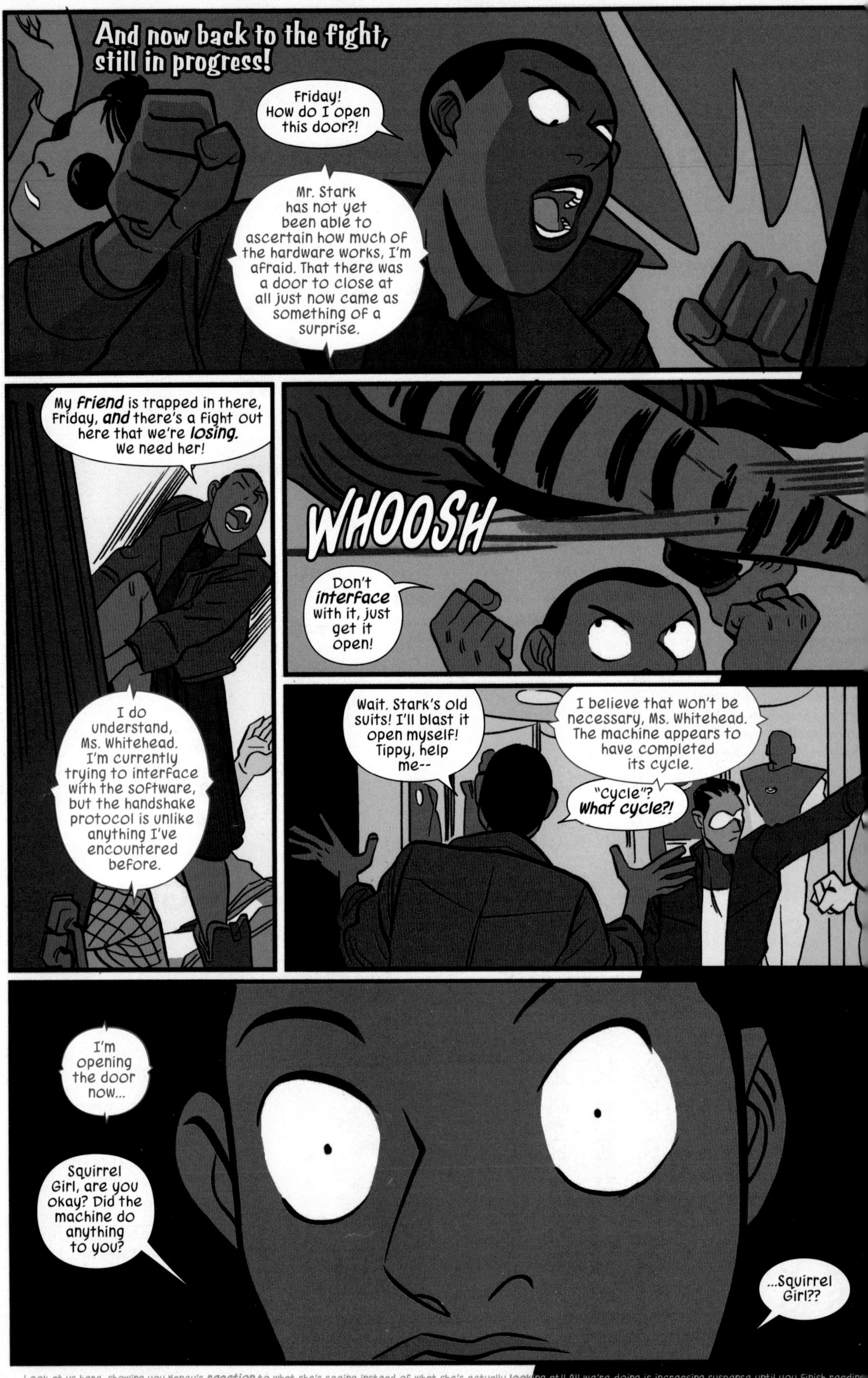
And now back to the fight, still in progress!
Friday! How do I open this door?!
Mr. Stark has not yet been able to ascertain how much of the hardware works, I'm afraid. That there was a door to close at all just now came as something of a surprise.
My *friend* is trapped in there, Friday, *and* there's a fight out here that we're *losing.* We need her!
WHOOSH
Don't *interface* with it, just get it open!
I do understand, Ms. Whitehead. I'm currently trying to interface with the software, but the handshake protocol is unlike anything I've encountered before.
Wait. Stark's old suits! I'll blast it open myself! Tippy, help me--
I believe that won't be necessary, Ms. Whitehead. The machine appears to have completed its cycle.
"Cycle"? *What cycle?!*
I'm opening the door now...
Squirrel Girl, are you okay? Did the machine do anything to you?
...Squirrel Girl??

Look at us here, showing you Nancy's ***reaction*** to what she's seeing instead of what she's actually **look**ing at!! All we're doing is increasing suspense until you finish readin this text and then continue on with the comic! Okay, everything should be pretty suspenseful right about now. Thank you for reading all this text before taking even a quic glance to the right. You can go ahead now.

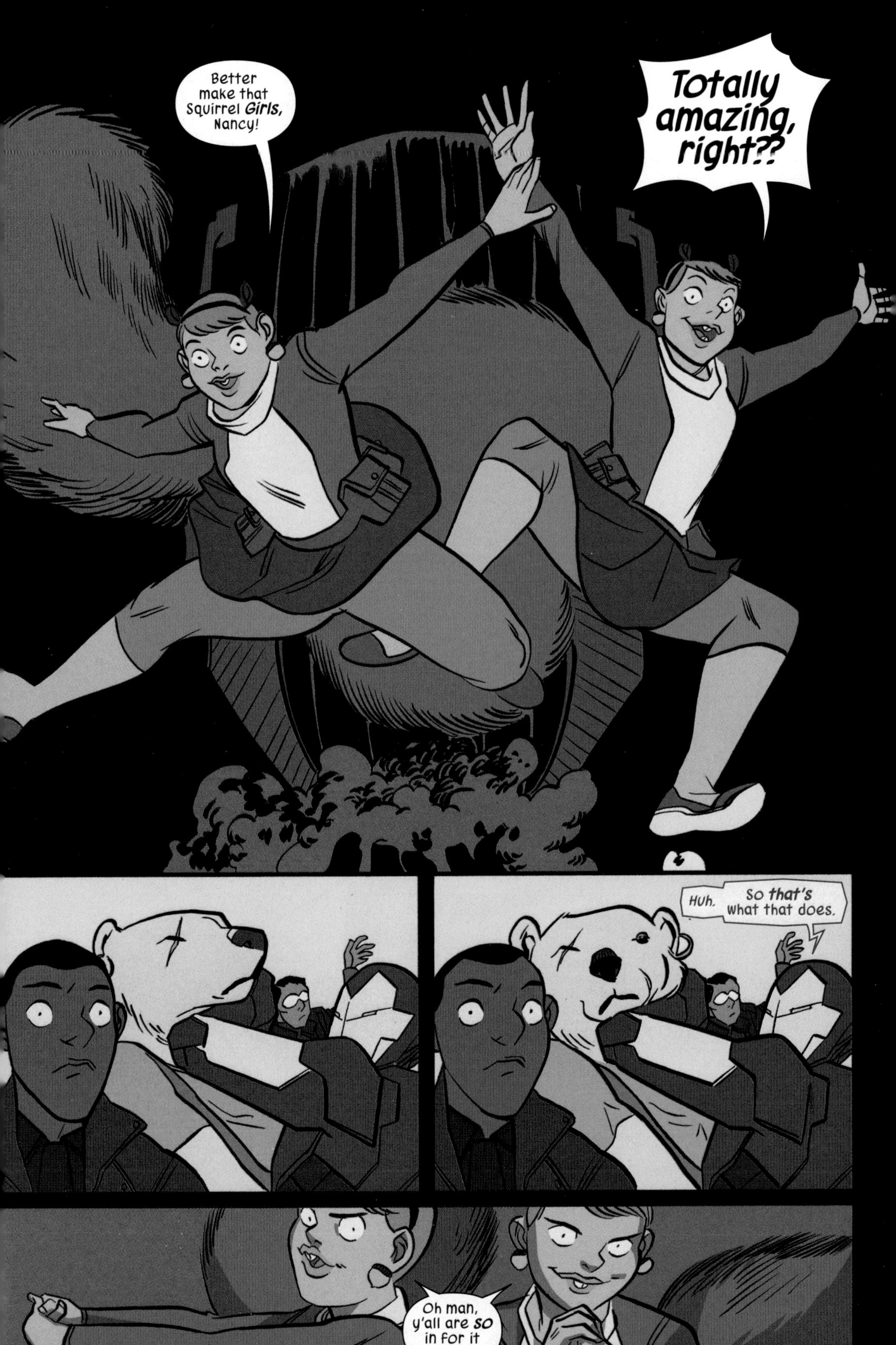
Better make that Squirrel *Girls*, Nancy!
Totally amazing, right??
HUh.
So *that's* what that does.
Oh man, y'all are *SO* in for it now.

pe you did a good job doing the connect-the-dots Squirrel Girl on the last page, because ***you made her!!*** And I don't want to explicitly ***say*** that now if anything goes wrong with her it's your fault since you're the one who drew her into existence, so instead I'll just let you...connect the dots.

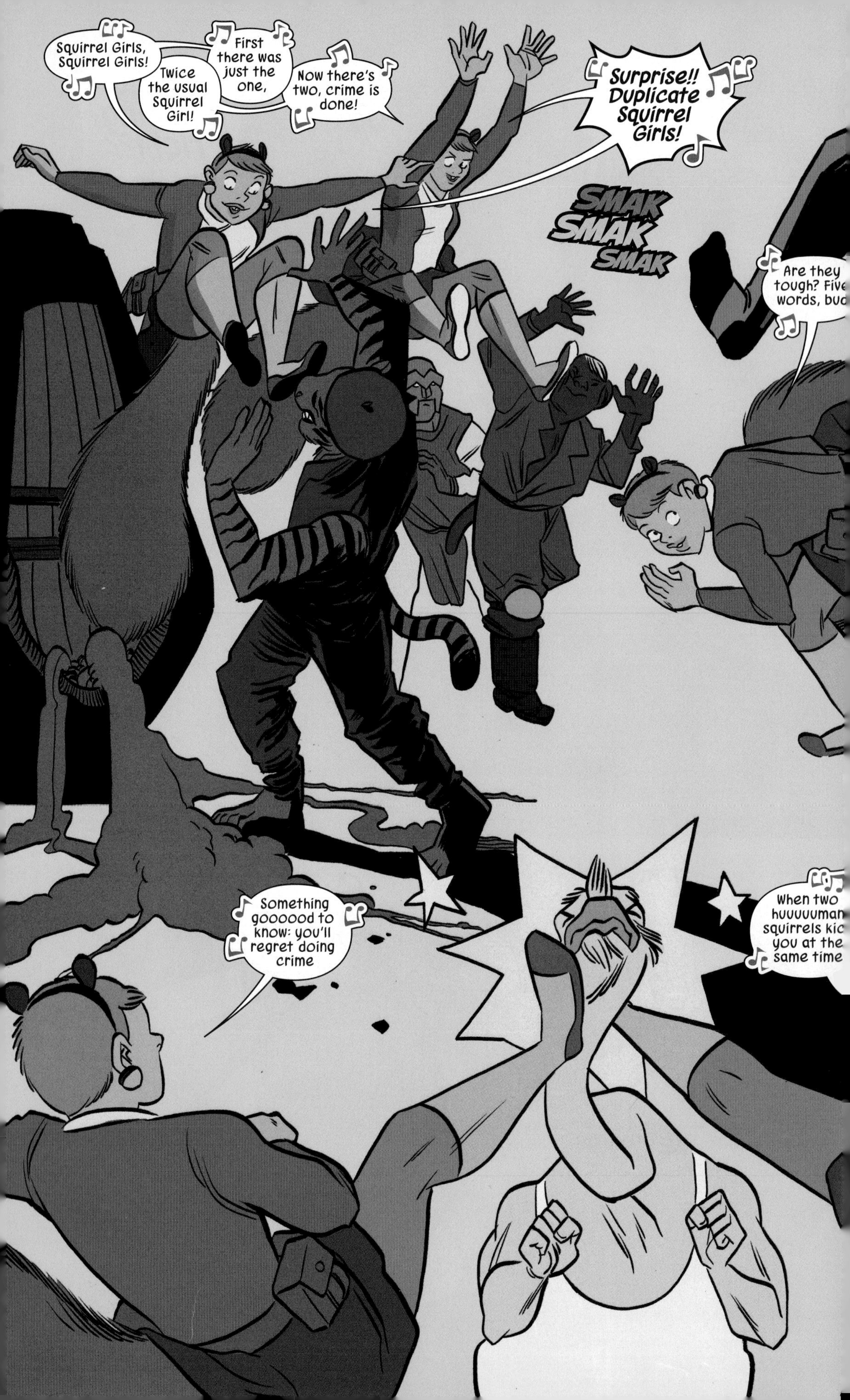
Squirrel Girls, Squirrel Girls!
First there was just the one,
Twice the usual Squirrel Girl!
Now there's two, crime is done!
Surprise!! Duplicate Squirrel Girls!
SMAK SMAK SMAK
Are they tough? Five words, bud
Something gooooood to know: you'll regret doing crime
When two huuuuuman squirrels kic you at the same time

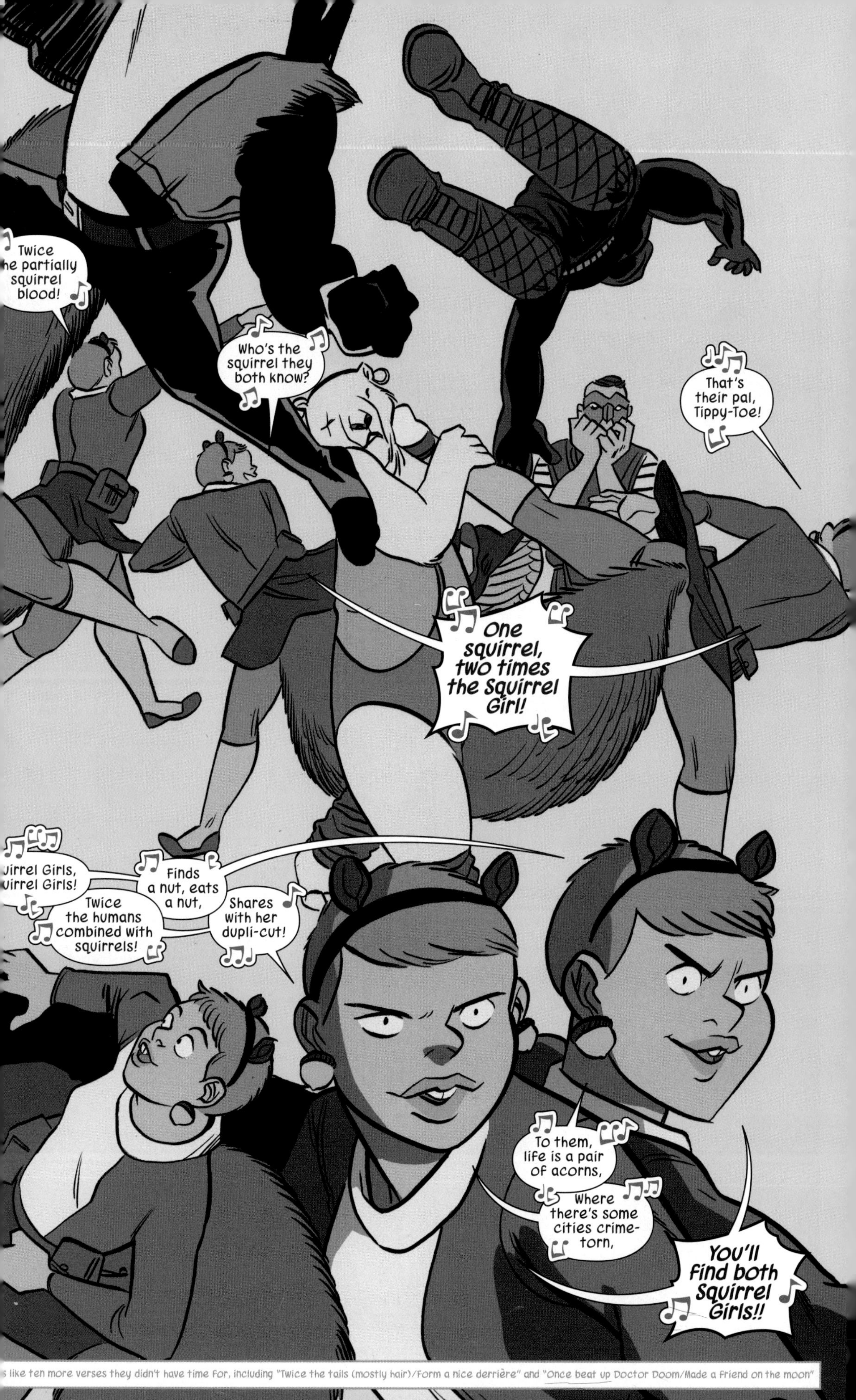
Twice he partially squirrel blood!
Who's the squirrel they both know?
That's their pal, Tippy-Toe!
One squirrel, two times the Squirrel Girl!
uirrel Girls, uirrel Girls!
Finds a nut, eats a nut,
Twice the humans combined with squirrels!
Shares with her dupli-cut!
To them, life is a pair of acorns,
Where there's some cities crime-torn,
You'll find both Squirrel Girls!!
s like ten more verses they didn't have time for, including "Twice the tails (mostly hair)/Form a nice derrière" and "Once beat up Doctor Doom/Made a friend on the moon"

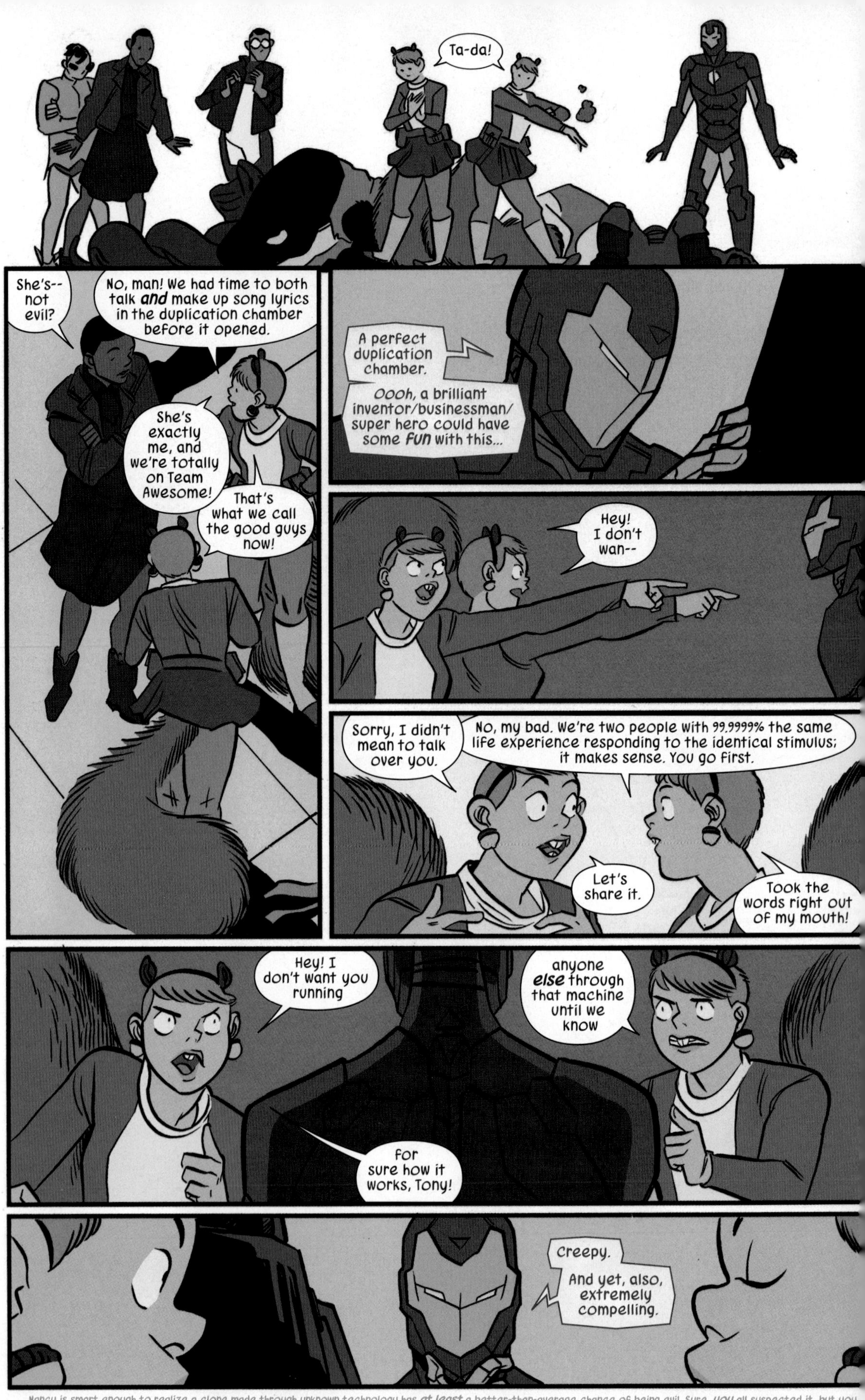
Ta-da!
She's--not evil?
No, man! We had time to both talk and make up song lyrics in the duplication chamber before it opened.
She's exactly me, and we're totally on Team Awesome!
That's what we call the good guys now!
A perfect duplication chamber.
Oooh, a brilliant inventor/businessman/super hero could have some fun with this...
Hey! I don't wan--
Sorry, I didn't mean to talk over you.
No, my bad. We're two people with 99.9999% the same life experience responding to the identical stimulus; it makes sense. You go first.
Let's share it.
Took the words right out of my mouth!
Hey! I don't want you running
anyone else through that machine until we know
for sure how it works, Tony!
Creepy.
And yet, also, extremely compelling.

Nancy is smart enough to realize a clone made through unknown technology has *at least* a better-than-average chance of being evil. Sure, *you* all suspected it, but you know this book has "Squirrel Girl Beats Up The Marvel Universe!" on the cover! You were cheating before you even opened the book!

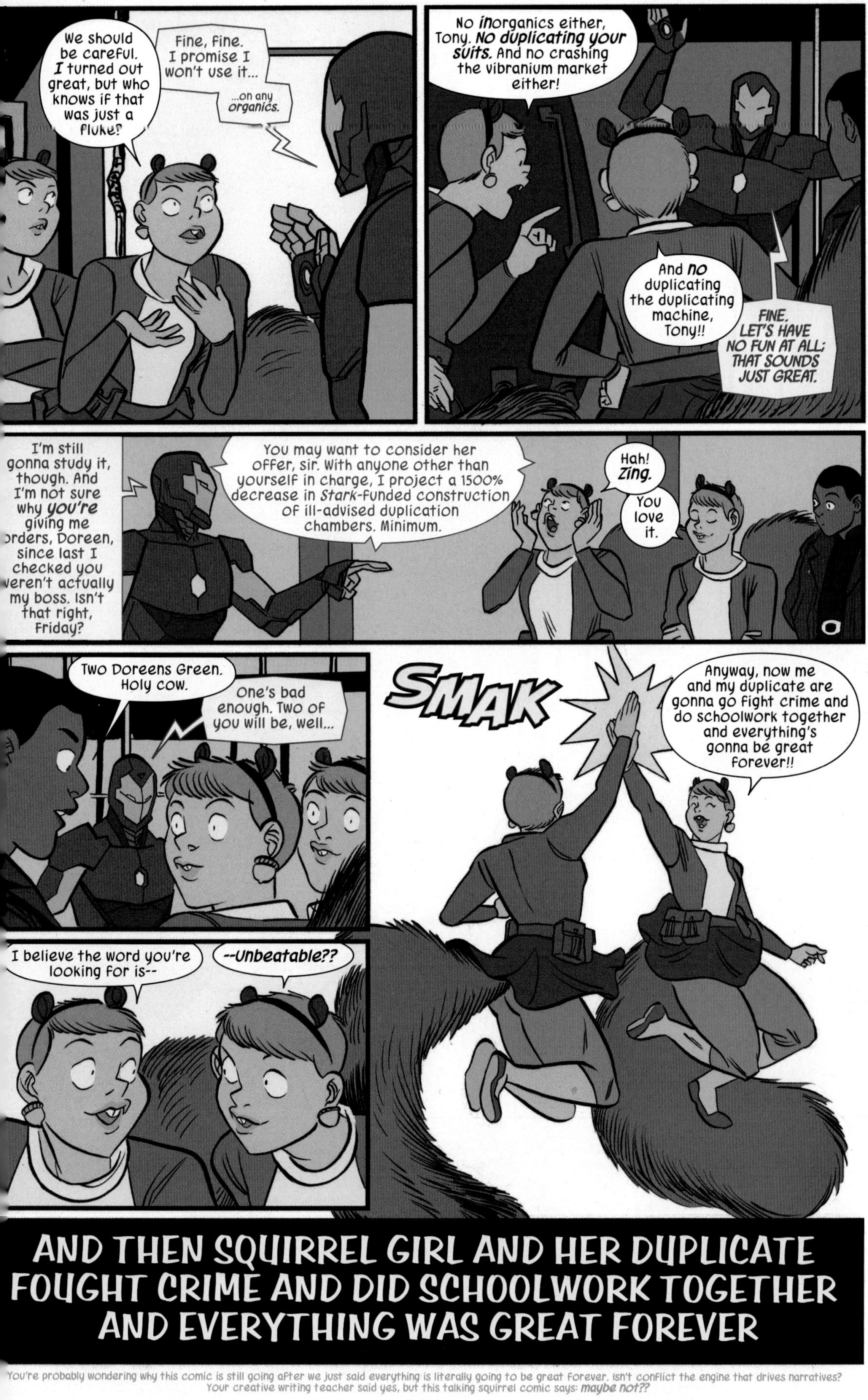
We should be careful. *I* turned out great, but who knows if that was just a fluke?
Fine, fine. I promise I won't use it...
...on any *organics.*
No *in*organics either, Tony. *No duplicating your suits.* And no crashing the vibranium market either!
And *no* duplicating the duplicating machine, Tony!!
FINE. LET'S HAVE NO FUN AT ALL; THAT SOUNDS JUST GREAT.
I'm still gonna study it, though. And I'm not sure why *you're* giving me rders, Doreen, since last I checked you eren't actually my boss. Isn't that right, Friday?
You may want to consider her offer, sir. With anyone other than yourself in charge, I project a 1500% decrease in *Stark*-funded construction of ill-advised duplication chambers. Minimum.
Hah! *Zing.*
You love it.
Two Doreens Green. Holy cow.
One's bad enough. Two of you will be, well...
I believe the word you're looking for is--
--Unbeatable??
SMAK
Anyway, now me and my duplicate are gonna go fight crime and do schoolwork together and everything's gonna be great forever!!
AND THEN SQUIRREL GIRL AND HER DUPLICATE FOUGHT CRIME AND DID SCHOOLWORK TOGETHER AND EVERYTHING WAS GREAT FOREVER

You're probably wondering why this comic is still going after we just said everything is literally going to be great forever. Isn't conflict the engine that drives narratives? Your creative writing teacher said yes, but this talking squirrel comic says: ***maybe not??***

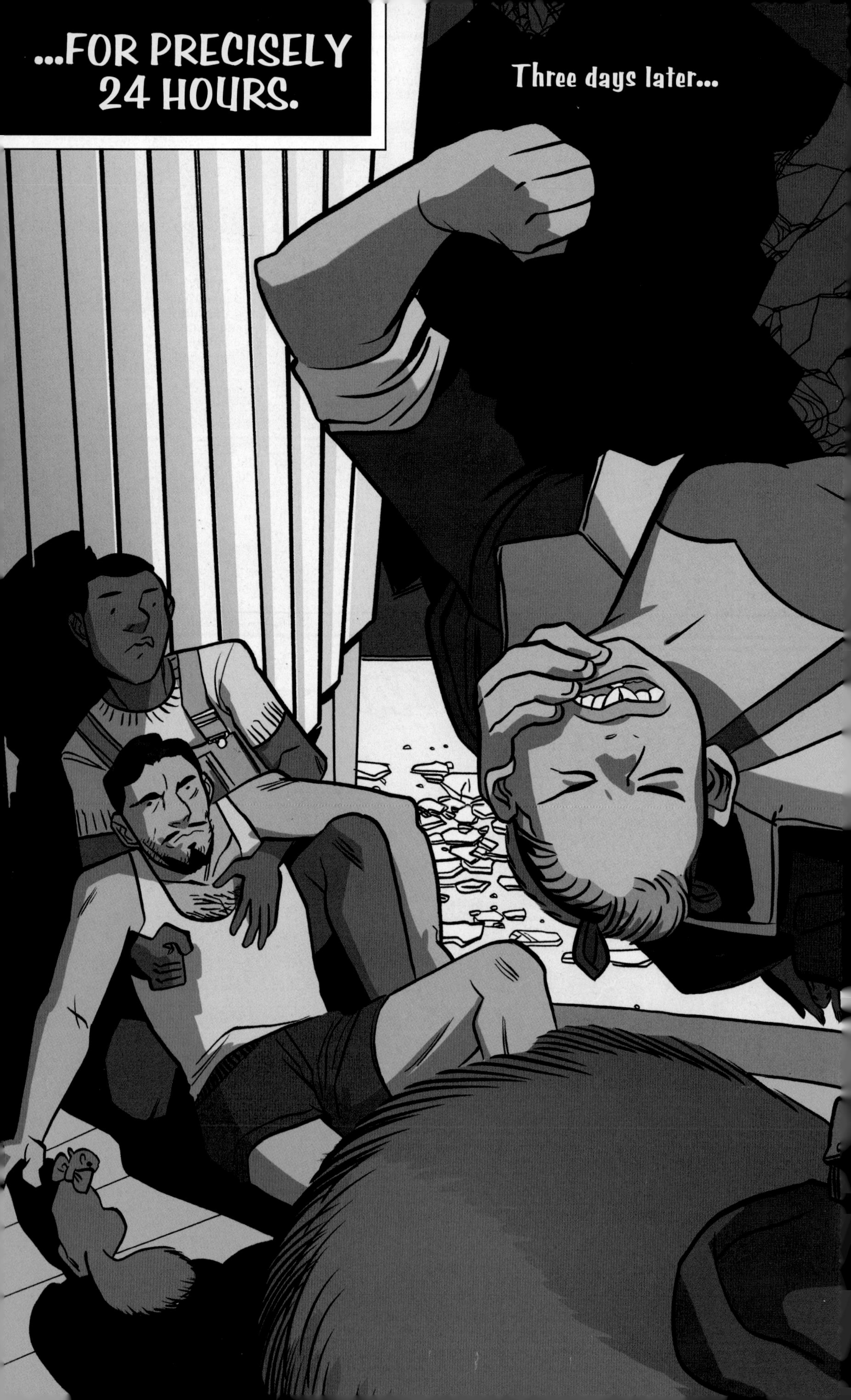
...FOR PRECISELY 24 HOURS.
Three days later...

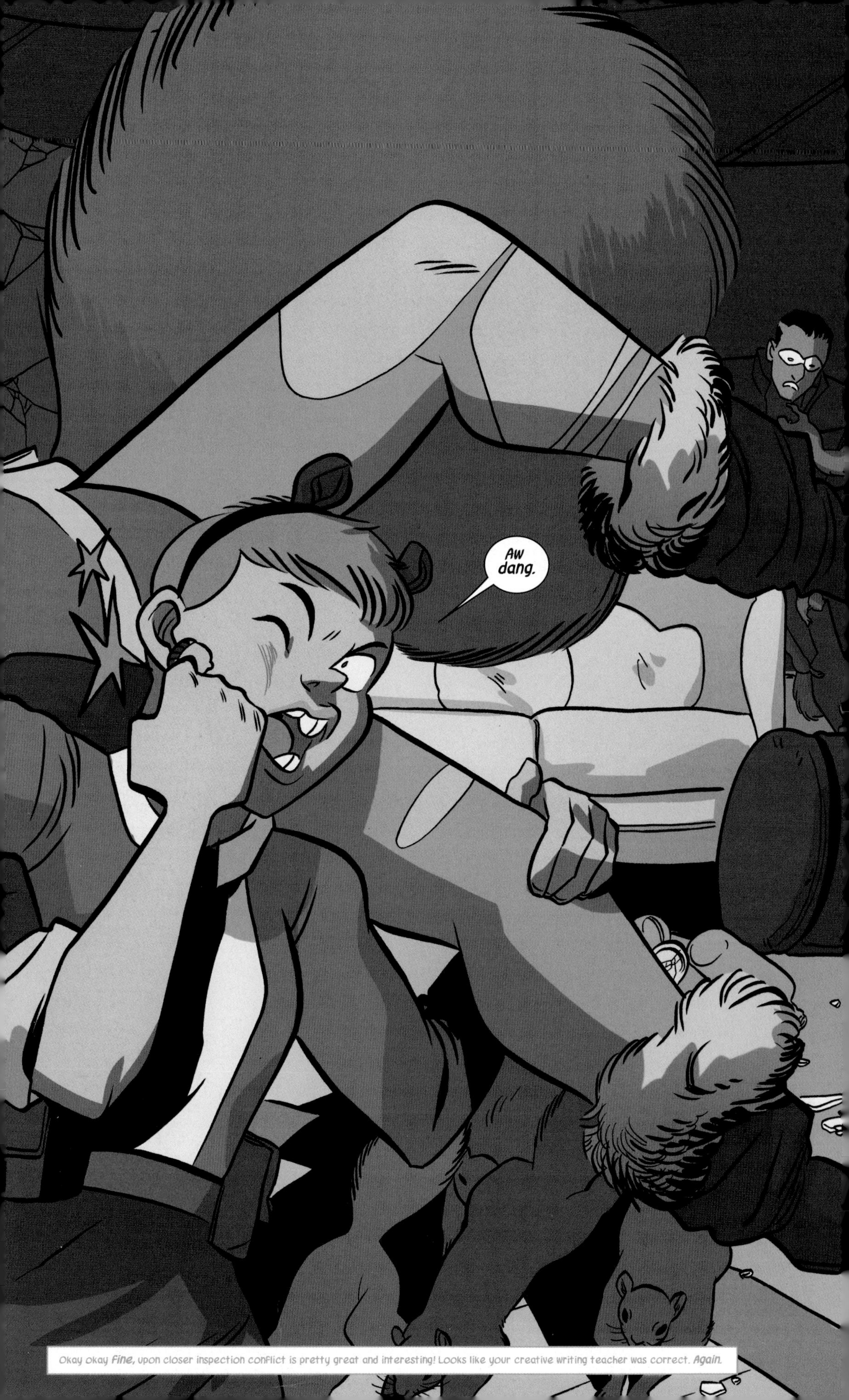
Aw dang.
Okay okay *Fine,* upon closer inspection conflict is pretty great and interesting! Looks like your creative writing teacher was correct. *Again.*

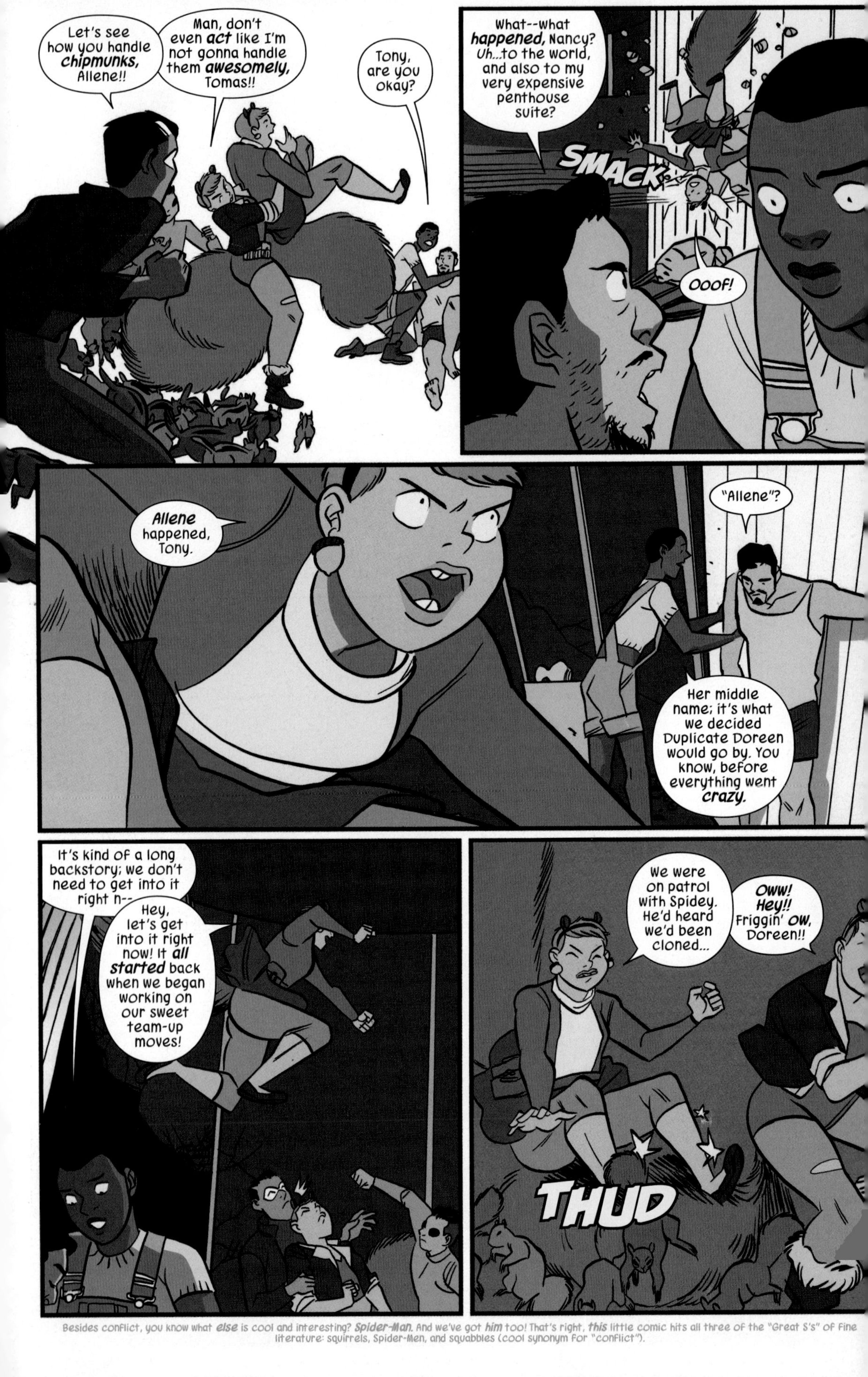
Let's see how you handle chipmunks, Allene!!
Man, don't even act like I'm not gonna handle them awesomely, Tomas!!
Tony, are you okay?
What--what happened, Nancy? Uh...to the world, and also to my very expensive penthouse suite?
SMACK
OOOF!
Allene happened, Tony.
"Allene"?
Her middle name; it's what we decided Duplicate Doreen would go by. You know, before everything went crazy.
It's kind of a long backstory; we don't need to get into it right n--
Hey, let's get into it right now! It all started back when we began working on our sweet team-up moves!
We were on patrol with Spidey. He'd heard we'd been cloned...
Oww! Hey!! Friggin' OW, Doreen!!
THUD

Besides conflict, you know what *else* is cool and interesting? *Spider-Man.* And we've got *him* too! That's right, *this* little comic hits all three of the "Great S's" of Fine literature: squirrels, Spider-Men, and squabbles (cool synonym for "conflict").

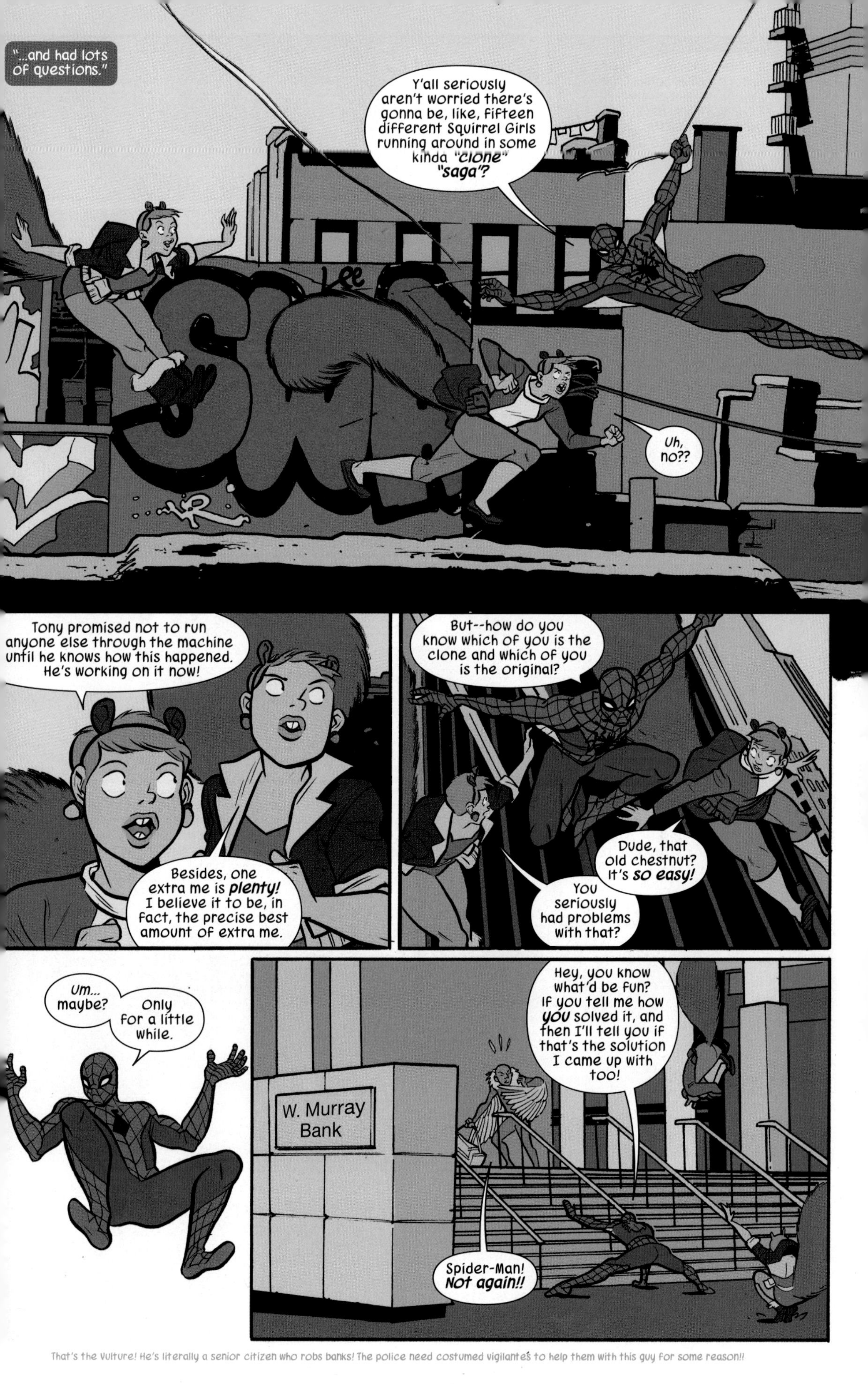
"...and had lots of questions."
Y'all seriously aren't worried there's gonna be, like, fifteen different Squirrel Girls running around in some kinda "clone" "saga"?
Uh, no??
Tony promised not to run anyone else through the machine until he knows how this happened. He's working on it now!
Besides, one extra me is plenty! I believe it to be, in fact, the precise best amount of extra me.
But--how do you know which of you is the clone and which of you is the original?
Dude, that old chestnut? It's so easy!
You seriously had problems with that?
Um... maybe?
Only for a little while.
W. Murray Bank
Hey, you know what'd be fun? If you tell me how you solved it, and then I'll tell you if that's the solution I came up with too!
Spider-Man! Not again!!

That's the Vulture! He's literally a senior citizen who robs banks! The police need costumed vigilantes to help them with this guy for some reason!!

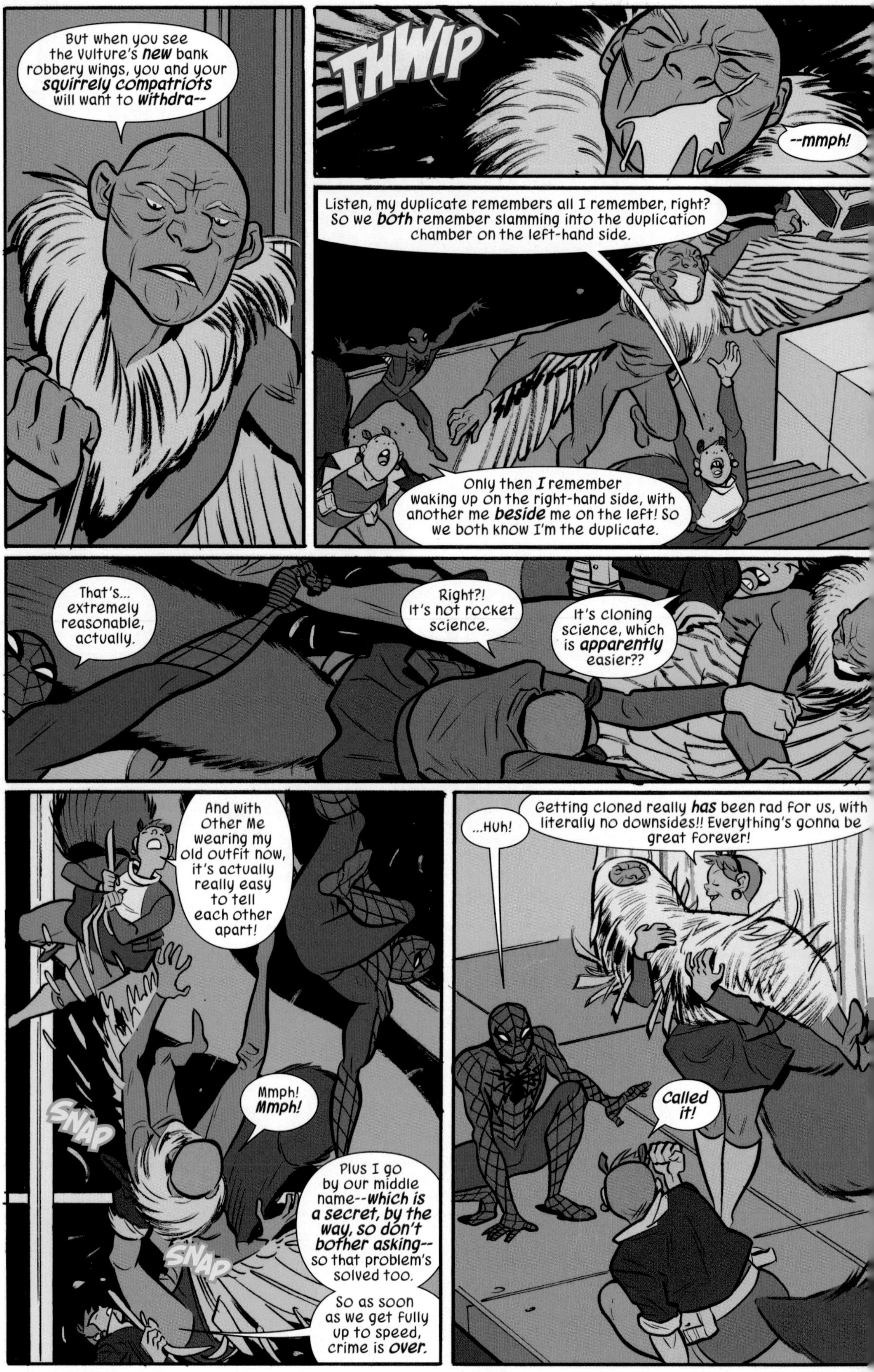
But when you see the Vulture's *new* bank robbery wings, you and your *squirrely compatriots* will want to *withdra--*
THWIP
--mmph!
Listen, my duplicate remembers all I remember, right? So we *both* remember slamming into the duplication chamber on the left-hand side.
Only then *I* remember waking up on the right-hand side, with another me *beside* me on the left! So we both know I'm the duplicate.
That's... extremely reasonable, actually.
Right?! It's not rocket science.
It's cloning science, which is *apparently* easier??
And with Other Me wearing my old outfit now, it's actually really easy to tell each other apart!
SNAP
Mmph! *Mmph!*
SNAP
Plus I go by our middle name--*which is a secret, by the way, so don't bother asking--* so that problem's solved too.
So as soon as we get fully up to speed, crime is *over.*
...Huh!
Getting cloned really *has* been rad for us, with literally no downsides!! Everything's gonna be great forever!
Called it!

The reason rocket science has a reputation for being hard is that it's *real difficult* to focus on the actual work of science when there's all those fun rockets lying aroun

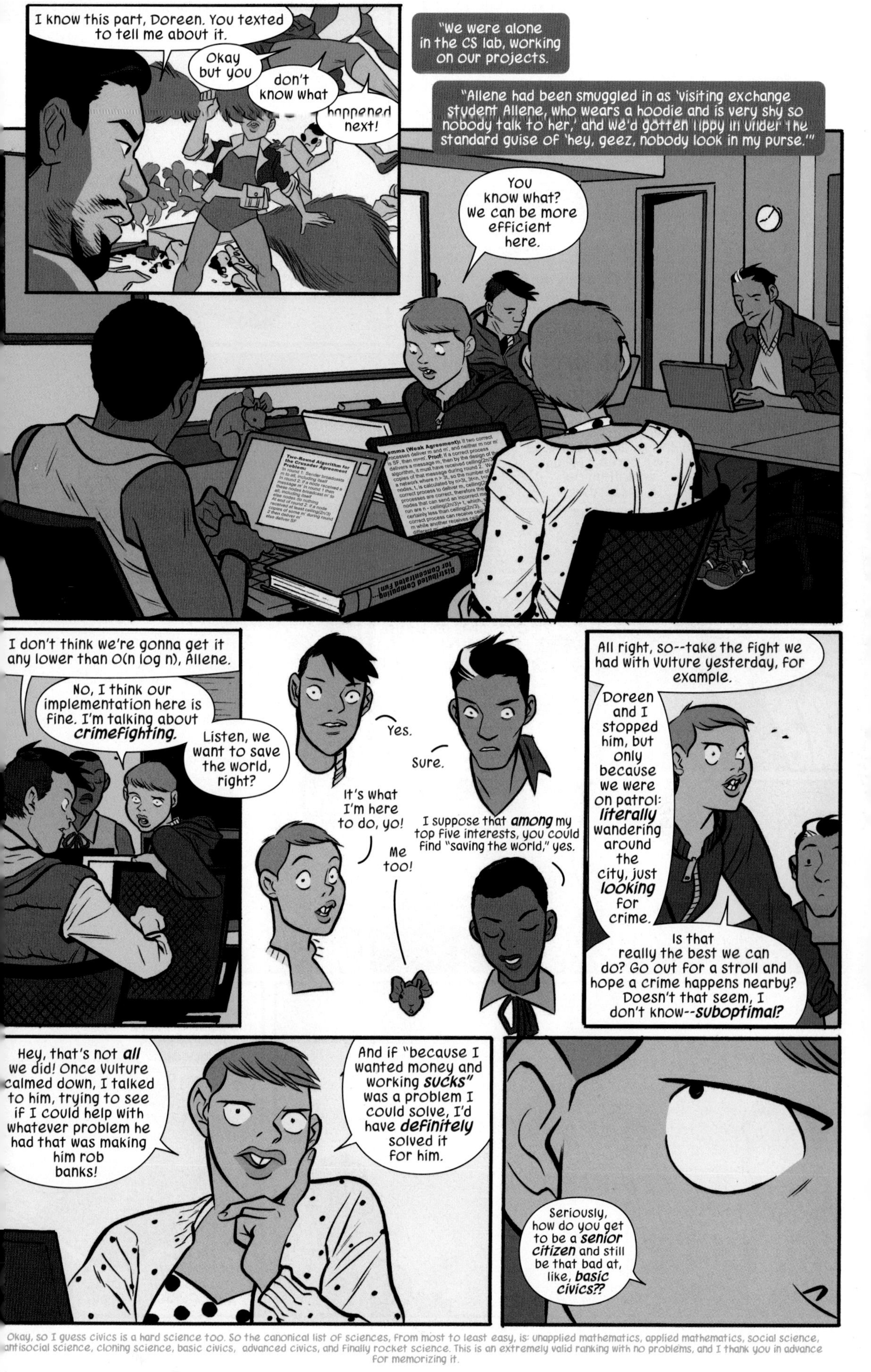
I know this part, Doreen. You texted to tell me about it.
Okay but you
don't know what
happened next!
"We were alone in the CS lab, working on our projects.
"Allene had been smuggled in as 'visiting exchange student Allene, who wears a hoodie and is very shy so nobody talk to her,' and we'd gotten Tippy in under the standard guise of 'hey, geez, nobody look in my purse.'"
You know what? We can be more efficient here.
Two-Round Algorithm for the Crusader Agreement Problem:
Lemma (Weak Agreement):
I don't think we're gonna get it any lower than O(n log n), Allene.
No, I think our implementation here is fine. I'm talking about *crimefighting.*
Listen, we want to save the world, right?
Yes.
Sure.
It's what I'm here to do, yo!
Me too!
I suppose that *among* my top five interests, you could find "saving the world," yes.
All right, so--take the fight we had with Vulture yesterday, for example.
Doreen and I stopped him, but only because we were on patrol: *literally* wandering around the city, just *looking* for crime.
Is that really the best we can do? Go out for a stroll and hope a crime happens nearby? Doesn't that seem, I don't know--*suboptimal?*
Hey, that's not *all* we did! Once Vulture calmed down, I talked to him, trying to see if I could help with whatever problem he had that was making him rob banks!
And if "because I wanted money and working *sucks*" was a problem I could solve, I'd have *definitely* solved it for him.
Seriously, how do you get to be a *senior citizen* and still be that bad at, like, *basic civics??*

Okay, so I guess civics is a hard science too. So the canonical list of sciences, from most to least easy, is: unapplied mathematics, applied mathematics, social science, antisocial science, cloning science, basic civics, advanced civics, and finally rocket science. This is an extremely valid ranking with no problems, and I thank you in advance for memorizing it.

You've got a better idea, Allene?

I do! The way we're fighting crime out there? It can be done better.

We **have** authority, but we're not using it. Not as much as we could.

```
IF ($status==REACTIVE){
        bad_and_sucky();
}ELSE IF ($status==PROACTIVE){
        well_NOW_we're_talking();
}
```

Up to now, we've been **reactive**: we wait for something bad to happen, and then we fix it.

```
IF ($status==REACTIVE){
    bad_and_sucky();
}ELSE IF ($stat...ACTIVE){
    we...talking
}
```

It's like our first run at our networking assignment: we were doing work we didn't **need** to, because we weren't fully exploiting our resources.

...Holy crap, I see where you're going with this! Efficiency, right? Saving the world by **preventing** the bad things from happening in the first place?

Exactly. And we do **that** by **leveling ourselves up.** We use the squirrel scouts, chipmunk corps, and fish navy like what they actually **are**...

...a worldwide, universal collection of invisible, always-on **peacekeepers.**

```
well_NOW_we're_talking(){
    //Squirrel Avengers Initiative
    while (can_talk_to_squirrels()){
        worldwide_squirrel_humanitarian_aid();
        worldwide_squirrel_environmental_se...
        worldwide_squirrel_public_health...
        worldwide_squirrel_waste_disposal...
        shell(and_MORE.exe);
```

No way. Shut up.

This just might **work.**

WRITE WRITE WRITE

Ta-da!

Uh, can you explain that for the squirrels here who **don't** know pseudocode?

Oh my gosh, Tippy! I'm so sorry! **OF course!**

Sorry, Tippy!

I have two degrees in computer science and I am here to tell you that this is completely valid pseudocode and programmers actually do model programs like this. Most do tend to use fewer squirrels in their function names, but pobody's nerfect.

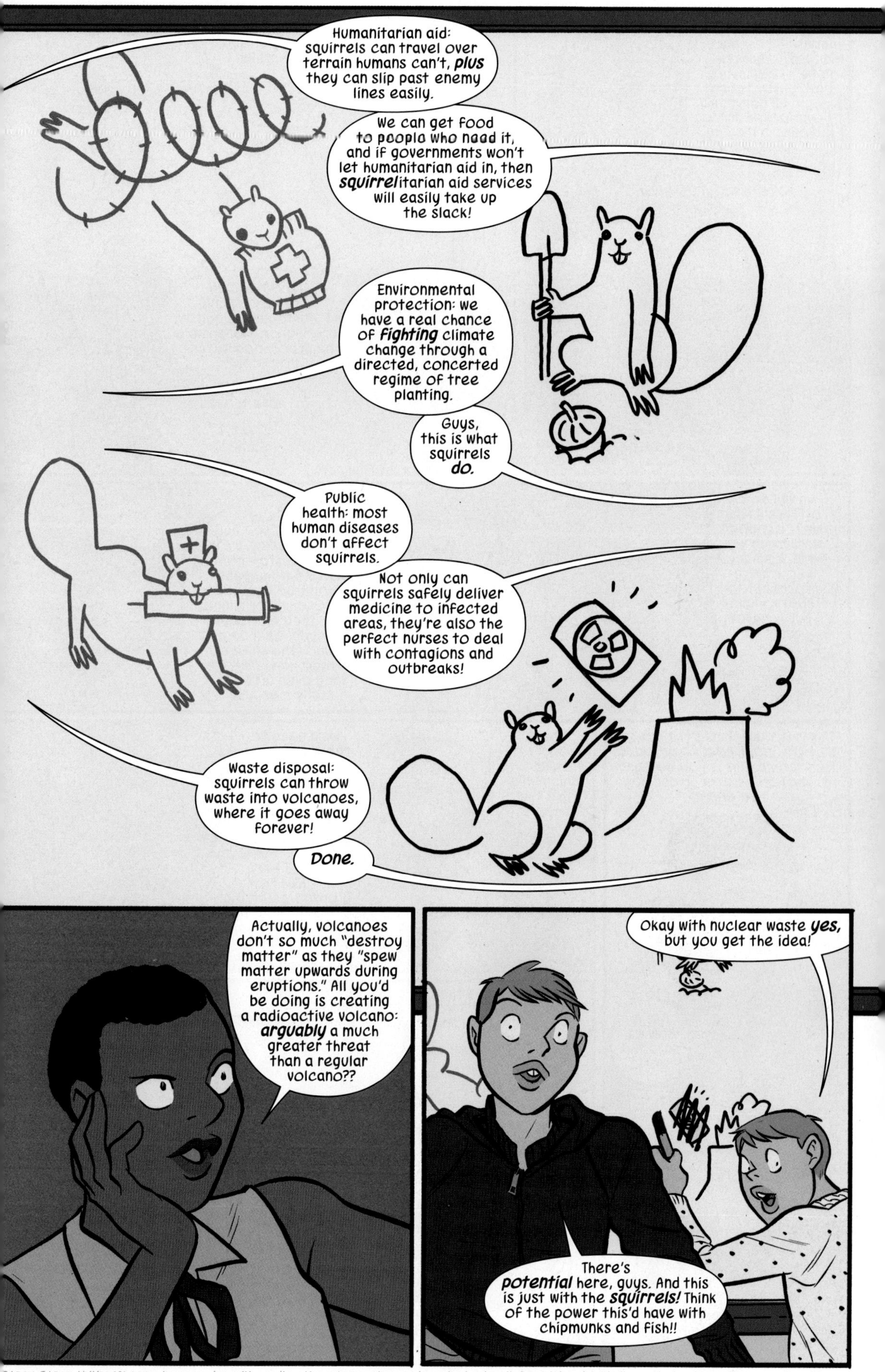
Humanitarian aid: squirrels can travel over terrain humans can't, *plus* they can slip past enemy lines easily.
We can get food to people who need it, and if governments won't let humanitarian aid in, then *squirrel*itarian aid services will easily take up the slack!
Environmental protection: we have a real chance of *fighting* climate change through a directed, concerted regime of tree planting.
Guys, this is what squirrels *do.*
Public health: most human diseases don't affect squirrels.
Not only can squirrels safely deliver medicine to infected areas, they're also the perfect nurses to deal with contagions and outbreaks!
Waste disposal: squirrels can throw waste into volcanoes, where it goes away forever!
Done.
Actually, volcanoes don't so much "destroy matter" as they "spew matter upwards during eruptions." All you'd be doing is creating a radioactive volcano: *arguably* a much greater threat than a regular volcano??
Okay with nuclear waste *yes,* but you get the idea!
There's *potential* here, guys. And this is just with the *squirrels!* Think of the power this'd have with chipmunks and fish!!

I know, I know, Writing 101: never tease readers with a radioactive volcano unless you're going to show it. So at this point I invite you to imagine a volcano erupting with a stick figure running away shouting "why? why did our political leaders think this was a good idea??"

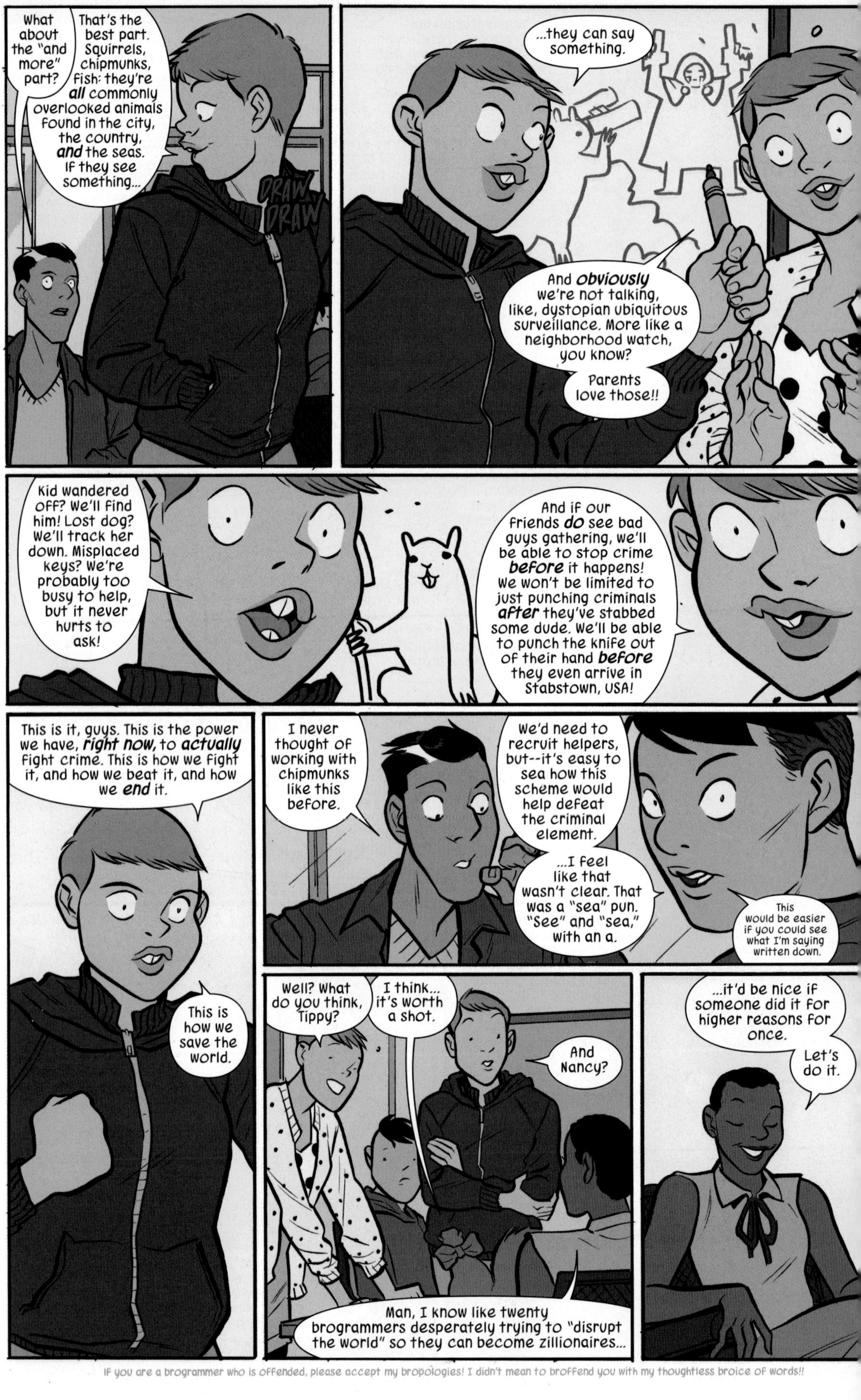
What about the "and more" part?
That's the best part. Squirrels, chipmunks, fish: they're **all** commonly overlooked animals found in the city, the country, **and** the seas. If they see something...
DRAW DRAW
...they can say something.
And **obviously** we're not talking, like, dystopian ubiquitous surveillance. More like a neighborhood watch, you know?
Parents love those!!
Kid wandered off? We'll find him! Lost dog? We'll track her down. Misplaced keys? We're probably too busy to help, but it never hurts to ask!
And if our friends **do** see bad guys gathering, we'll be able to stop crime **before** it happens! We won't be limited to just punching criminals **after** they've stabbed some dude. We'll be able to punch the knife out of their hand **before** they even arrive in Stabstown, USA!
This is it, guys. This is the power we have, **right now,** to **actually** fight crime. This is how we fight it, and how we beat it, and how we **end** it.
This is how we save the world.
I never thought of working with chipmunks like this before.
We'd need to recruit helpers, but--it's easy to sea how this scheme would help defeat the criminal element.
...I feel like that wasn't clear. That was a "sea" pun. "See" and "sea," with an a.
This would be easier if you could see what I'm saying written down.
Well? What do you think, Tippy?
I think... it's worth a shot.
And Nancy?
Man, I know like twenty brogrammers desperately trying to "disrupt the world" so they can become zillionaires...
...it'd be nice if someone did it for higher reasons for once.
Let's do it.

If you are a brogrammer who is offended, please accept my bropologies! I didn't mean to broffend you with my thoughtless broice of words!!

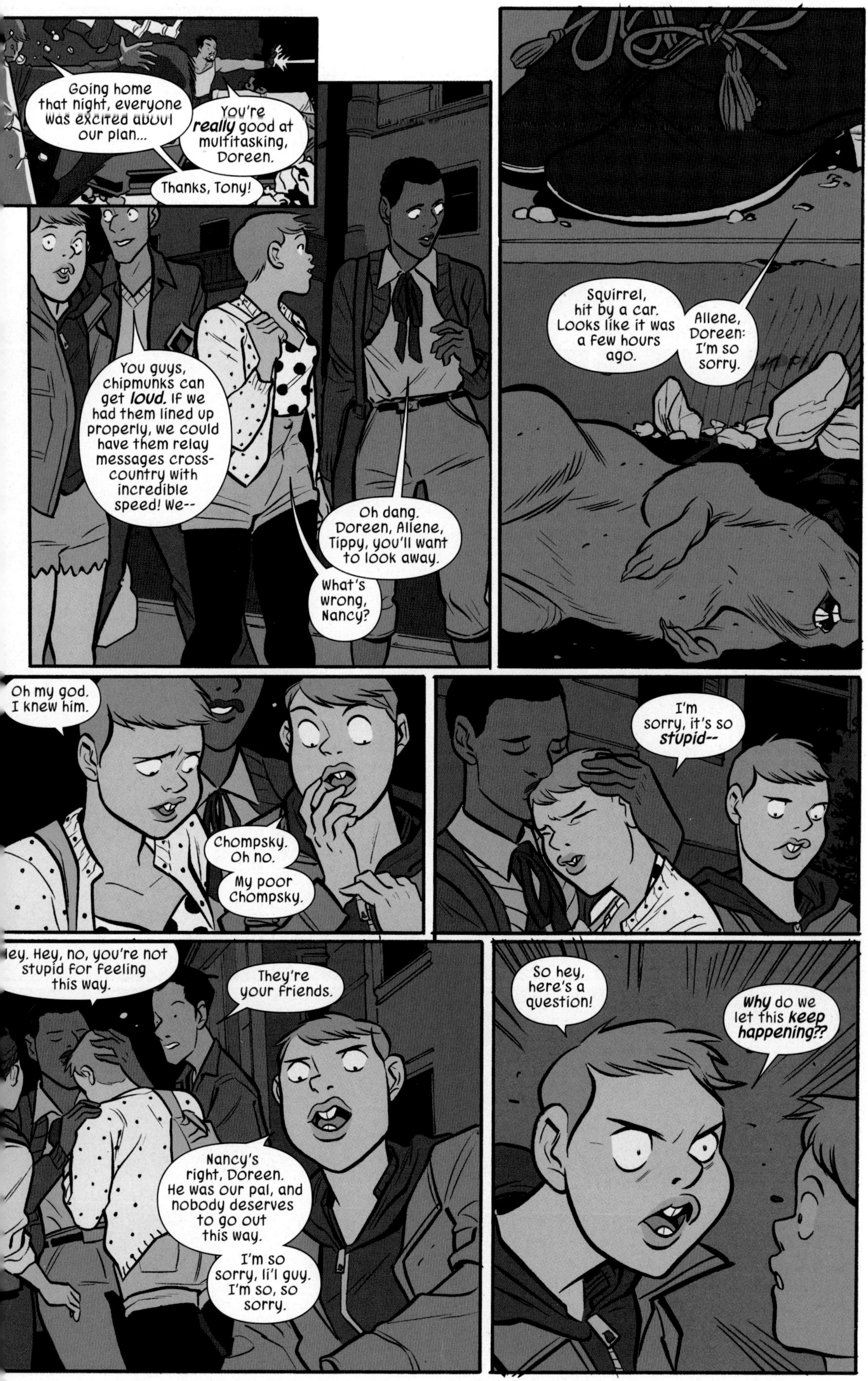

Going home that night, everyone was excited about our plan...
You're *really* good at multitasking, Doreen.
Thanks, Tony!
You guys, chipmunks can get *loud.* If we had them lined up properly, we could have them relay messages cross-country with incredible speed! We--
Oh dang. Doreen, Allene, Tippy, you'll want to look away.
What's wrong, Nancy?
Squirrel, hit by a car. Looks like it was a few hours ago.
Allene, Doreen: I'm so sorry.
Oh my god. I knew him.
Chompsky. Oh no.
My poor Chompsky.
I'm sorry, it's so *stupid--*
Hey. Hey, no, you're not stupid for feeling this way.
They're your friends.
Nancy's right, Doreen. He was our pal, and nobody deserves to go out this way.
I'm so sorry, li'l guy. I'm so, so sorry.
So hey, here's a question!
Why do we let this *keep happening??*

Chompsky is a squirrel who bit a guy named "Bonehead" in the butt in a previous issue. Bonehead had appeared in other comics, but clearly the ultimate expression of this dynamic character was to get bit in the butt by a squirrel. RIP Chompsky.

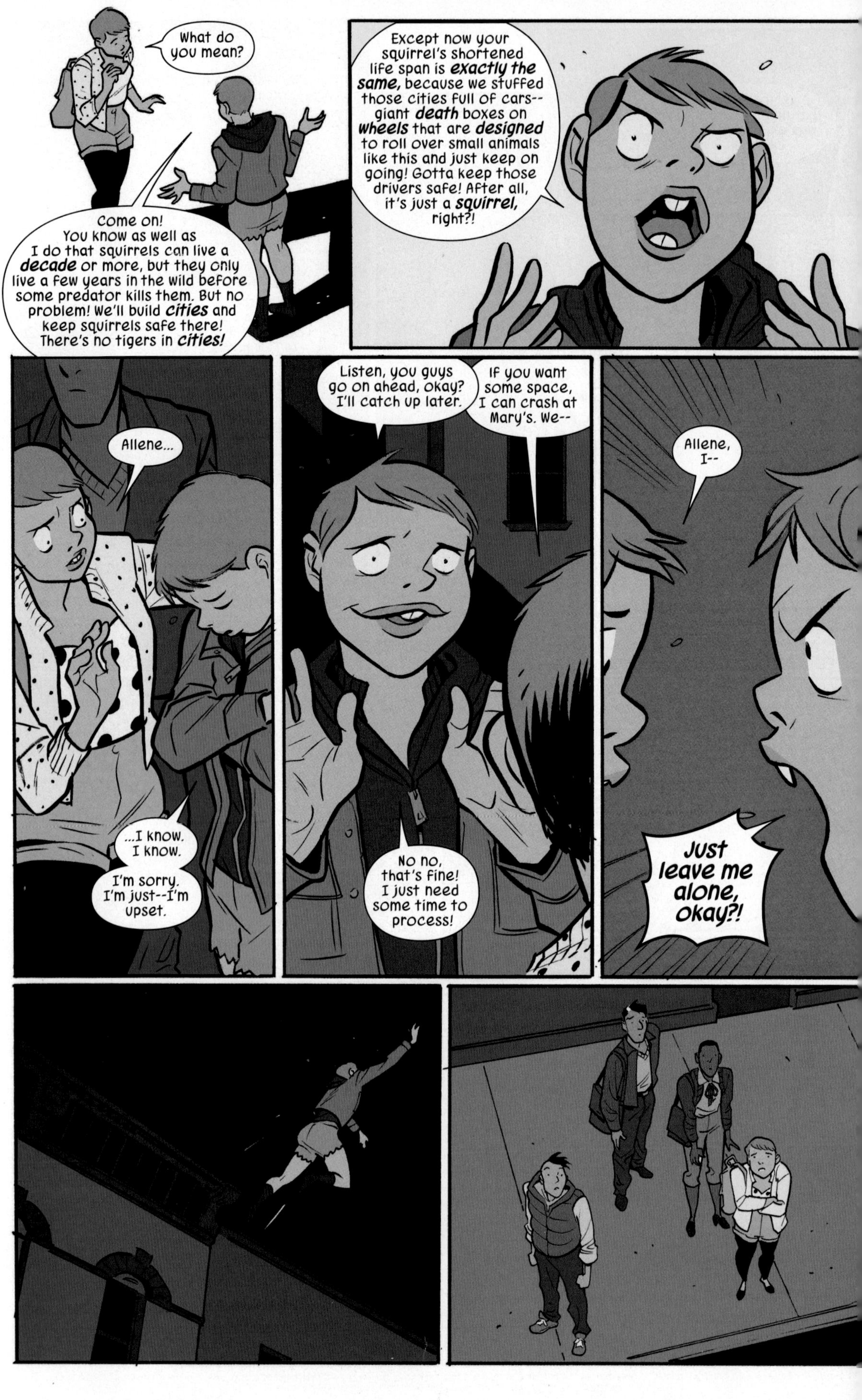
What do you mean?
Come on! You know as well as I do that squirrels can live a *decade* or more, but they only live a few years in the wild before some predator kills them. But no problem! We'll build *cities* and keep squirrels safe there! There's no tigers in *cities!*
Except now your squirrel's shortened life span is *exactly the same,* because we stuffed those cities full of cars-- giant *death* boxes on *wheels* that are *designed* to roll over small animals like this and just keep on going! Gotta keep those drivers safe! After all, it's just a *squirrel,* right?!
Allene...
...I know. I know.
I'm sorry. I'm just--I'm upset.
Listen, you guys go on ahead, okay? I'll catch up later.
If you want some space, I can crash at Mary's. We--
No no, that's fine! I just need some time to process!
Allene, I--
Just leave me alone, okay?!

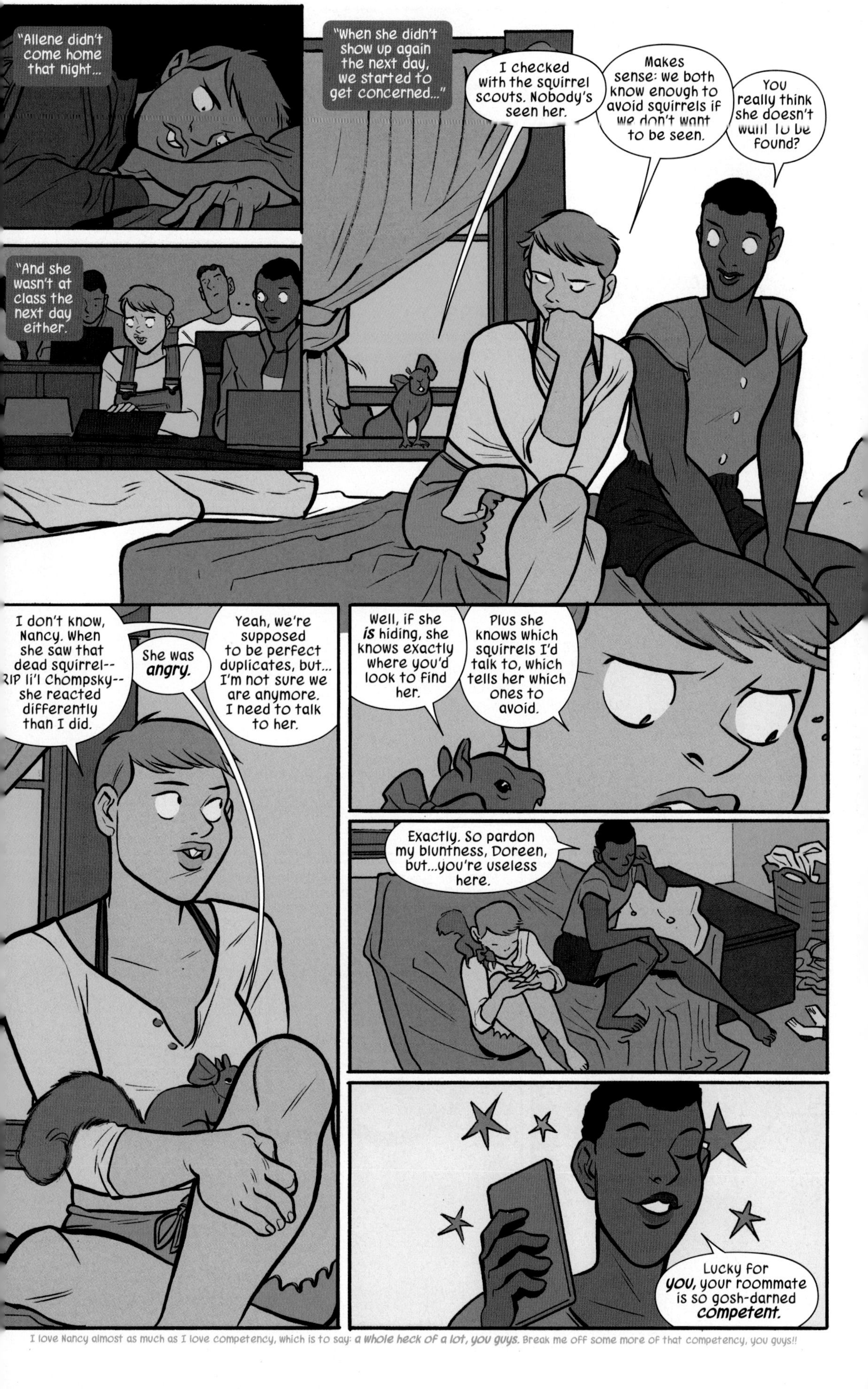
"Allene didn't come home that night...
"And she wasn't at class the next day either.
"When she didn't show up again the next day, we started to get concerned..."
I checked with the squirrel scouts. Nobody's seen her.
Makes sense: we both know enough to avoid squirrels if we don't want to be seen.
You really think she doesn't want to be found?
I don't know, Nancy. When she saw that dead squirrel-- RIP li'l Chompsky-- she reacted differently than I did.
She was angry.
Yeah, we're supposed to be perfect duplicates, but... I'm not sure we are anymore. I need to talk to her.
Well, if she is hiding, she knows exactly where you'd look to find her.
Plus she knows which squirrels I'd talk to, which tells her which ones to avoid.
Exactly. So pardon my bluntness, Doreen, but...you're useless here.
Lucky for you, your roommate is so gosh-darned competent.

I love Nancy almost as much as I love competency, which is to say: ***a whole heck of a lot, you guys.*** Break me off some more of that competency, you guys!!

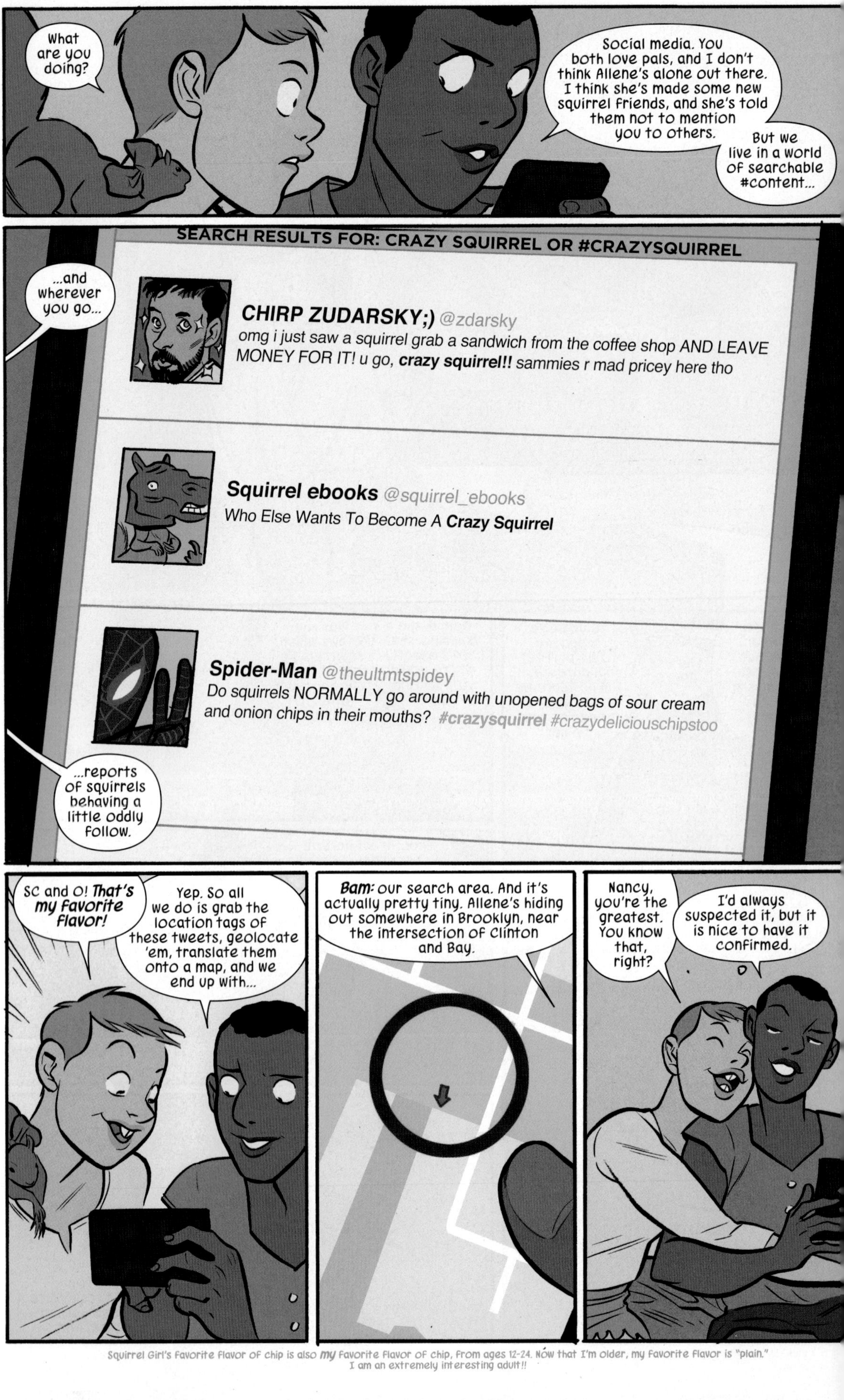
What are you doing?
Social media. You both love pals, and I don't think Allene's alone out there. I think she's made some new squirrel friends, and she's told them not to mention you to others.
But we live in a world of searchable #content...
SEARCH RESULTS FOR: CRAZY SQUIRREL OR #CRAZYSQUIRREL
...and wherever you go...
CHIRP ZUDARSKY;) @zdarsky
omg i just saw a squirrel grab a sandwich from the coffee shop AND LEAVE MONEY FOR IT! u go, crazy squirrel!! sammies r mad pricey here tho
Squirrel ebooks @squirrel_ebooks
Who Else Wants To Become A Crazy Squirrel
Spider-Man @theultmtspidey
Do squirrels NORMALLY go around with unopened bags of sour cream and onion chips in their mouths? #crazysquirrel #crazydeliciouschipstoo
...reports of squirrels behaving a little oddly follow.
SC and O! That's my favorite flavor!
Yep. So all we do is grab the location tags of these tweets, geolocate 'em, translate them onto a map, and we end up with...
Bam: our search area. And it's actually pretty tiny. Allene's hiding out somewhere in Brooklyn, near the intersection of Clinton and Bay.
Nancy, you're the greatest. You know that, right?
I'd always suspected it, but it is nice to have it confirmed.

Squirrel Girl's favorite flavor of chip is also *my* favorite flavor of chip, from ages 12-24. Now that I'm older, my favorite flavor is "plain."
I am an extremely interesting adult!!

That night...

Okay, come on. This is by *far* the most likely secret hideout on the block.

But it's so *dour.*

If I were gonna run away from home, I'd like to think I'd find someplace that didn't look like an abandoned *nightmare factory.*

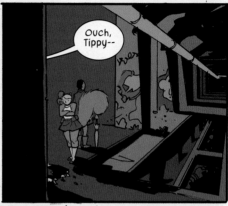

I like it! Lots of places to hide nuts.

Ouch, Tippy--

--who you calling a nut?

Allene!!

We were so *worried* about you, Allene!!

Right. Sorry for running off like that earlier. I needed to, I don't know...

...do some thinking.

And have you done it? Your thinking? You've thought everything over and everything's great forever now and you're gonna come home?

Not quite. I've had a breakthrough, Doreen.

And *this* you'll really want to see.

ON Klik

Why does everyone always set up their secret bases in the abandoned nightmare factories? Why couldn't they use the well-lit artisanal cupcake depositories instead?? This is *Brooklyn.* There's like fifty of 'em right around the block!!

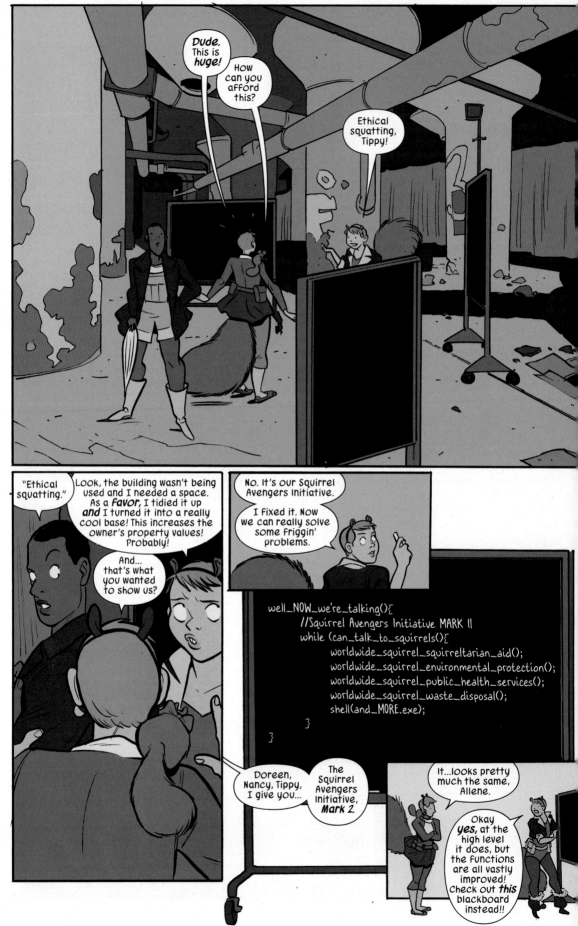

Dude. This is *huge!*

How can you afford this?

Ethical squatting, Tippy!

"Ethical squatting."

Look, the building wasn't being used and I needed a space. As a *favor,* I tidied it up *and* I turned it into a really cool base! This increases the owner's property values! Probably!

And... that's what you wanted to show us?

No. It's our Squirrel Avengers Initiative.

I fixed it. Now we can really solve some friggin' problems.

```
well_NOW_we're_talking(){
        //Squirrel Avengers Initiative MARK II
        while (can_talk_to_squirrels(){
                worldwide_squirrel_squirreltarian_aid();
                worldwide_squirrel_environmental_protection();
                worldwide_squirrel_public_health_services();
                worldwide_squirrel_waste_disposal();
                shell(and_MORE.exe);

        }
}
```

Doreen, Nancy, Tippy, I give you...

The Squirrel Avengers Initiative, *Mark 2.*

It...looks pretty much the same, Allene.

Okay *yes,* at the high level it does, but the functions are all vastly improved! Check out *this* blackboard instead!!

Ethical squatting is the idea that it's okay to live for free in an empty building if the owner isn't using it. This is a not-uncontroversial idea, *especially* among owners of empty buildings!!

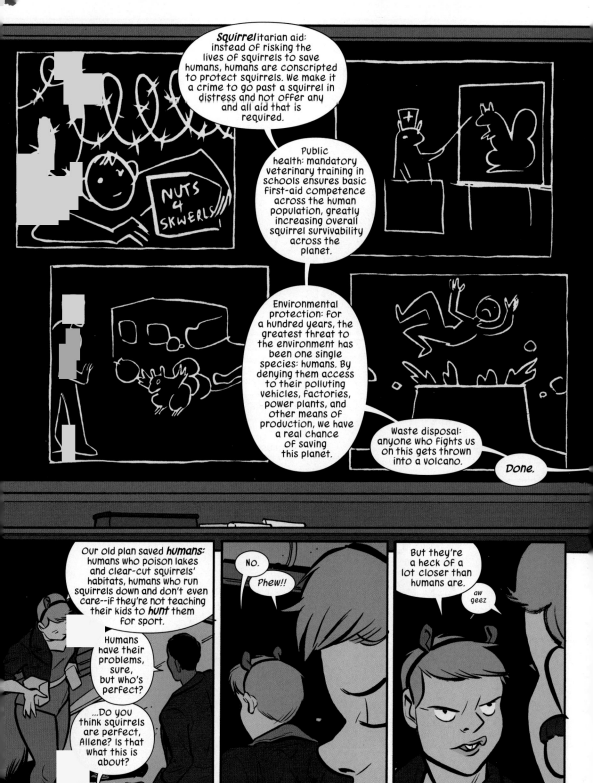

*Squirrel*itarian aid: instead of risking the lives of squirrels to save humans, humans are conscripted to protect squirrels. We make it a crime to go past a squirrel in distress and not offer any and all aid that is required.

Public health: mandatory veterinary training in schools ensures basic first-aid competence across the human population, greatly increasing overall squirrel survivability across the planet.

Environmental protection: For a hundred years, the greatest threat to the environment has been one single species: humans. By denying them access to their polluting vehicles, factories, power plants, and other means of production, we have a real chance of saving this planet.

Waste disposal: anyone who fights us on this gets thrown into a volcano.

Done.

NUTS 4 SKWERLS!

Our old plan saved *humans:* humans who poison lakes and clear-cut squirrels' habitats, humans who run squirrels down and don't even care--if they're not teaching their kids to *hunt* them for sport.

Humans have their problems, sure, but who's perfect?

...Do you think squirrels are perfect, Allene? Is that what this is about?

NO.

Phew!!

But they're a heck of a lot closer than humans are.

aw geez

ONLY HUMANS READ THIS PART: please keep reading! I promise this comic isn't anti-human propaganda forever.
ONLY SQUIRRELS READ THIS PART: squirrels, I am on your side; please look upon me with kindness in the coming revolution ;)

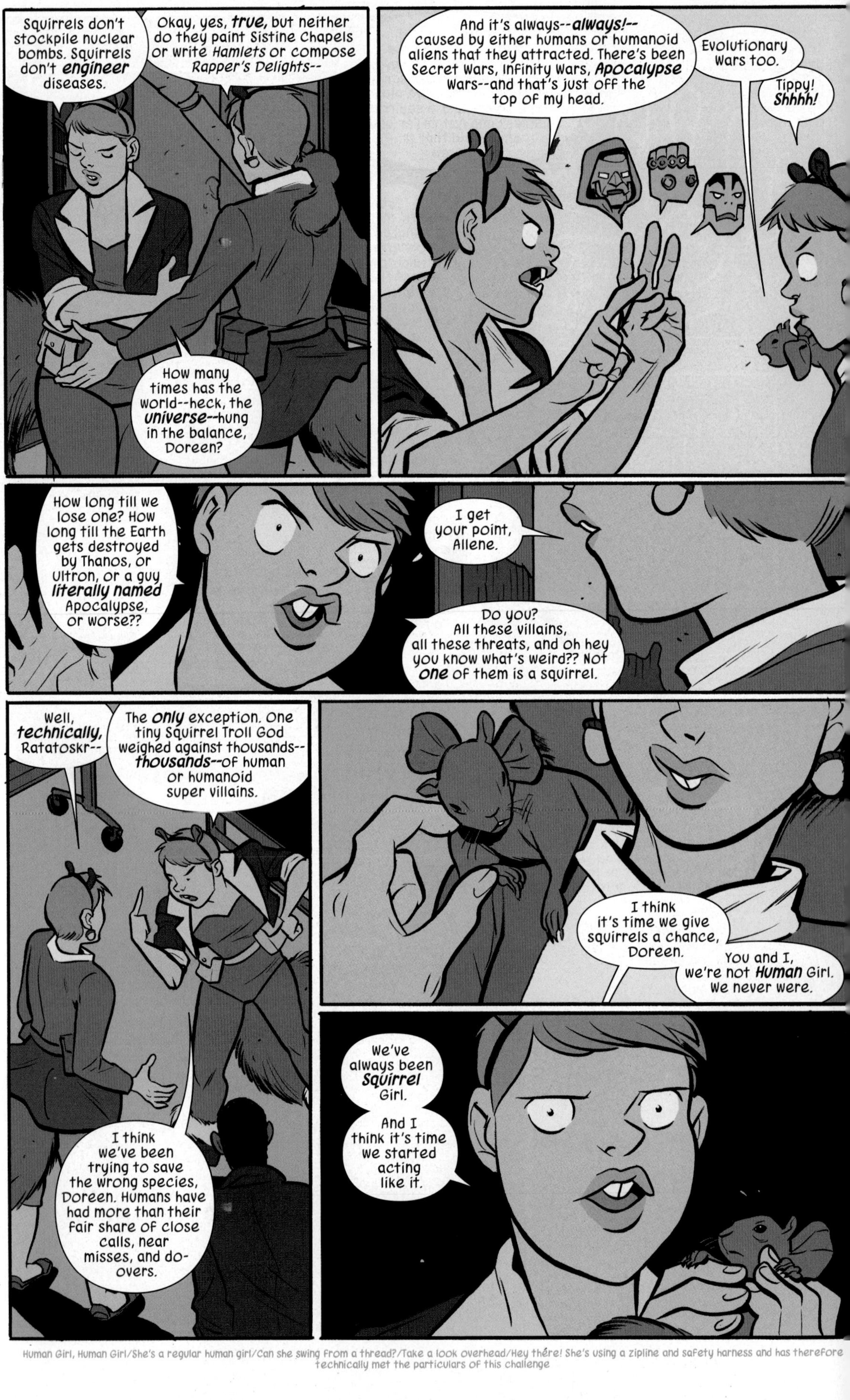
Squirrels don't stockpile nuclear bombs. Squirrels don't engineer diseases.
Okay, yes, true, but neither do they paint Sistine Chapels or write Hamlets or compose Rapper's Delights--
How many times has the world--heck, the universe--hung in the balance, Doreen?
And it's always--always!--caused by either humans or humanoid aliens that they attracted. There's been Secret Wars, Infinity Wars, Apocalypse Wars--and that's just off the top of my head.
Evolutionary Wars too.
Tippy! Shhhh!
How long till we lose one? How long till the Earth gets destroyed by Thanos, or Ultron, or a guy literally named Apocalypse, or worse??
I get your point, Allene.
Do you? All these villains, all these threats, and oh hey you know what's weird?? Not one of them is a squirrel.
Well, technically, Ratatoskr--
The only exception. One tiny Squirrel Troll God weighed against thousands--thousands--of human or humanoid super villains.
I think we've been trying to save the wrong species, Doreen. Humans have had more than their fair share of close calls, near misses, and do-overs.
I think it's time we give squirrels a chance, Doreen.
You and I, we're not Human Girl. We never were.
We've always been Squirrel Girl.
And I think it's time we started acting like it.

Human Girl, Human Girl/She's a regular human girl/Can she swing from a thread?/Take a look overhead/Hey thére! She's using a zipline and safety harness and has therefore technically met the particulars of this challenge

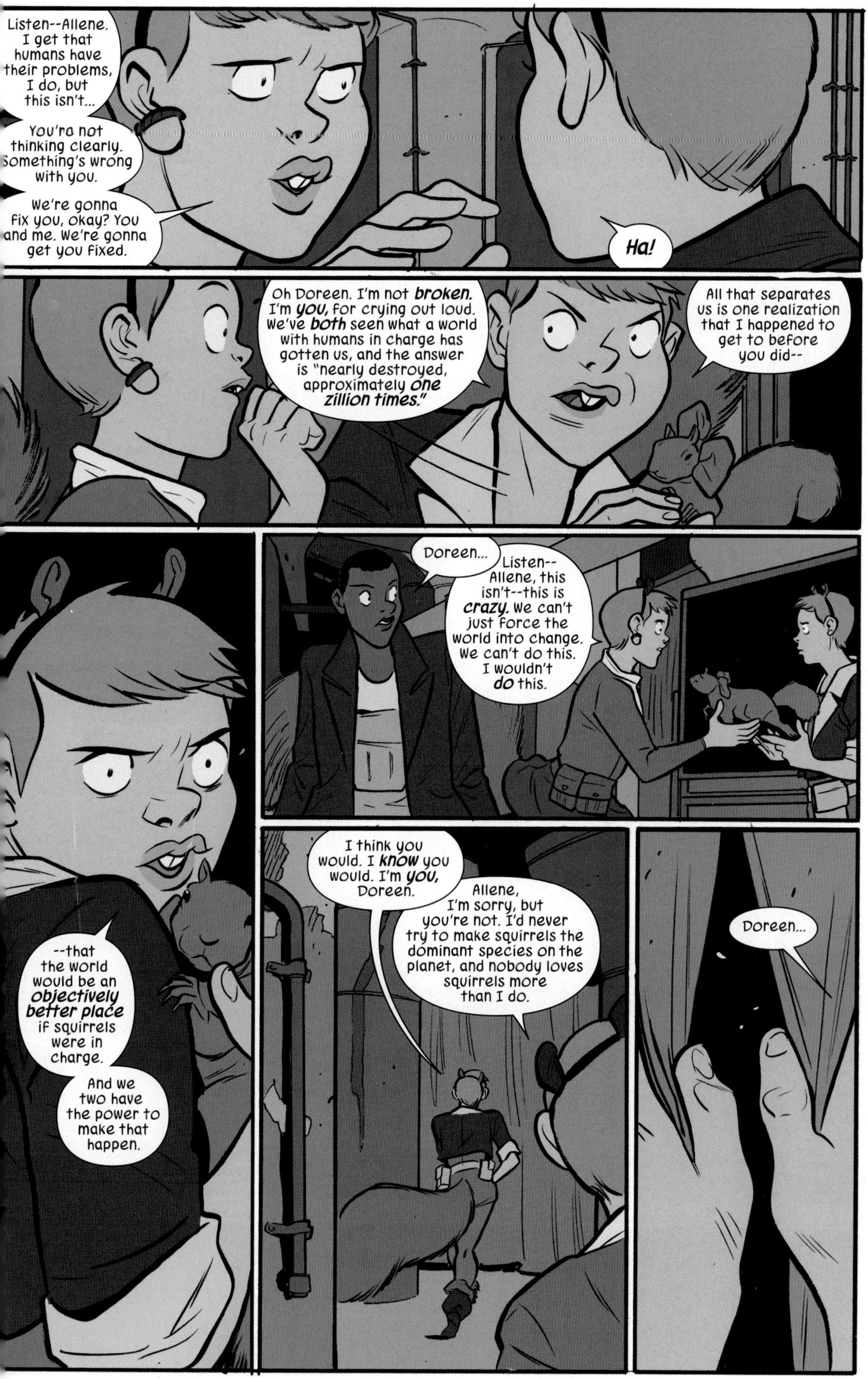
Listen--Allene. I get that humans have their problems, I do, but this isn't...
You're not thinking clearly. Something's wrong with you.
We're gonna fix you, okay? You and me. We're gonna get you fixed.
Ha!
Oh Doreen. I'm not broken. I'm you, for crying out loud. We've both seen what a world with humans in charge has gotten us, and the answer is "nearly destroyed, approximately one zillion times."
All that separates us is one realization that I happened to get to before you did--
--that the world would be an objectively better place if squirrels were in charge.
And we two have the power to make that happen.
Doreen...
Listen--Allene, this isn't--this is crazy. We can't just force the world into change. We can't do this. I wouldn't do this.
I think you would. I know you would. I'm you, Doreen.
Allene, I'm sorry, but you're not. I'd never try to make squirrels the dominant species on the planet, and nobody loves squirrels more than I do.
Doreen...

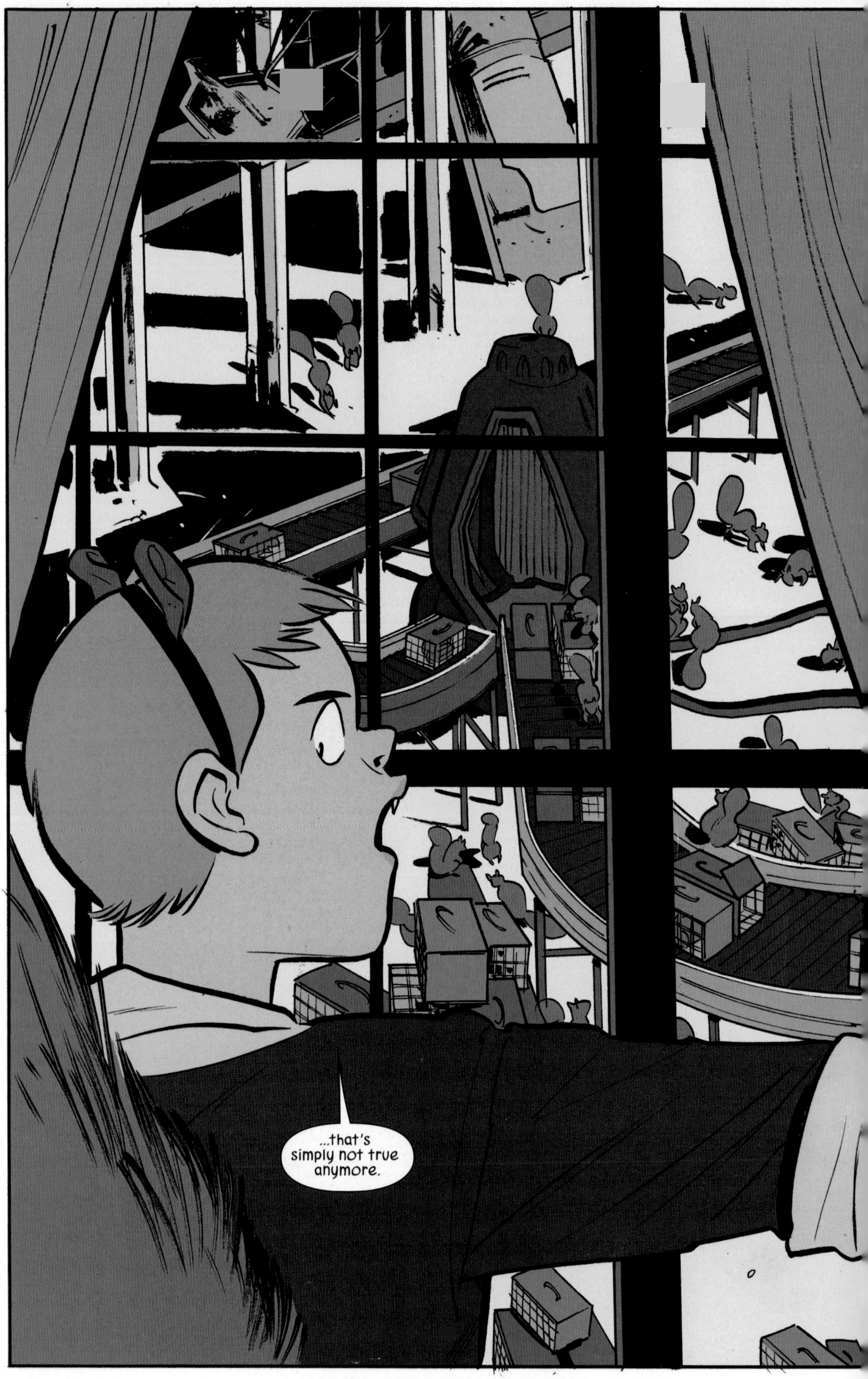
...that's simply not true anymore.

Now *those* are what I call "unbeatable squirrels," girl!

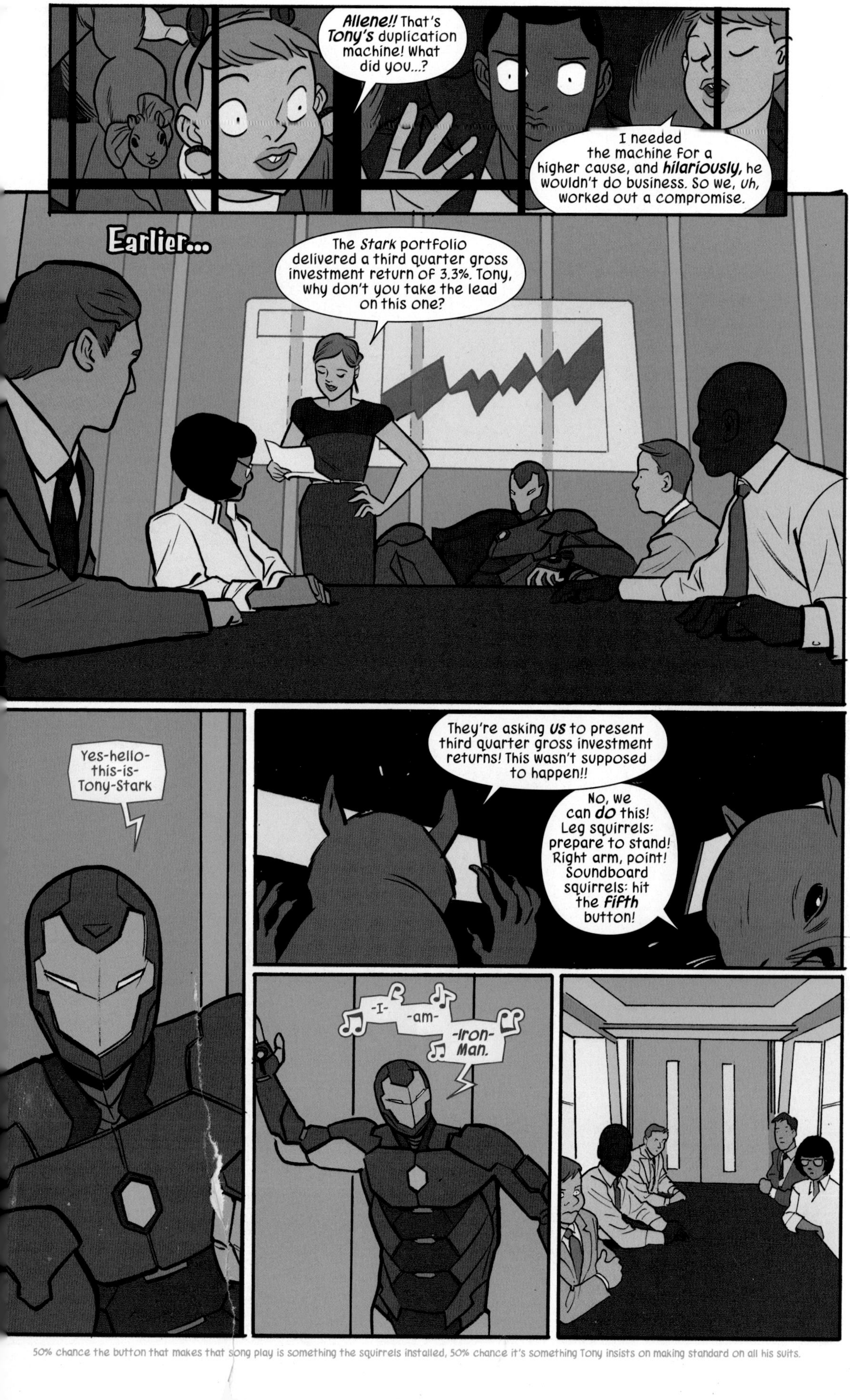
Allene!! That's Tony's duplication machine! What did you...?
I needed the machine for a higher cause, and hilariously, he wouldn't do business. So we, uh, worked out a compromise.
Earlier...
The Stark portfolio delivered a third quarter gross investment return of 3.3%. Tony, why don't you take the lead on this one?
Yes-hello-this-is-Tony-Stark
They're asking US to present third quarter gross investment returns! This wasn't supposed to happen!!
No, we can do this! Leg squirrels: prepare to stand! Right arm, point! Soundboard squirrels: hit the fifth button!
-I- -am- -Iron- Man.
50% chance the button that makes that song play is something the squirrels installed, 50% chance it's something Tony insists on making standard on all his suits.

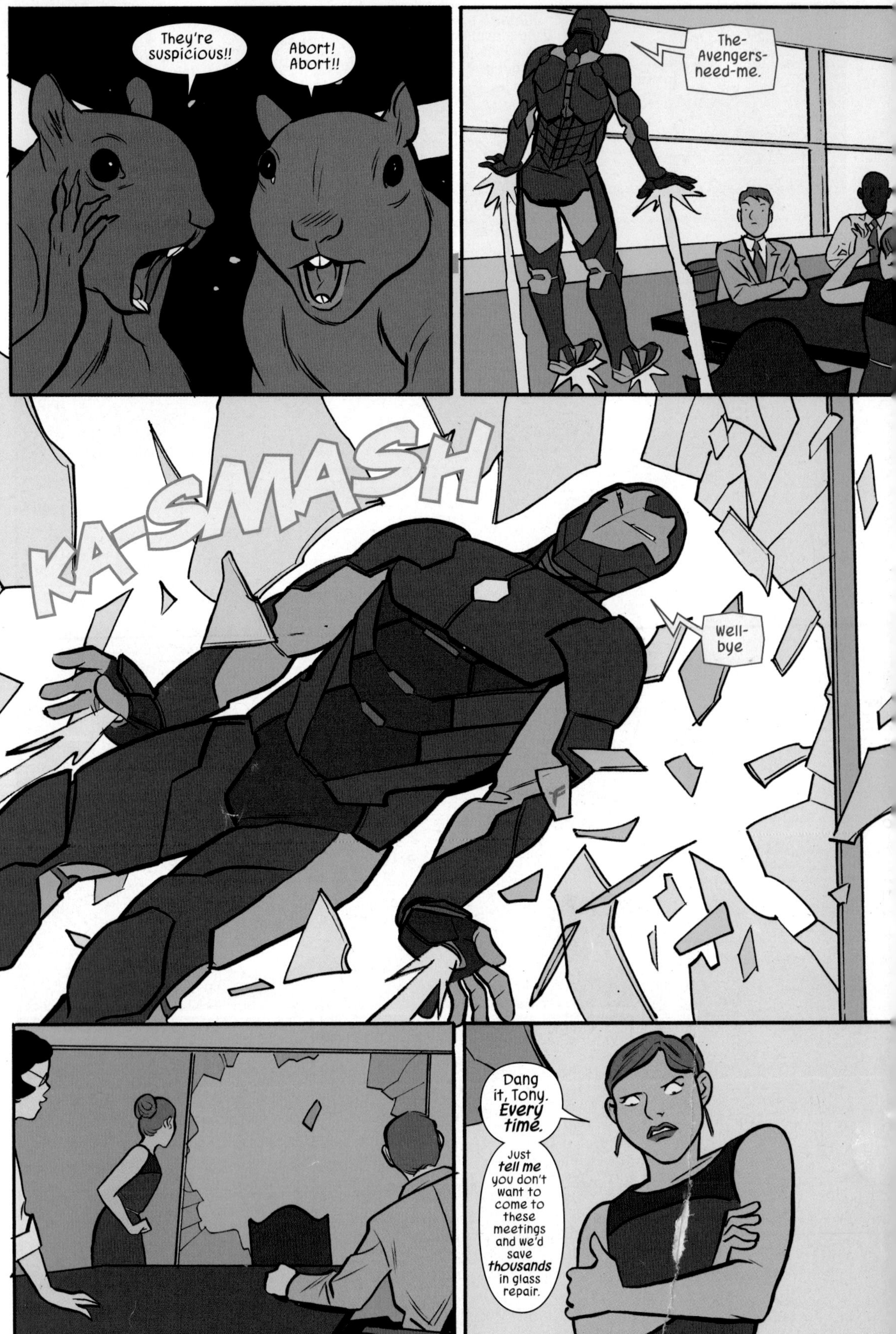
They're suspicious!!
Abort! Abort!!
The-Avengers-need-me.
KA-SMASH
Well-bye
Dang it, Tony. *Every time.*
Just *tell me* you don't want to come to these meetings and we'd save *thousands* in glass repair.

See, *this* is what you get for cultivating a personality in which you could be replaced by a bunch of squirrels in a robot suit and *nobody would ever notice.* If you are an unpredictable, egocentric, unreasonably rich reader who has become insulated to all consequences of their actions: *take heed!!*

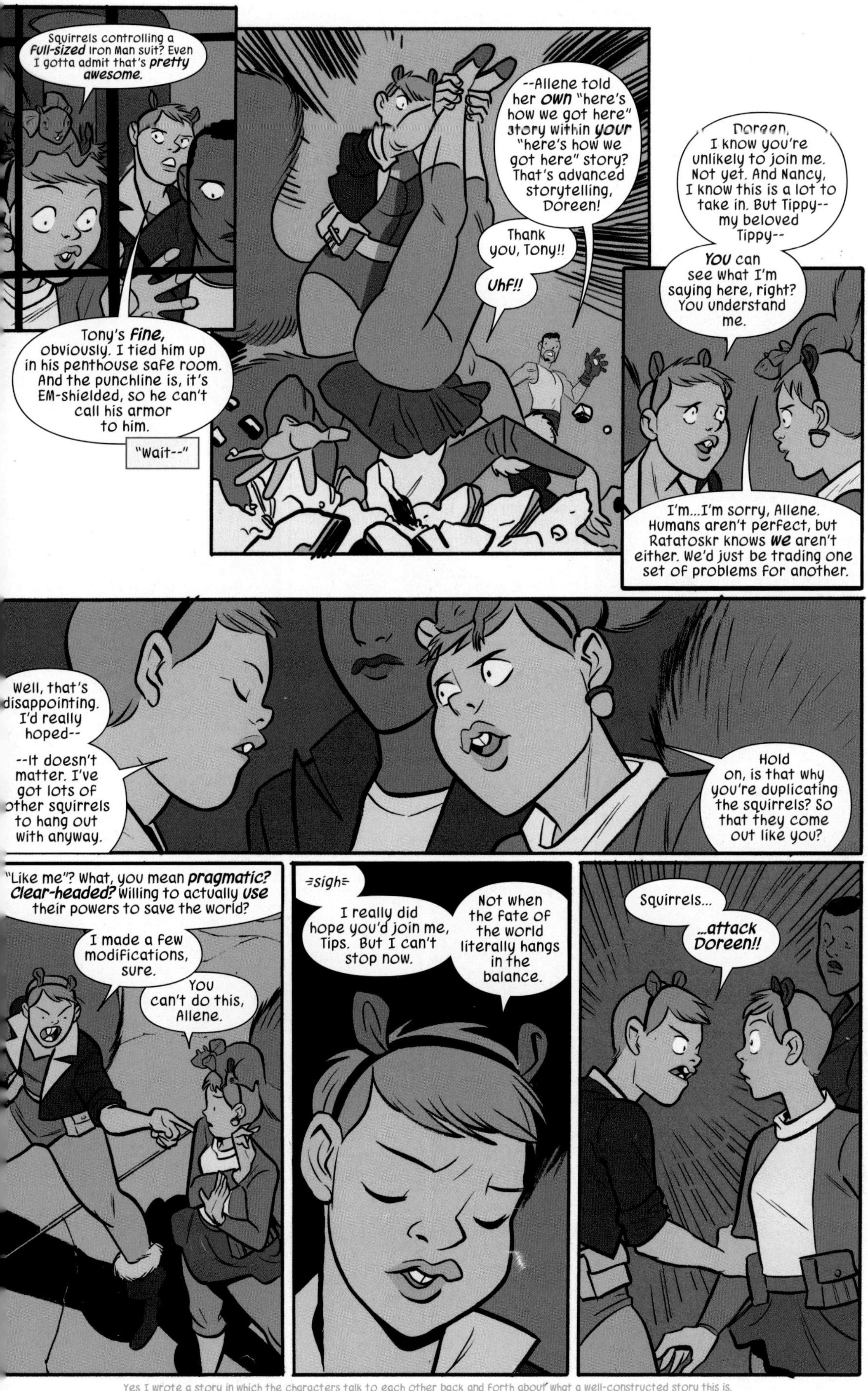
Squirrels controlling a Full-sized Iron Man suit? Even I gotta admit that's pretty awesome.
Tony's Fine, obviously. I tied him up in his penthouse safe room. And the punchline is, it's EM-shielded, so he can't call his armor to him.
"Wait--"
--Allene told her OWN "here's how we got here" story within YOUR "here's how we got here" story? That's advanced storytelling, Doreen!
Thank you, Tony!!
Uhf!!
Doreen, I know you're unlikely to join me. Not yet. And Nancy, I know this is a lot to take in. But Tippy-- my beloved Tippy--
YOU can see what I'm saying here, right? You understand me.
I'm...I'm sorry, Allene. Humans aren't perfect, but Ratatoskr knows WE aren't either. We'd just be trading one set of problems for another.
Well, that's disappointing. I'd really hoped--
--It doesn't matter. I've got lots of other squirrels to hang out with anyway.
Hold on, is that why you're duplicating the squirrels? So that they come out like you?
"Like me"? What, you mean pragmatic? Clear-headed? Willing to actually use their powers to save the world?
I made a few modifications, sure.
You can't do this, Allene.
=sigh=
I really did hope you'd join me, Tips. But I can't stop now.
Not when the fate of the world literally hangs in the balance.
Squirrels...
...attack Doreen!!

Yes I wrote a story in which the characters talk to each other back and forth about what a well-constructed story this is.
Why would you become a writer and not do this, is my question??

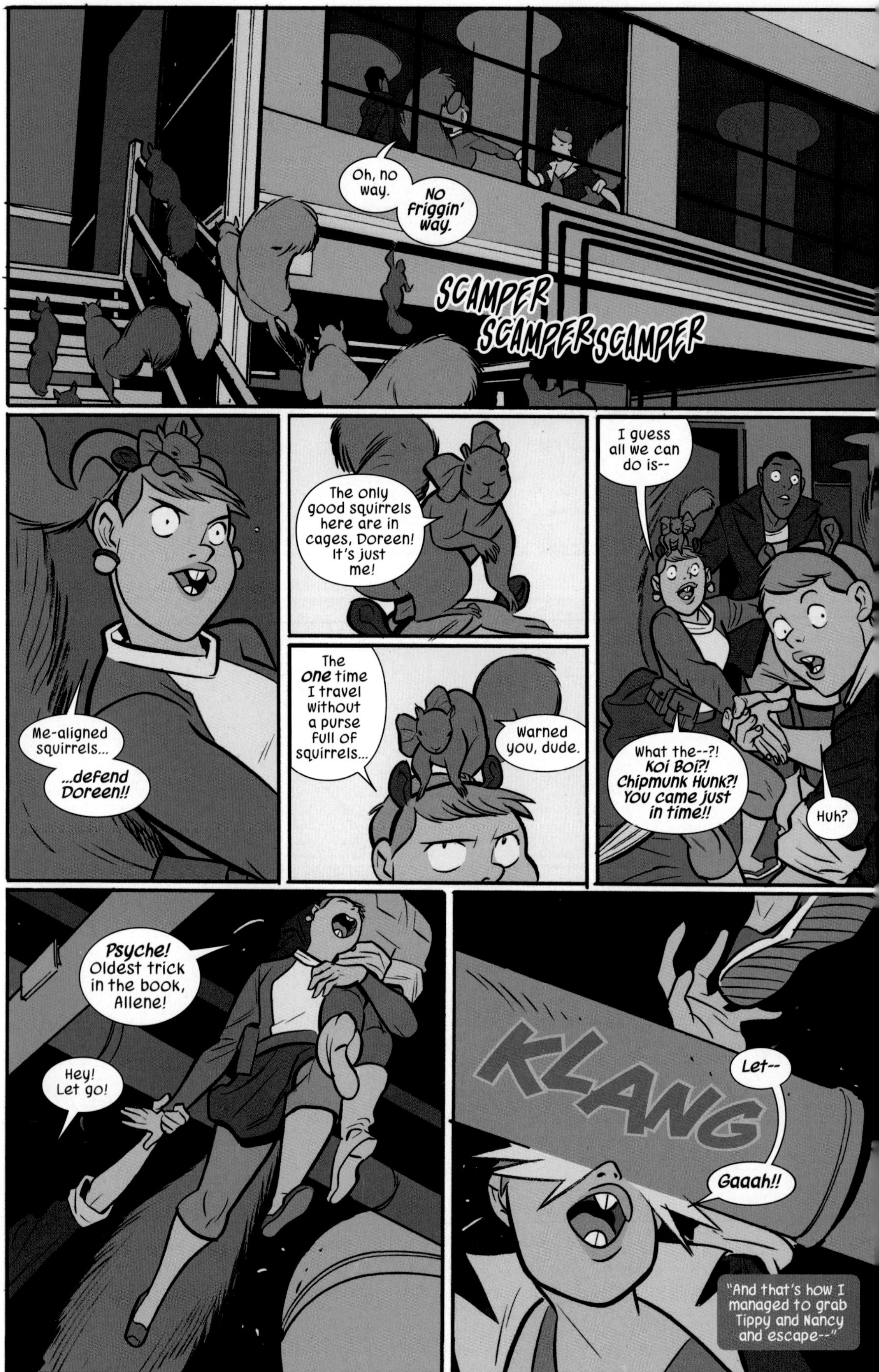
Oh, no way.
NO friggin' way.
SCAMPER SCAMPER SCAMPER
Me-aligned squirrels...
...defend Doreen!!
The only good squirrels here are in cages, Doreen! It's just me!
The one time I travel without a purse full of squirrels...
Warned you, dude.
I guess all we can do is--
What the--?! Koi Boi?! Chipmunk Hunk?! You came just in time!!
Huh?
Psyche! Oldest trick in the book, Allene!
Hey! Let go!
KLANG
Let--
Gaaah!!
"And that's how I managed to grab Tippy and Nancy and escape--"

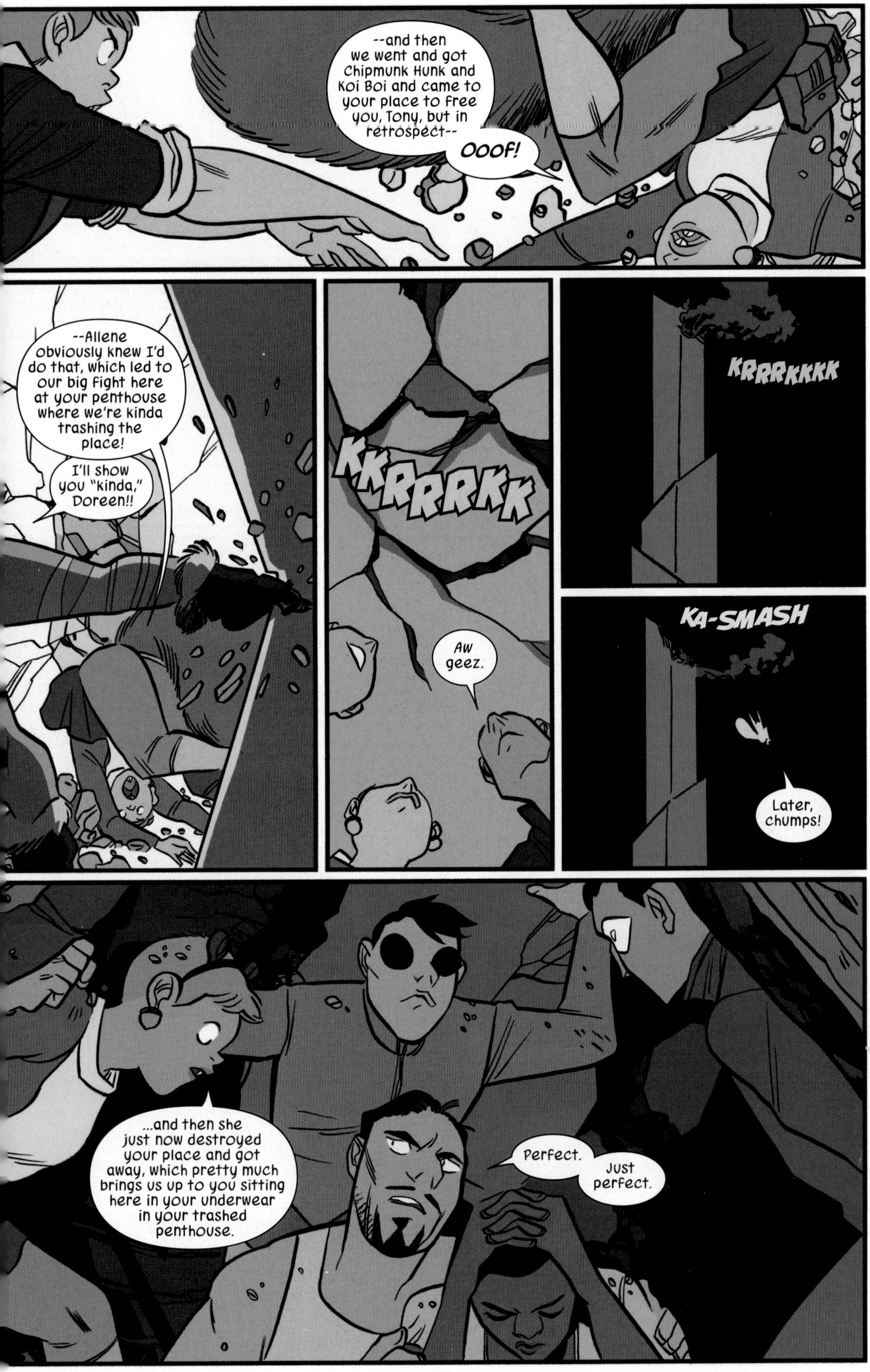
--and then we went and got Chipmunk Hunk and Koi Boi and came to your place to free you, Tony, but in retrospect--
OOOF!
--Allene obviously knew I'd do that, which led to our big fight here at your penthouse where we're kinda trashing the place!
I'll show you "kinda," Doreen!!
KKRRRRKK
Aw geez.
KRRRKKKK
KA-SMASH
Later, chumps!
...and then she just now destroyed your place and got away, which pretty much brings us up to you sitting here in your underwear in your trashed penthouse.
Perfect.
Just perfect.

I really wanted to get that ultramodern "rubble chic" look at the top of my multinational company's flagship tower, so things are working out just great for Team Iron Man over here.

Tony, I gotta say: I think the machine maybe messed up a little when it duplicated me.

YOU think?

Look, for once, this is a problem I can't fix in my underwear. Help me look for suit parts.

...ent over the machine's design while I was locked up in there, and I think I found the flaw.

In-- in your *head*?

Genius billionaire playboy philanthropist, remember?

Squirrel Girl looks for compromise, for solutions that make everyone happy. That's her *thing*.

Allene didn't get that part. She doesn't see the point in compromise when you *know* you're right, especially when you're strong enough to ensure what you want to happen *actually happens*.

Someone with all her power and none of the restraint. That's, uh... concerning?

Our only advantage right now is so far she's only duplicating squirrels, not herself.

She can control her squirrels, and that keeps her power with her. She wouldn't trust another self. She clearly no longer trusts *you*, Doreen.

Man! This *sucks*. I loved the idea of another me! We were gonna battle crime *and* homework at greater efficiency!

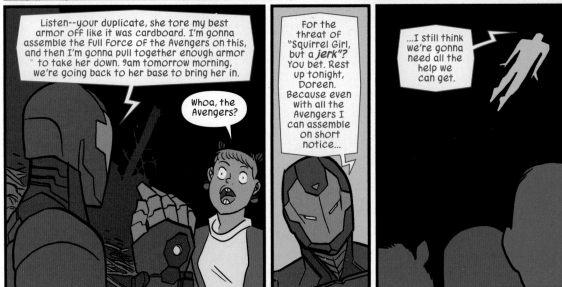

Listen--your duplicate, she tore my best armor off like it was cardboard. I'm gonna assemble the full force of the Avengers on this, and then I'm gonna pull together enough armor to take her down. 9am tomorrow morning, we're going back to her base to bring her in.

Whoa, the Avengers?

For the threat of "Squirrel Girl," but a *jerk*? You bet. Rest up tonight, Doreen. Because even with all the Avengers I can assemble on short notice...

...I still think we're gonna need all the help we can get.

Tony's line in panel one really raises a lot of questions. For answers, maybe check out the Iron Man comics! There's always a chance the Iron Man writers feature him there fighting crime in his underwear. (P.S. Iron Man writers: this is an excellent free idea and you should definitely use it)

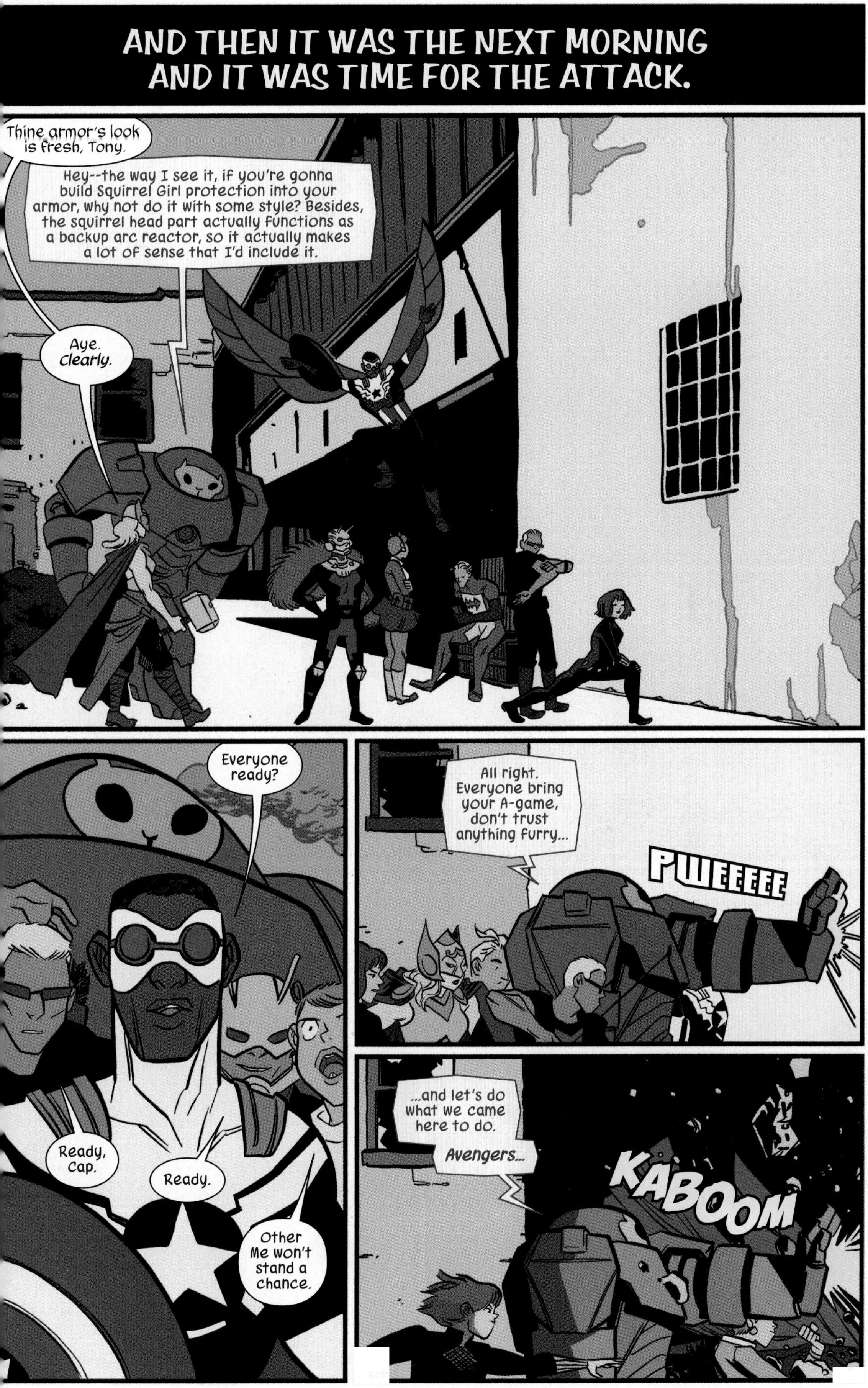
AND THEN IT WAS THE NEXT MORNING AND IT WAS TIME FOR THE ATTACK.
Thine armor's look is fresh, Tony.
Hey--the way I see it, if you're gonna build Squirrel Girl protection into your armor, why not do it with some style? Besides, the squirrel head part actually functions as a backup arc reactor, so it actually makes a lot of sense that I'd include it.
Aye. Clearly.
Everyone ready?
Ready, Cap.
Ready.
Other Me won't stand a chance.
All right. Everyone bring your A-game, don't trust anything furry...
PWEEEEE
...and let's do what we came here to do.
Avengers...
KABOOM

s is Tony's first crossover AU cosplay and he's big into it, but he's shy. It's okay, Tony! I like your suit! You built a giant squirrel that fires missiles! That's sincerely amazing!!

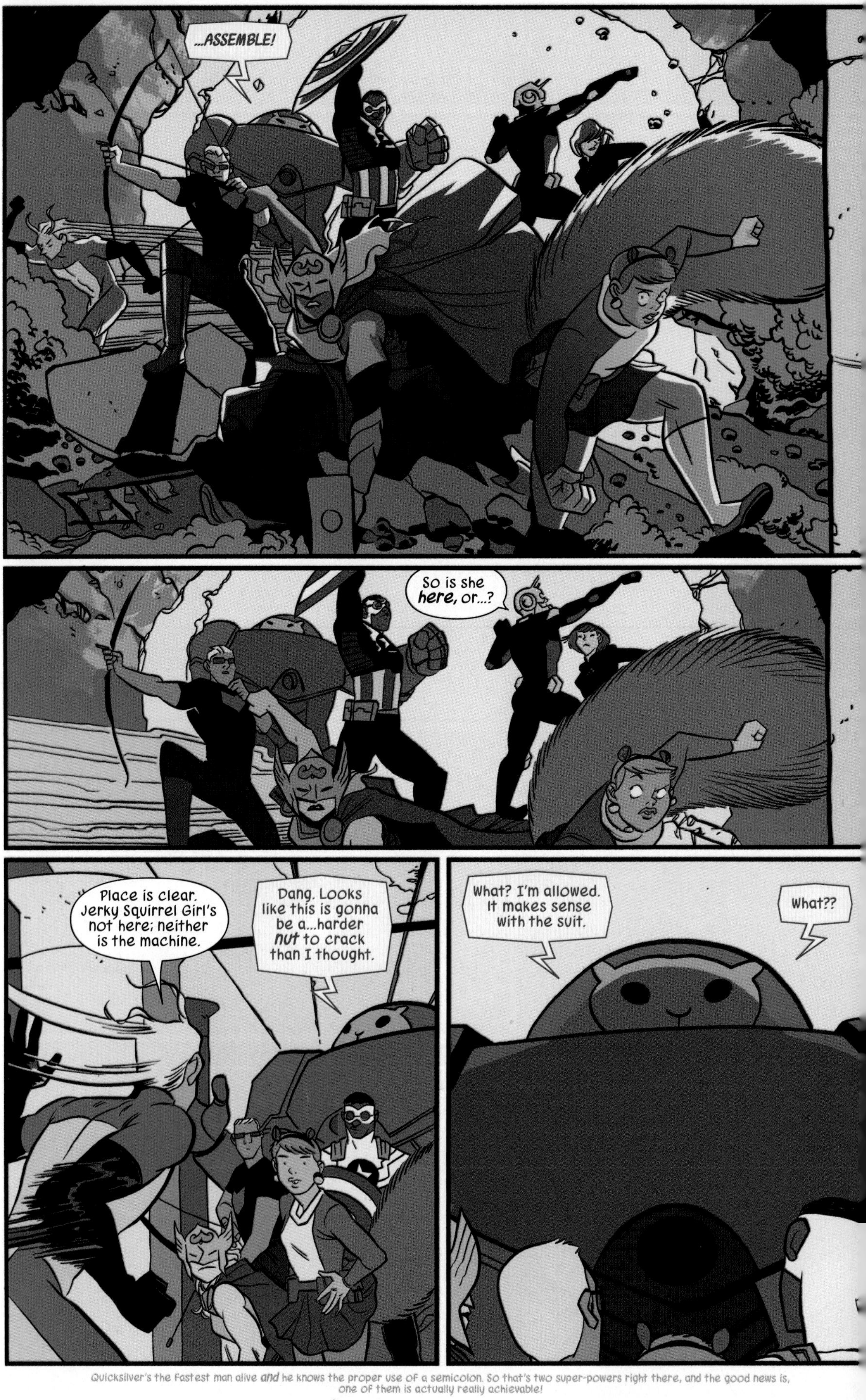
...ASSEMBLE!
So is she *here,* or...?
Place is clear. Jerky Squirrel Girl's not here; neither is the machine.
Dang. Looks like this is gonna be a...harder *nut* to crack than I thought.
What? I'm allowed. It makes sense with the suit.
What??

Quicksilver's the fastest man alive *and* he knows the proper use of a semicolon. So that's two super-powers right there, and the good news is, one of them is actually really achievable!

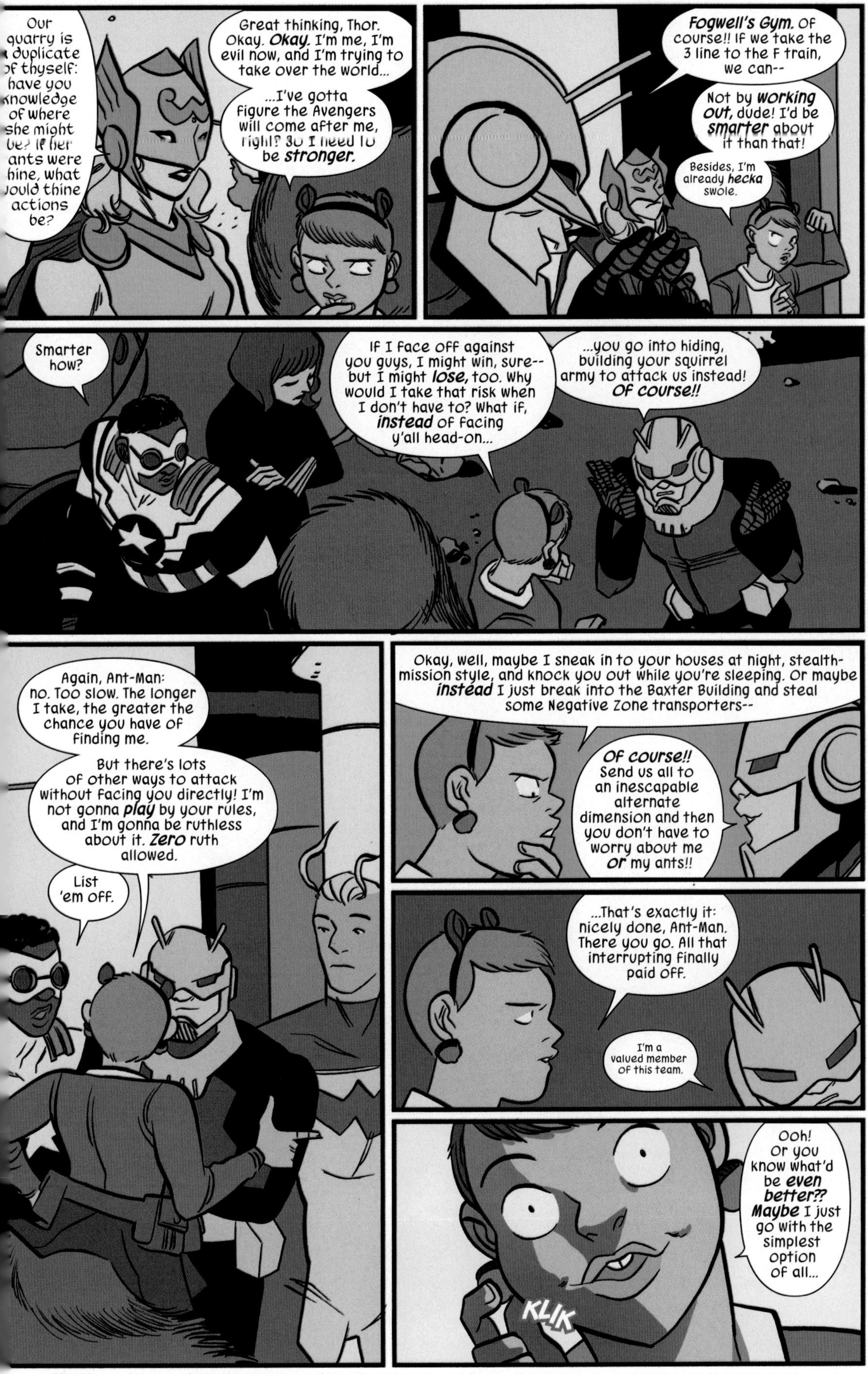

Our quarry is a duplicate of thyself: have you knowledge of where she might be? If her ants were thine, what would thine actions be?
Great thinking, Thor. Okay. Okay. I'm me, I'm evil now, and I'm trying to take over the world...
...I've gotta figure the Avengers will come after me, right? So I need to be stronger.
Fogwell's Gym. Of course!! If we take the 3 line to the F train, we can--
Not by working out, dude! I'd be smarter about it than that!
Besides, I'm already hecka swole.
Smarter how?
If I face off against you guys, I might win, sure-- but I might lose, too. Why would I take that risk when I don't have to? What if, instead of facing y'all head-on...
...you go into hiding, building your squirrel army to attack us instead! Of course!!
Again, Ant-Man: no. Too slow. The longer I take, the greater the chance you have of finding me.
But there's lots of other ways to attack without facing you directly! I'm not gonna play by your rules, and I'm gonna be ruthless about it. Zero ruth allowed.
List 'em off.
Okay, well, maybe I sneak in to your houses at night, stealth-mission style, and knock you out while you're sleeping. Or maybe instead I just break into the Baxter Building and steal some Negative Zone transporters--
Of course!! Send us all to an inescapable alternate dimension and then you don't have to worry about me or my ants!!
...That's exactly it: nicely done, Ant-Man. There you go. All that interrupting finally paid off.
I'm a valued member of this team.
Ooh! Or you know what'd be even better?? Maybe I just go with the simplest option of all...
KLIK

"Ruth" is one of those words that we only keep around because another form of it ("ruthless") is way more popular. These are called "unpaired words," and while they may leave *you* couth, sheveled, and kempt, they don't leave *me* gruntled at all!!

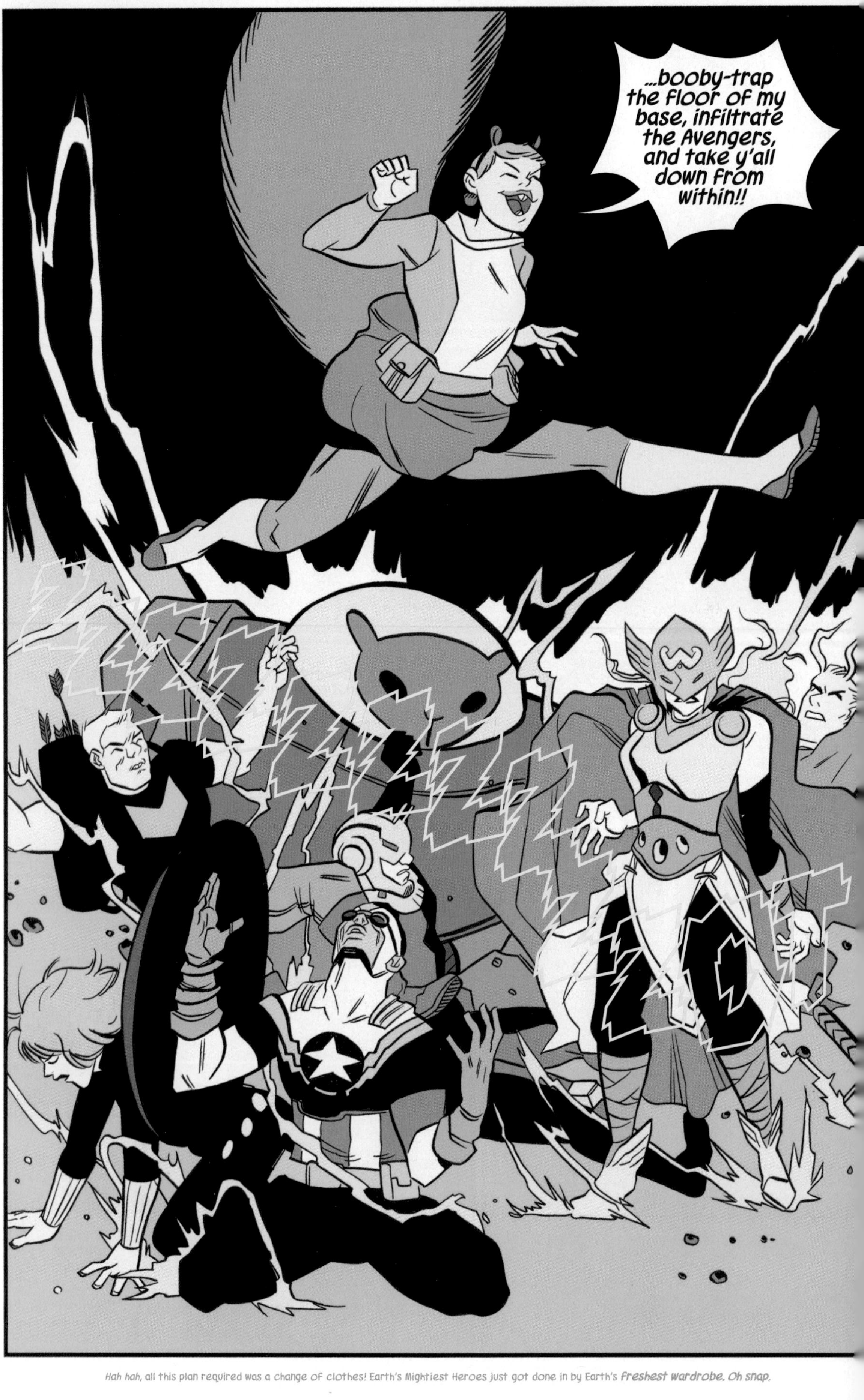
...booby-trap the floor of my base, infiltrate the Avengers, and take y'all down from within!!

Hah hah, all this plan required was a change of clothes! Earth's Mightiest Heroes just got done in by Earth's ***freshest wardrobe. Oh snap.***

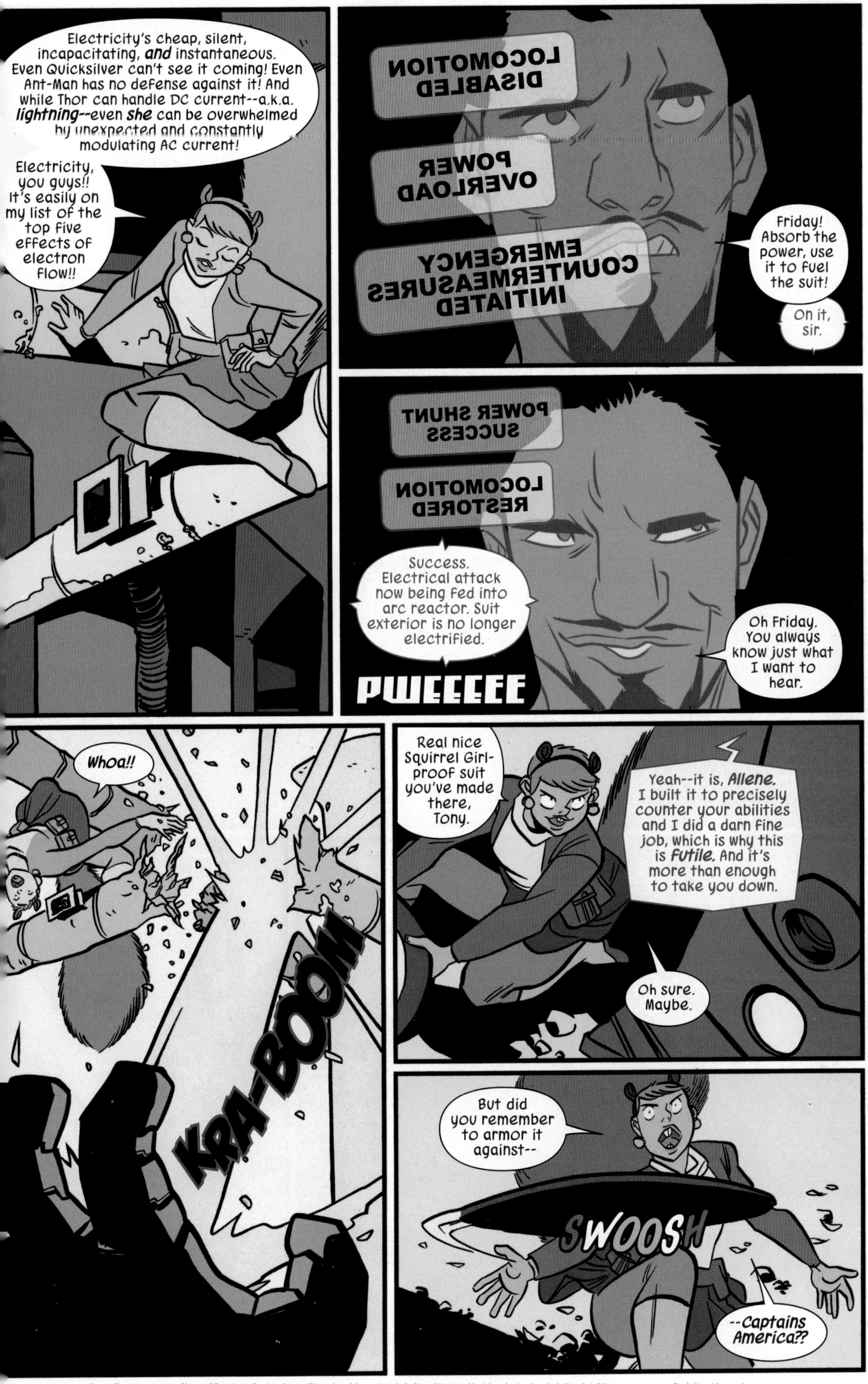
Electricity's cheap, silent, incapacitating, *and* instantaneous. Even Quicksilver can't see it coming! Even Ant-Man has no defense against it! And while Thor can handle DC current--a.k.a. *lightning*--even *she* can be overwhelmed by unexpected and constantly modulating AC current!
Electricity, you guys!! It's easily on my list of the top five effects of electron flow!!
LOCOMOTION DISABLED
POWER OVERLOAD
EMERGENCY COUNTERMEASURES INITIATED
Friday! Absorb the power, use it to fuel the suit!
On it, sir.
POWER SHUNT SUCCESS
LOCOMOTION RESTORED
Success. Electrical attack now being fed into arc reactor. Suit exterior is no longer electrified.
PWEEEEE
Oh Friday. You always know just what I want to hear.
Whoa!!
KRA-BOOM
Real nice Squirrel Girl-proof suit you've made there, Tony.
Yeah--it is, *Allene.* I built it to precisely counter your abilities and I did a darn fine job, which is why this is *futile.* And it's more than enough to take you down.
Oh sure. Maybe.
But did you remember to armor it against--
SWOOSH
--*Captains America??*

I can't even name five effects of electron flow besides electricity. Allene, that's what electricity is! Allene, are you fudging the science for the benefit of your trash talk here or what?

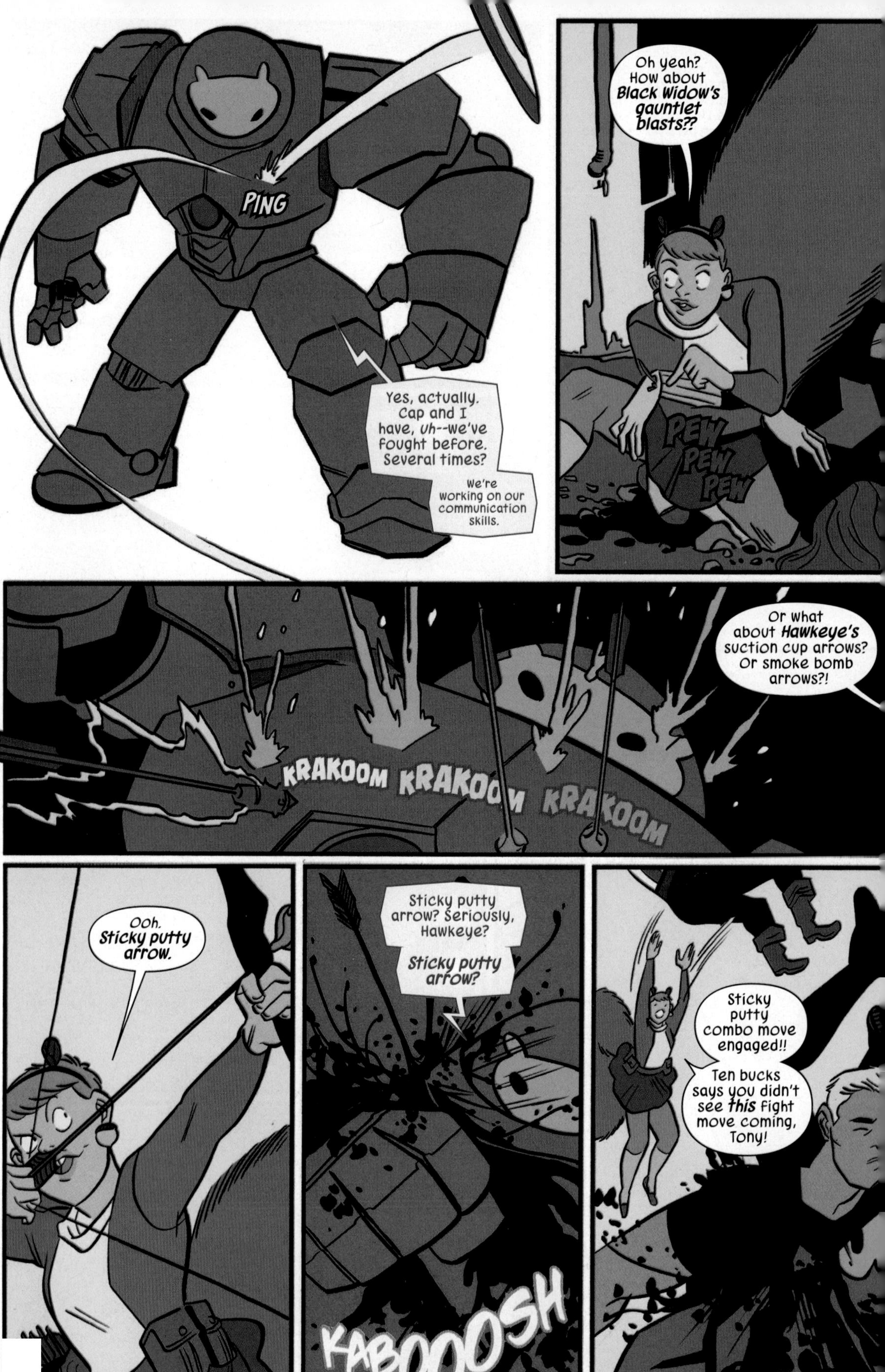
PING
Yes, actually. Cap and I have, *uh*--we've fought before. Several times?
We're working on our communication skills.
Oh yeah? How about **Black Widow's gauntlet blasts??**
PEW PEW PEW
Or what about **Hawkeye's** suction cup arrows? Or smoke bomb arrows?!
KRAKOOM KRAKOOM KRAKOOM
Ooh. **Sticky putty arrow.**
Sticky putty arrow? Seriously, Hawkeye?
Sticky putty arrow?
KABOOOSH
Sticky putty combo move engaged!!
Ten bucks says you didn't see **this** fight move coming, Tony!

FUN FACT: To be fair, it's hard to protect against ***every*** possible fight move, especially when those fight moves include "cover you in sticky putty, and then throw your knocked-out friends on you, so they stick to the sticky putty." This fun fact applies to both this comic ***and*** real life. Don't make the same mistakes I did!!

REPULSOR PORTS BLOCKED

AIR INTAKE BLOCKED

CLING ONE DETECTED
OFF STARBOARD ARM

All weapon ports have been blocked by one or more mighty Avengers, sir. We can't fire without--

I know, I know! Get them OFF!

Sir, I'm trying, but the arrow's polymer is extremely adhesive, and seems designed to resist our--

CRRK

HULL BREACH DETECTED

...What now?

UNEXPECTED LATERAL AND VERTICAL FORCES ON CHASSIS

CRRRRRK

aw geez

Tony.

Allene.

THWACK

Twenty-*two* seconds taking down the Avengers this time!

A *personal best!!*

the last time took her twenty-six seconds, and that was about a year ago. Practice makes perfect, everyone! *This is a motivational comic with a pro-practice message when it comes to beating up Avengers, everyone!*

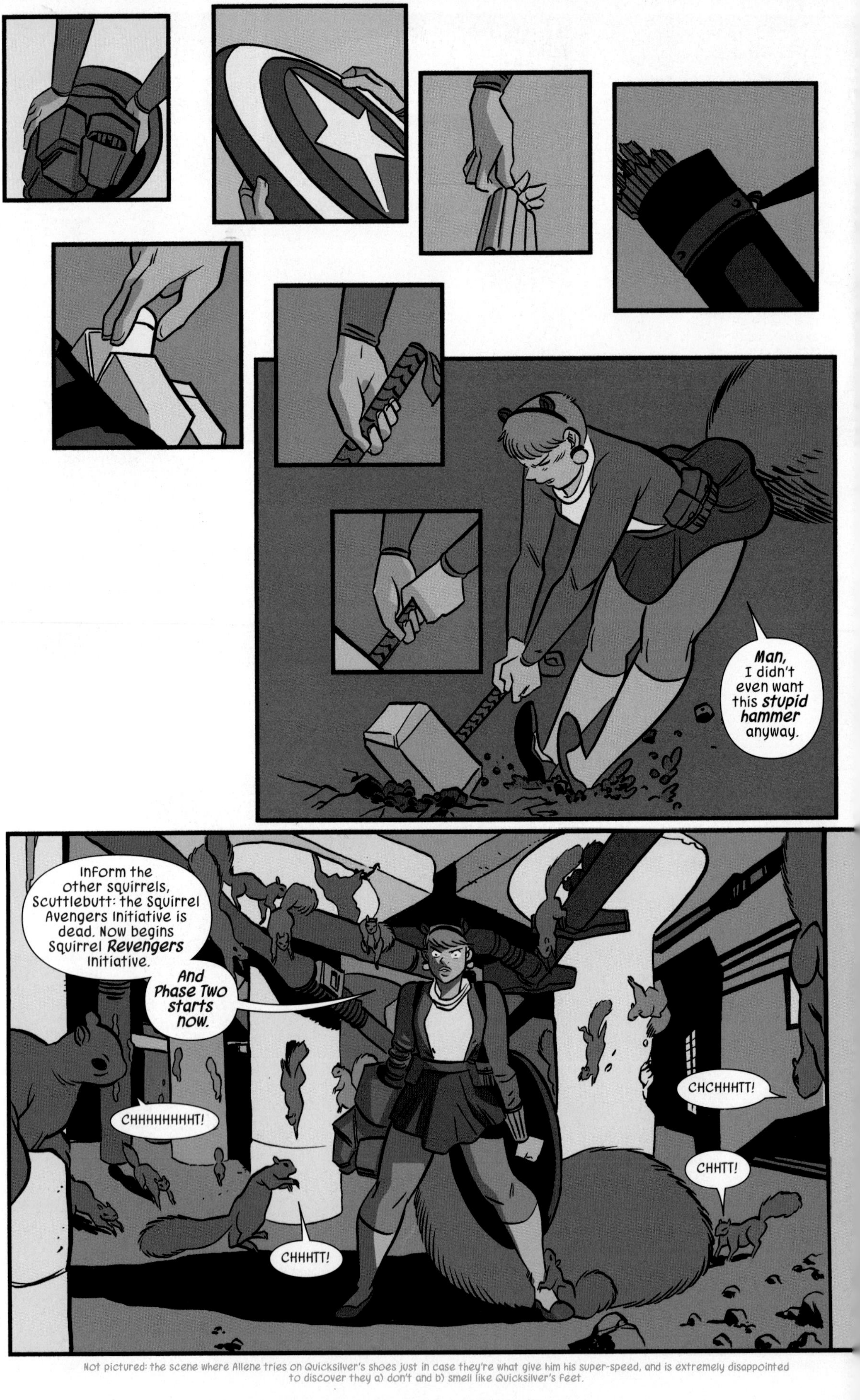
Man, I didn't even want this *stupid hammer* anyway.
Inform the other squirrels, Scuttlebutt: the Squirrel Avengers Initiative is dead. Now begins Squirrel *Revengers* Initiative.
And Phase Two starts now.
CHHHHHHHHT!
CHHHTT!
CHCHHHTT!
CHHTT!

Not pictured: the scene where Allene tries on Quicksilver's shoes just in case they're what give him his super-speed, and is extremely disappointed to discover they a) don't and b) smell like Quicksilver's feet.

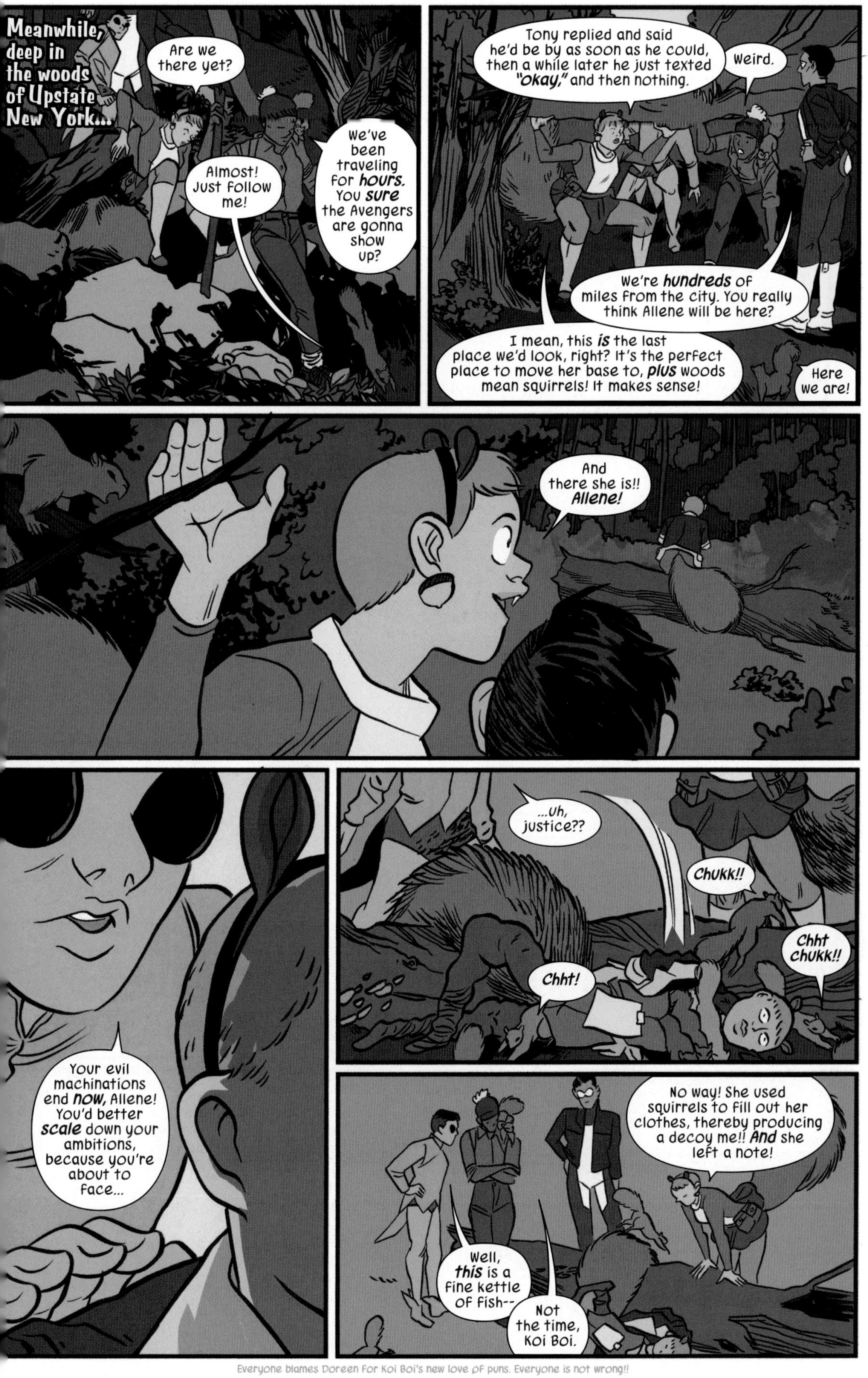
Meanwhile, deep in the woods of Upstate New York...
Are we there yet?
Almost! Just follow me!
We've been traveling for hours. You sure the Avengers are gonna show up?
Tony replied and said he'd be by as soon as he could, then a while later he just texted "okay," and then nothing.
Weird.
We're hundreds of miles from the city. You really think Allene will be here?
I mean, this is the last place we'd look, right? It's the perfect place to move her base to, plus woods mean squirrels! It makes sense!
Here we are!
And there she is!! Allene!
Your evil machinations end now, Allene! You'd better scale down your ambitions, because you're about to face...
...Uh, justice??
Chukk!!
Chht Chukk!!
Chht!
No way! She used squirrels to fill out her clothes, thereby producing a decoy me!! And she left a note!
Well, this is a fine kettle of fish--
Not the time, Koi Boi.

Everyone blames Doreen for Koi Boi's new love of puns. Everyone is not wrong!!

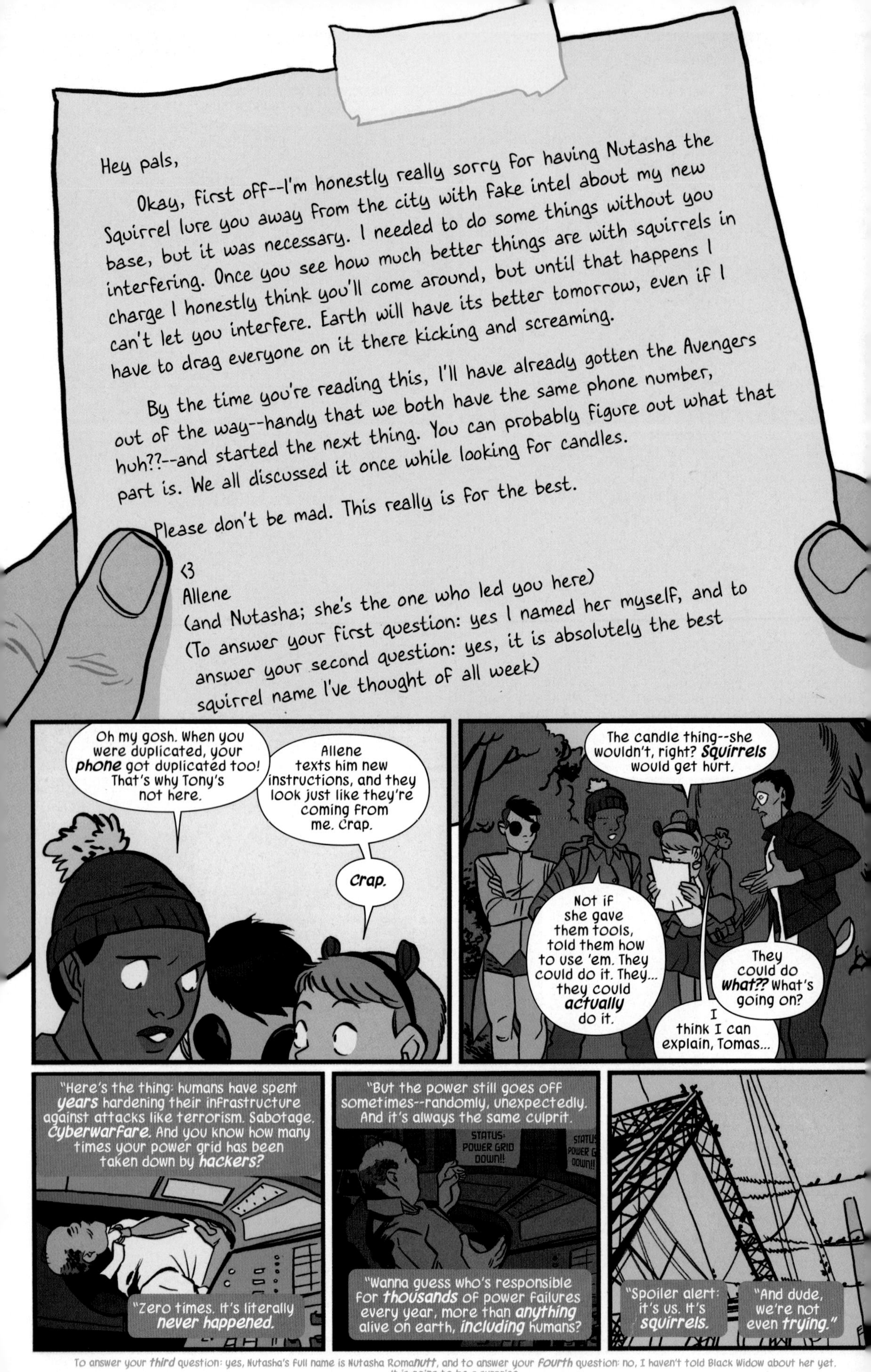
Hey pals,
Okay, first off--I'm honestly really sorry for having Nutasha the Squirrel lure you away from the city with fake intel about my new base, but it was necessary. I needed to do some things without you interfering. Once you see how much better things are with squirrels in charge I honestly think you'll come around, but until that happens I can't let you interfere. Earth will have its better tomorrow, even if I have to drag everyone on it there kicking and screaming.
By the time you're reading this, I'll have already gotten the Avengers out of the way--handy that we both have the same phone number, huh??--and started the next thing. You can probably figure out what that part is. We all discussed it once while looking for candles.
Please don't be mad. This really is for the best.
<3
Allene
(and Nutasha; she's the one who led you here)
(To answer your first question: yes I named her myself, and to answer your second question: yes, it is absolutely the best squirrel name I've thought of all week)
Oh my gosh. When you were duplicated, your *phone* got duplicated too! That's why Tony's not here.
Allene texts him new instructions, and they look just like they're coming from me. Crap.
Crap.
The candle thing--she wouldn't, right? *Squirrels* would get hurt.
Not if she gave them tools, told them how to use 'em. They could do it. They... they could *actually* do it.
They could do *what??* What's going on?
I think I can explain, Tomas...
"Here's the thing: humans have spent *years* hardening their infrastructure against attacks like terrorism. Sabotage. *Cyberwarfare.* And you know how many times your power grid has been taken down by *hackers?*
"Zero times. It's literally *never happened.*
"But the power still goes off sometimes--randomly, unexpectedly. And it's always the same culprit.
STATUS: POWER GRID DOWN!!
STATUS: POWER G DOWN!!
"Wanna guess who's responsible for *thousands* of power failures every year, more than *anything* alive on earth, *including* humans?
"Spoiler alert: it's us. It's *squirrels.*
"And dude, we're not even *trying.*"

To answer your *third* question: yes, Nutasha's full name is Nutasha Roma*nutt*, and to answer your *fourth* question: no, I haven't told Black Widow about her yet. It is going to be a surprise.

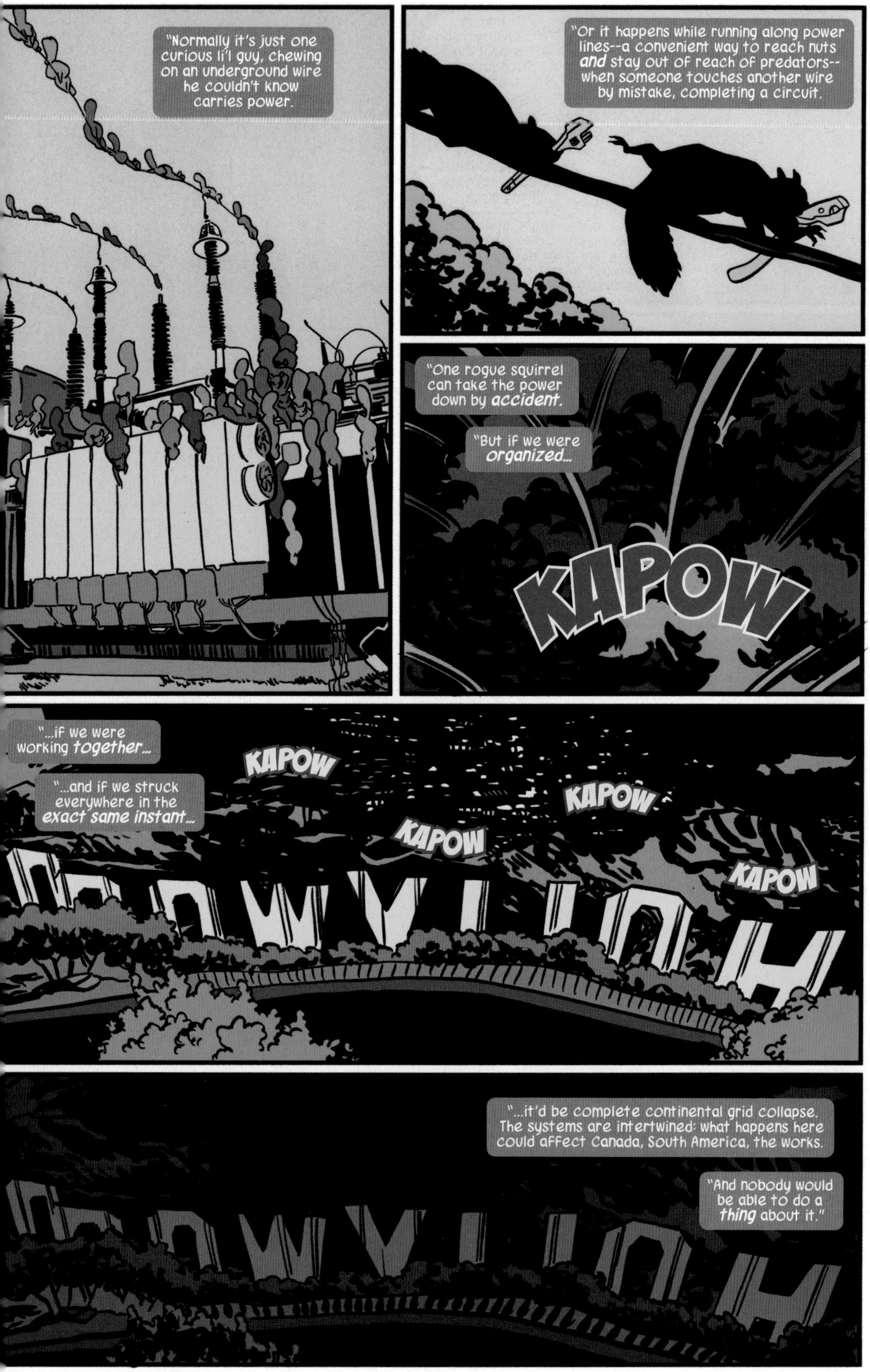
"Normally it's just one curious li'l guy, chewing on an underground wire he couldn't know carries power.
"Or it happens while running along power lines--a convenient way to reach nuts *and* stay out of reach of predators--when someone touches another wire by mistake, completing a circuit.
"One rogue squirrel can take the power down by *accident*.
"But if we were *organized*...
KAPOW
"...if we were working *together*...
"...and if we struck everywhere in the *exact same instant*...
KAPOW
KAPOW
KAPOW
KAPOW
"...it'd be complete continental grid collapse. The systems are intertwined: what happens here could affect Canada, South America, the works.
"And nobody would be able to do a *thing* about it."

his is all true, by the way: the number of outages caused by squirrels is well above those caused by rats and raccoons and snakes and birds all added together. Plus, any one of those animals causes more outages per year than those caused by humans. Maybe stay on your local squirrels' good side, huh??

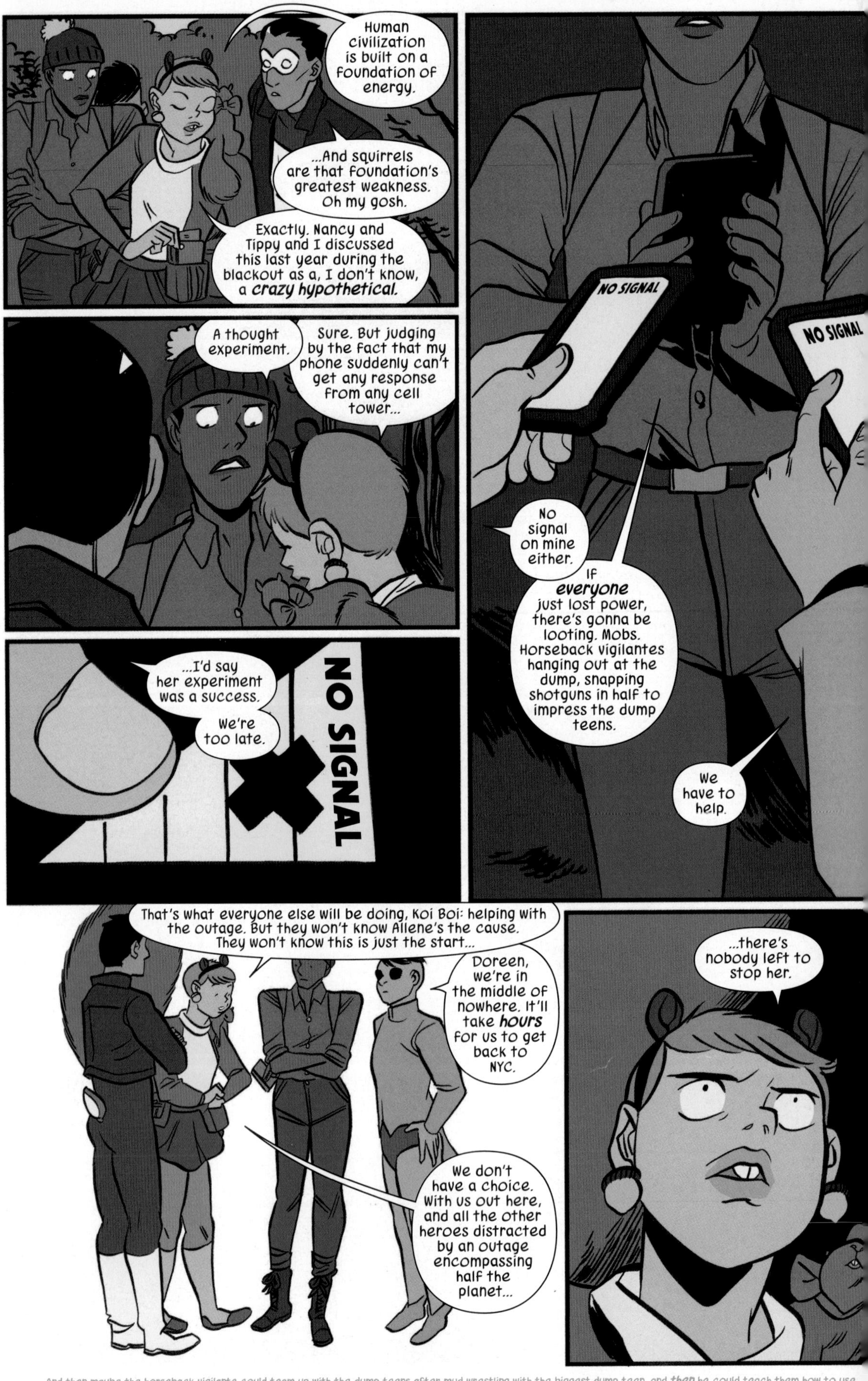
Human civilization is built on a foundation of energy.
...And squirrels are that foundation's greatest weakness. Oh my gosh.
Exactly. Nancy and Tippy and I discussed this last year during the blackout as a, I don't know, a *crazy hypothetical.*
A thought experiment.
Sure. But judging by the fact that my phone suddenly can't get any response from any cell tower...
...I'd say her experiment was a success.
We're too late.
NO SIGNAL
NO SIGNAL
NO SIGNAL
No signal on mine either.
If *everyone* just lost power, there's gonna be looting. Mobs. Horseback vigilantes hanging out at the dump, snapping shotguns in half to impress the dump teens.
We have to help.
That's what everyone else will be doing, Koi Boi: helping with the outage. But they won't know Allene's the cause. They won't know this is just the start...
Doreen, we're in the middle of nowhere. It'll take *hours* for us to get back to NYC.
We don't have a choice. With us out here, and all the other heroes distracted by an outage encompassing half the planet...
...there's nobody left to stop her.

And then maybe the horseback vigilante could team up with the dump teens after mud wrestling with the biggest dump teen, and *then* he could teach them how to use blue makeup to draw his logo across their faces before they all ride back into town to punch crime!!

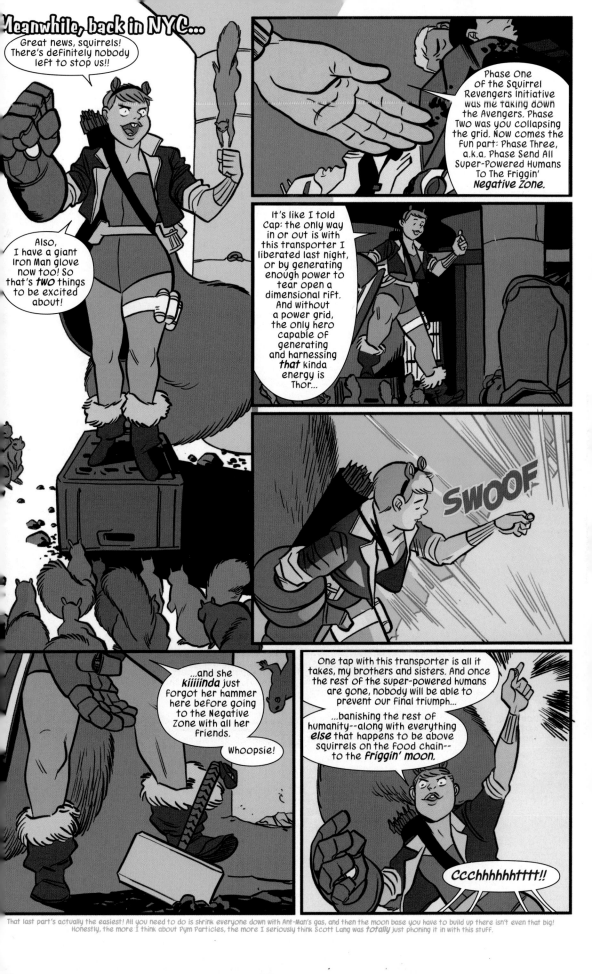

Great news, squirrels! There's definitely nobody left to stop us!!

Also, I have a giant Iron Man glove now too! So that's *two* things to be excited about!

Phase One of the Squirrel Revengers Initiative was me taking down the Avengers. Phase Two was you collapsing the grid. Now comes the fun part: Phase Three, a.k.a. Phase Send All Super-Powered Humans To The Friggin' **Negative Zone.**

It's like I told Cap: the only way in or out is with this transporter I liberated last night, or by generating enough power to tear open a dimensional rift. And without a power grid, the only hero capable of generating and harnessing *that* kinda energy is Thor...

SWOOF

...and she *kiiiiinda* just forgot her hammer here before going to the Negative Zone with all her friends.

Whoopsie!

One tap with this transporter is all it takes, my brothers and sisters. And once the rest of the super-powered humans are gone, nobody will be able to prevent our final triumph...

...banishing the rest of humanity--along with everything *else* that happens to be above squirrels on the food chain-- to the *friggin' moon.*

Ccchhhhhhtttt!!

That last part's actually the easiest! All you need to do is shrink everyone down with Ant-Man's gas, and then the moon base you have to build up there isn't even that big! Honestly, the more I think about Pym Particles, the more I seriously think Scott Lang was *totally* just phoning it in with this stuff.

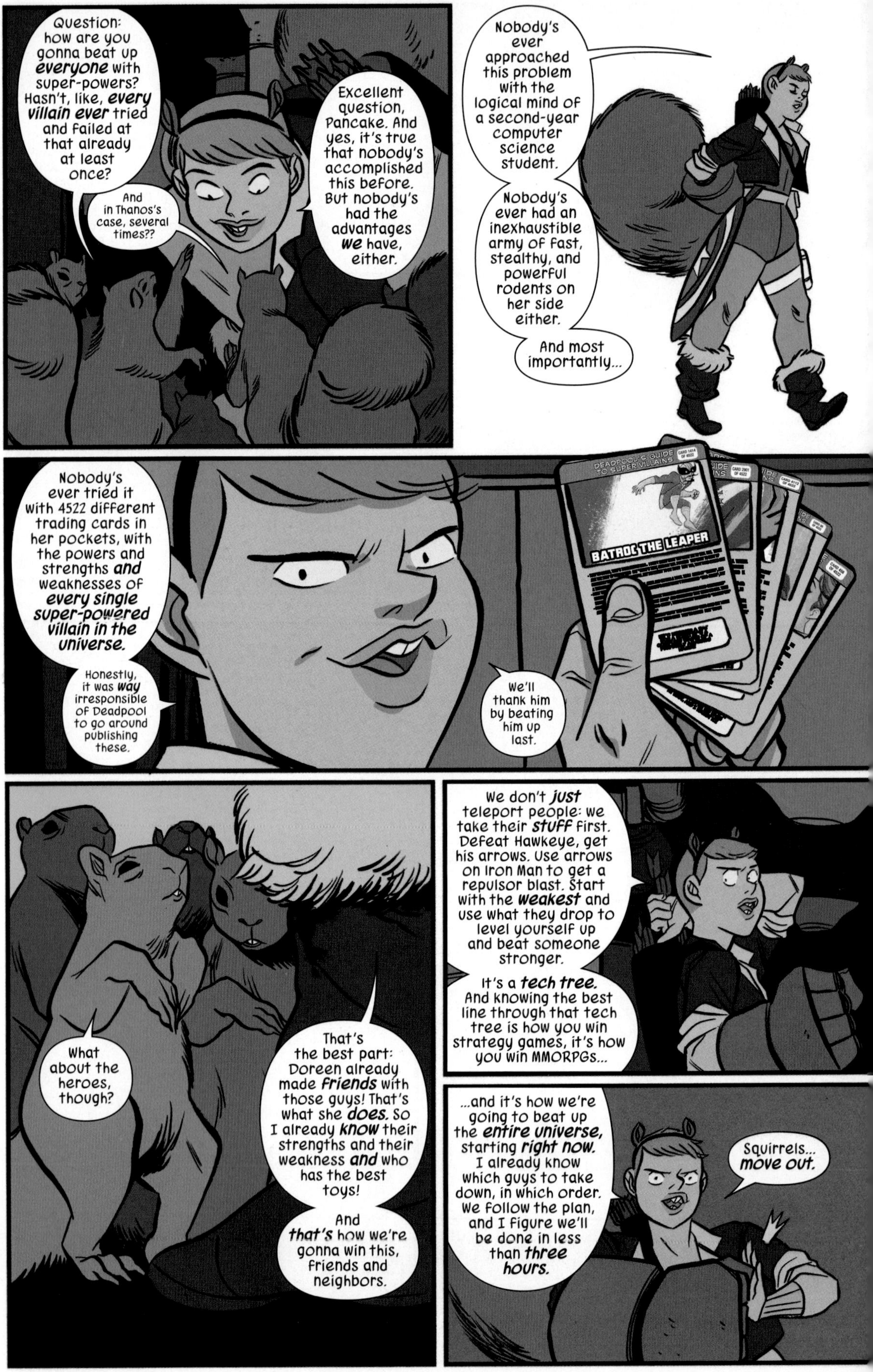

Question: how are you gonna beat up *everyone* with super-powers? Hasn't, like, *every villain ever* tried and failed at that already at least once?
And in Thanos's case, several times??
Excellent question, Pancake. And yes, it's true that nobody's accomplished this before. But nobody's had the advantages *we* have, either.
Nobody's ever approached this problem with the logical mind of a second-year computer science student.
Nobody's ever had an inexhaustible army of fast, stealthy, and powerful rodents on her side either.
And most importantly...
Nobody's ever tried it with 4522 different trading cards in her pockets, with the powers and strengths *and* weaknesses of *every single super-powered villain in the universe.*
Honestly, it was *way* irresponsible of Deadpool to go around publishing these.
DEADPOOL'S GUIDE TO SUPER VILLAINS
BATROC THE LEAPER
We'll thank him by beating him up last.
What about the heroes, though?
That's the best part: Doreen already made *friends* with those guys! That's what she *does.* So I already *know* their strengths and their weakness *and* who has the best toys!
And *that's* how we're gonna win this, friends and neighbors.
We don't *just* teleport people: we take their *stuff* first. Defeat Hawkeye, get his arrows. Use arrows on Iron Man to get a repulsor blast. Start with the *weakest* and use what they drop to level yourself up and beat someone stronger.
It's a *tech tree.* And knowing the best line through that tech tree is how you win strategy games, it's how you win MMORPGs...
...and it's how we're going to beat up the *entire universe,* starting *right now.* I already know which guys to take down, in which order. We follow the plan, and I figure we'll be done in less than *three hours.*
Squirrels... *move out.*

The Deadpool super villain cards were a bad enough idea, and that's without even *mentioning* the supplementary set of 1622 cards that cover their accessories. Deadpool, th
is an even worse idea than your *"Deadpool's Guide to Popular Cryptological Ciphers and Their Hitherto Undisclosed Vulnerabilities"* cards! *Sheesh!!*

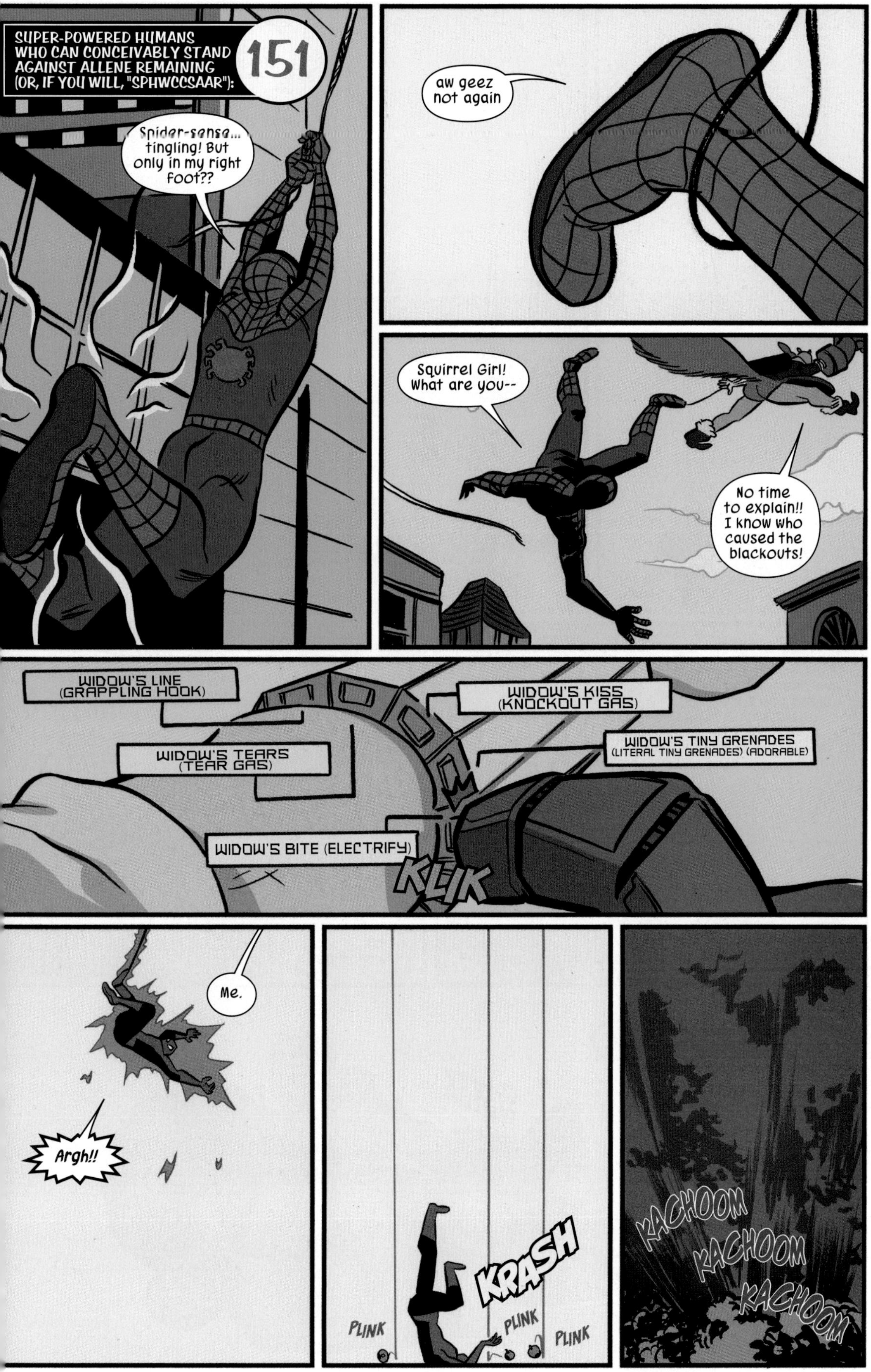

SUPER-POWERED HUMANS WHO CAN CONCEIVABLY STAND AGAINST ALLENE REMAINING (OR, IF YOU WILL, "SPHWCCSAAR"):
151
Spider-sense... tingling! But only in my right foot??
aw geez not again
Squirrel Girl! What are you--
No time to explain!! I know who caused the blackouts!
WIDOW'S LINE (GRAPPLING HOOK)
WIDOW'S KISS (KNOCKOUT GAS)
WIDOW'S TEARS (TEAR GAS)
WIDOW'S TINY GRENADES (LITERAL TINY GRENADES) (ADORABLE)
WIDOW'S BITE (ELECTRIFY)
KLIK
Me.
Argh!!
KRASH
PLINK
PLINK
PLINK
KACHOOM
KACHOOM
KACHOOM

And *that's* for preemptively ripping off the melody of my theme song before I even had a chance to think of it!

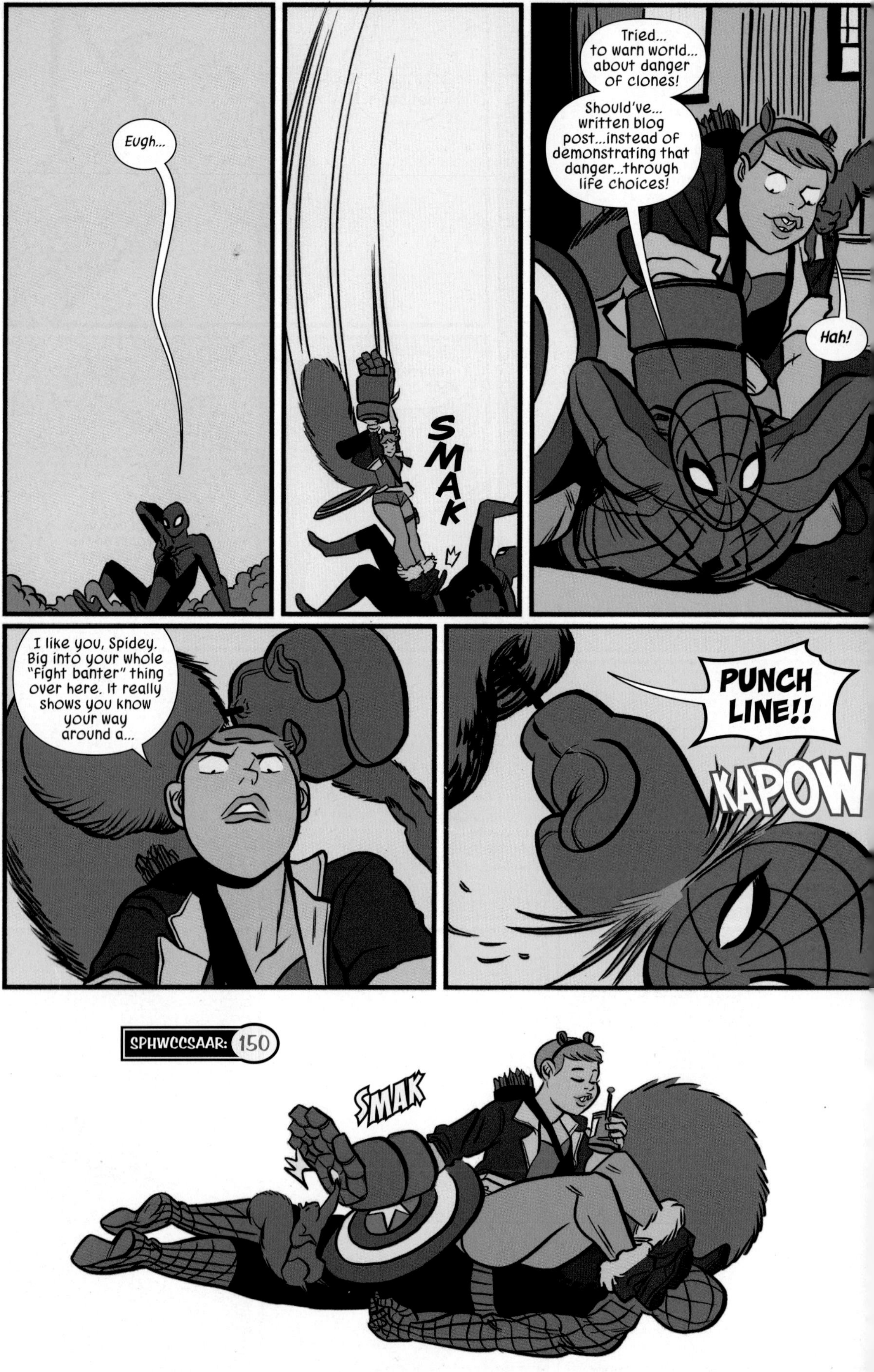
Eugh...
SMAK
Tried... to warn world... about danger of clones!
Should've... written blog post...instead of demonstrating that danger...through life choices!
Hah!
I like you, Spidey. Big into your whole "fight banter" thing over here. It really shows you know your way around a...
PUNCH LINE!!
KAPOW
SPHWCCSAAR: 150
SMAK

Spider-Man *claims* that he "spins a web, any size" which he then uses in the service of "[catching] thieves, just like flies." But the ability of a web to catch thieves doesn't scale linearly with size, which *necessarily* implies that Spider-Man could then spin a web so large that even *he* couldn't catch thieves in it! What's going on, Spider-Man?! Are you bragging so hard that you forgot about *logic??*

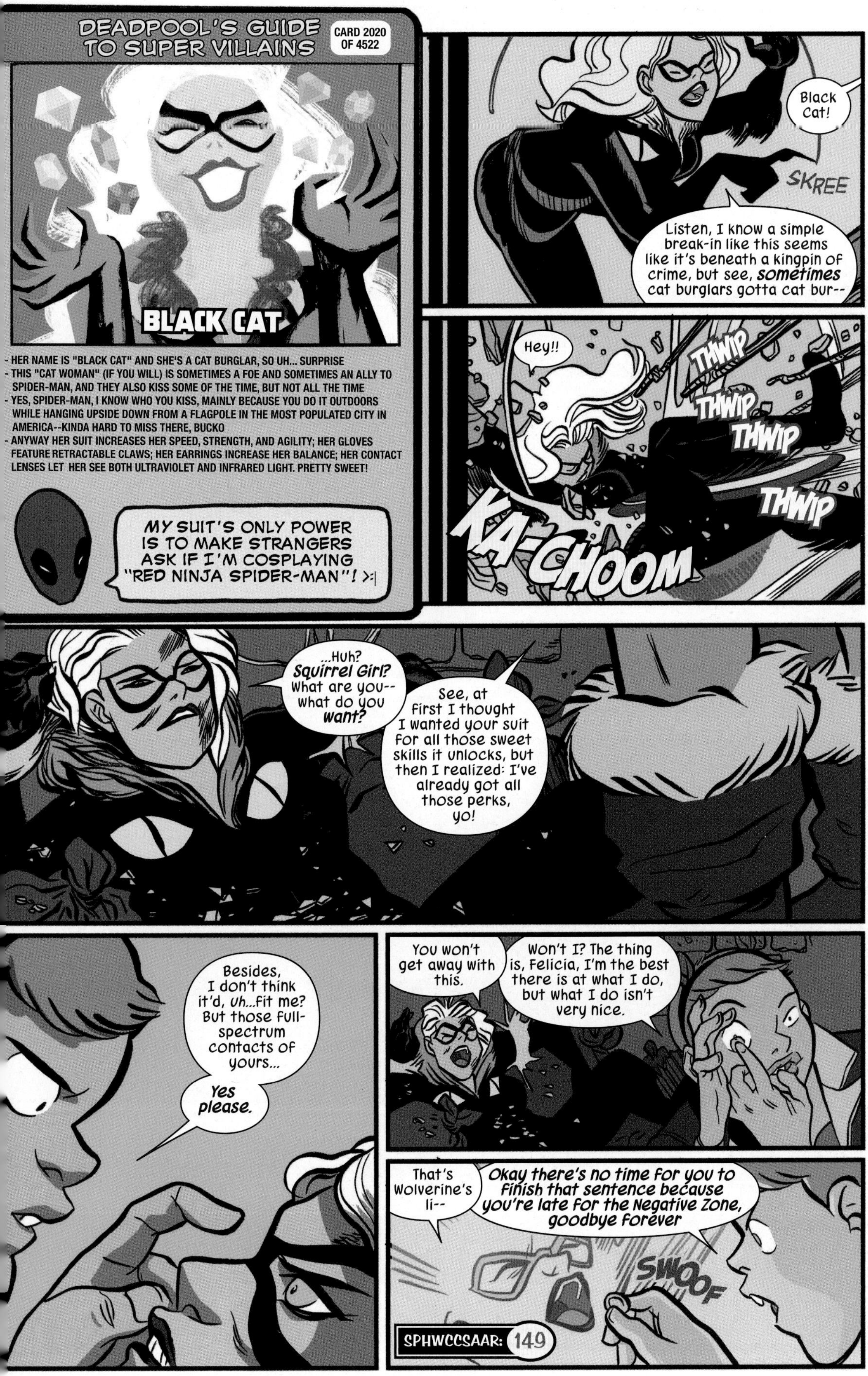

DEADPOOL'S GUIDE TO SUPER VILLAINS
CARD 2020 OF 4522
BLACK CAT
- HER NAME IS "BLACK CAT" AND SHE'S A CAT BURGLAR, SO UH... SURPRISE
- THIS "CAT WOMAN" (IF YOU WILL) IS SOMETIMES A FOE AND SOMETIMES AN ALLY TO SPIDER-MAN, AND THEY ALSO KISS SOME OF THE TIME, BUT NOT ALL THE TIME
- YES, SPIDER-MAN, I KNOW WHO YOU KISS, MAINLY BECAUSE YOU DO IT OUTDOORS WHILE HANGING UPSIDE DOWN FROM A FLAGPOLE IN THE MOST POPULATED CITY IN AMERICA--KINDA HARD TO MISS THERE, BUCKO
- ANYWAY HER SUIT INCREASES HER SPEED, STRENGTH, AND AGILITY; HER GLOVES FEATURE RETRACTABLE CLAWS; HER EARRINGS INCREASE HER BALANCE; HER CONTACT LENSES LET HER SEE BOTH ULTRAVIOLET AND INFRARED LIGHT. PRETTY SWEET!
MY SUIT'S ONLY POWER IS TO MAKE STRANGERS ASK IF I'M COSPLAYING "RED NINJA SPIDER-MAN"! >:|
Black Cat!
SKREE
Listen, I know a simple break-in like this seems like it's beneath a kingpin of crime, but see, *sometimes* cat burglars gotta cat bur--
Hey!!
THWIP
THWIP
THWIP
THWIP
KA-CHOOM
...Huh? *Squirrel Girl?* What are you-- what do you *want?*
See, at first I thought I wanted your suit for all those sweet skills it unlocks, but then I realized: I've already got all those perks, yo!
Besides, I don't think it'd, *uh*...fit me? But those full-spectrum contacts of yours...
Yes please.
You won't get away with this.
Won't I? The thing is, Felicia, I'm the best there is at what I do, but what I do isn't very nice.
That's Wolverine's li--
Okay there's no time for you to finish that sentence because you're late for the Negative Zone, goodbye forever
SWOOF
SPHWCCSAAR: 149

I'm the best at what I do too, but what I do isn't very hard (what I do is fall asleep watching movies).

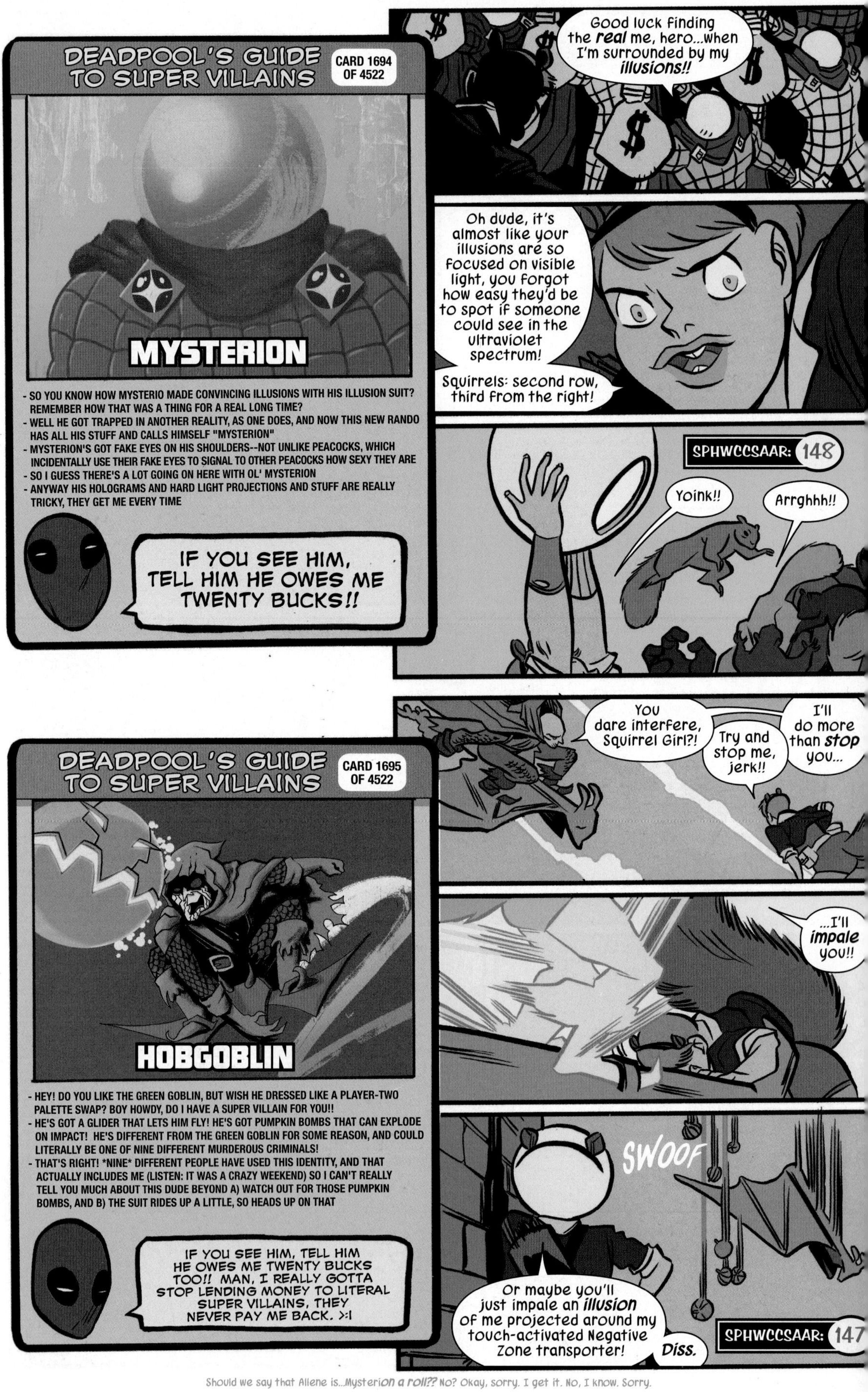
DEADPOOL'S GUIDE TO SUPER VILLAINS
CARD 1694 OF 4522
MYSTERION
- SO YOU KNOW HOW MYSTERIO MADE CONVINCING ILLUSIONS WITH HIS ILLUSION SUIT? REMEMBER HOW THAT WAS A THING FOR A REAL LONG TIME?
- WELL HE GOT TRAPPED IN ANOTHER REALITY, AS ONE DOES, AND NOW THIS NEW RANDO HAS ALL HIS STUFF AND CALLS HIMSELF "MYSTERION"
- MYSTERION'S GOT FAKE EYES ON HIS SHOULDERS--NOT UNLIKE PEACOCKS, WHICH INCIDENTALLY USE THEIR FAKE EYES TO SIGNAL TO OTHER PEACOCKS HOW SEXY THEY ARE
- SO I GUESS THERE'S A LOT GOING ON HERE WITH OL' MYSTERION
- ANYWAY HIS HOLOGRAMS AND HARD LIGHT PROJECTIONS AND STUFF ARE REALLY TRICKY, THEY GET ME EVERY TIME
IF YOU SEE HIM, TELL HIM HE OWES ME TWENTY BUCKS!!
Good luck finding the *real* me, hero...when I'm surrounded by my *illusions!!*
Oh dude, it's almost like your illusions are so focused on visible light, you forgot how easy they'd be to spot if someone could see in the ultraviolet spectrum!
Squirrels: second row, third from the right!
SPHWCCSAAR: 148
Yoink!!
Arrghhh!!
DEADPOOL'S GUIDE TO SUPER VILLAINS
CARD 1695 OF 4522
HOBGOBLIN
- HEY! DO YOU LIKE THE GREEN GOBLIN, BUT WISH HE DRESSED LIKE A PLAYER-TWO PALETTE SWAP? BOY HOWDY, DO I HAVE A SUPER VILLAIN FOR YOU!!
- HE'S GOT A GLIDER THAT LETS HIM FLY! HE'S GOT PUMPKIN BOMBS THAT CAN EXPLODE ON IMPACT! HE'S DIFFERENT FROM THE GREEN GOBLIN FOR SOME REASON, AND COULD LITERALLY BE ONE OF NINE DIFFERENT MURDEROUS CRIMINALS!
- THAT'S RIGHT! *NINE* DIFFERENT PEOPLE HAVE USED THIS IDENTITY, AND THAT ACTUALLY INCLUDES ME (LISTEN: IT WAS A CRAZY WEEKEND) SO I CAN'T REALLY TELL YOU MUCH ABOUT THIS DUDE BEYOND A) WATCH OUT FOR THOSE PUMPKIN BOMBS, AND B) THE SUIT RIDES UP A LITTLE, SO HEADS UP ON THAT
IF YOU SEE HIM, TELL HIM HE OWES ME TWENTY BUCKS TOO!! MAN, I REALLY GOTTA STOP LENDING MONEY TO LITERAL SUPER VILLAINS, THEY NEVER PAY ME BACK. >:I
You dare interfere, Squirrel Girl?!
Try and stop me, jerk!!
I'll do more than *stop* you...
...I'll *impale* you!!
SWOOF
Or maybe you'll just impale an *illusion* of me projected around my touch-activated Negative Zone transporter!
Diss.
SPHWCCSAAR: 147

Should we say that Allene is...Mysteri*on a roll??* No? Okay, sorry. I get it. No, I know. Sorry.

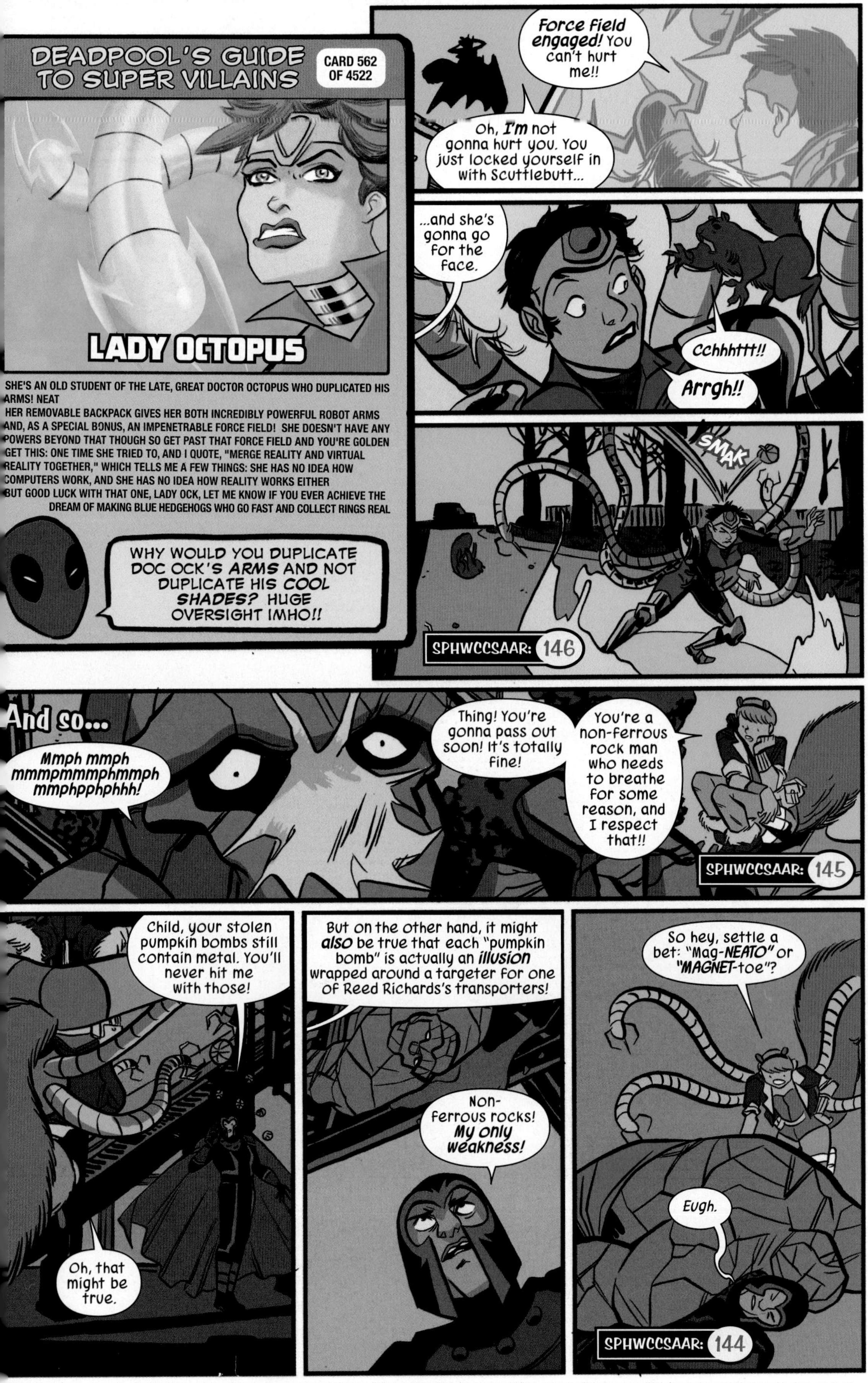
DEADPOOL'S GUIDE TO SUPER VILLAINS
CARD 562 OF 4522
LADY OCTOPUS
SHE'S AN OLD STUDENT OF THE LATE, GREAT DOCTOR OCTOPUS WHO DUPLICATED HIS ARMS! NEAT
HER REMOVABLE BACKPACK GIVES HER BOTH INCREDIBLY POWERFUL ROBOT ARMS AND, AS A SPECIAL BONUS, AN IMPENETRABLE FORCE FIELD! SHE DOESN'T HAVE ANY POWERS BEYOND THAT THOUGH SO GET PAST THAT FORCE FIELD AND YOU'RE GOLDEN
GET THIS: ONE TIME SHE TRIED TO, AND I QUOTE, "MERGE REALITY AND VIRTUAL REALITY TOGETHER," WHICH TELLS ME A FEW THINGS: SHE HAS NO IDEA HOW COMPUTERS WORK, AND SHE HAS NO IDEA HOW REALITY WORKS EITHER
BUT GOOD LUCK WITH THAT ONE, LADY OCK, LET ME KNOW IF YOU EVER ACHIEVE THE DREAM OF MAKING BLUE HEDGEHOGS WHO GO FAST AND COLLECT RINGS REAL
WHY WOULD YOU DUPLICATE DOC OCK'S ARMS AND NOT DUPLICATE HIS COOL SHADES? HUGE OVERSIGHT IMHO!!
Force field engaged! You can't hurt me!!
Oh, I'm not gonna hurt you. You just locked yourself in with Scuttlebutt...
...and she's gonna go for the face.
Cchhhttt!!
Arrgh!!
SMAK
SPHWCCSAAR: 146
And so...
Mmph mmph mmmpmmmphmmph mmphpphphhh!
Thing! You're gonna pass out soon! It's totally fine!
You're a non-ferrous rock man who needs to breathe for some reason, and I respect that!!
SPHWCCSAAR: 145
Child, your stolen pumpkin bombs still contain metal. You'll never hit me with those!
Oh, that might be true.
But on the other hand, it might also be true that each "pumpkin bomb" is actually an illusion wrapped around a targeter for one of Reed Richards's transporters!
Non-ferrous rocks! My only weakness!
So hey, settle a bet: "Mag-NEATO" or "MAGNET-toe"?
Eugh.
SPHWCCSAAR: 144

JN FACT: Did you know the full version of the Thing's famous catchphrase, "What a revoltin' development" is actually "What a revoltin' development! First my hip-hop project 'It's Clobbering Rhyme' breaks up, and now *this?*"

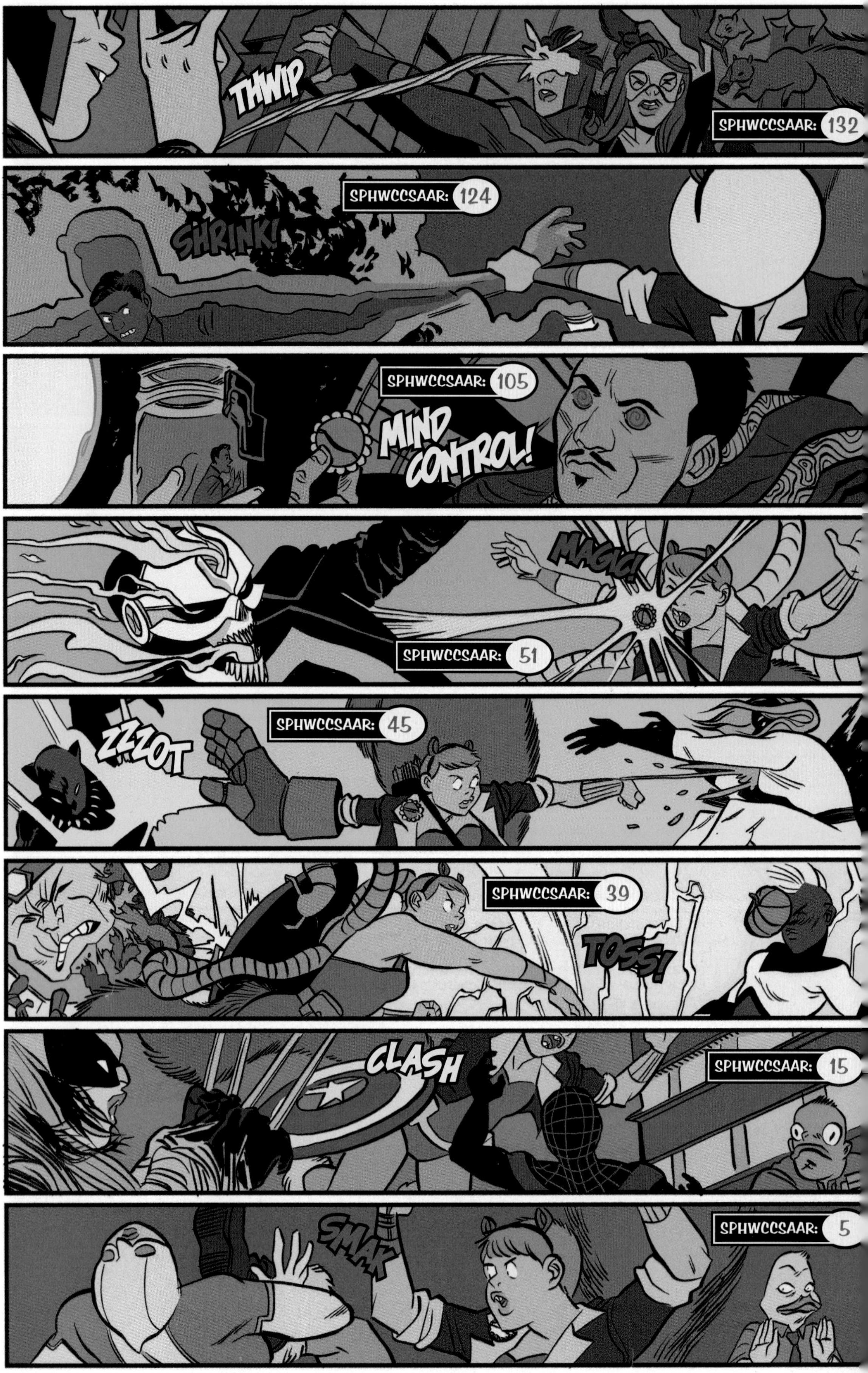
THWIP
SPHWCCSAAR: 132
SPHWCCSAAR: 124
SHRINK!
SPHWCCSAAR: 105
MIND CONTROL!
MAGIC!
SPHWCCSAAR: 51
ZZZOT
SPHWCCSAAR: 45
SPHWCCSAAR: 39
TOSS!
CLASH
SPHWCCSAAR: 15
SMAK
SPHWCCSAAR: 5

There he is, just like I promised: ***Johnny Fishlips!!*** Also featured on this page are Purple Man (whose body squirts out mind-control gas), Doctor Strange (who seems a fair sight stranger than any actual doctor ***I've*** ever seen, that's for darn sure), Gwenpool (who I can only assume has all the powers of both Gwens ***and*** pools) and Ghost Rider (half ghost, half rider).

Chht chhht cht!

Wait wait wait!! I was under the impression this was the *nonviolent* comi--

SPHWCCSAAR!

Aaaaand... *done.*

Unf!

PLOPP

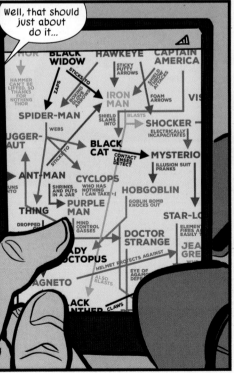

Well, that should just about do it...

THOR   BLACK WIDOW   HAWKEYE   CAPTAIN AMERICA

HAMMER CAN'T BE LIFTED, SO THANKS FOR NOTHING THOR

STICKS TO

ZAPS

STICKY PUTTY ARROWS

FOLDS REMOTELY ATTACKS

IRON MAN

VIS

FOAM ARROWS

BLASTS

SPIDER-MAN

WEBS

SHIELD SLAMS INTO

SHOCKER

ELECTRICALLY INCAPACITATES

UGGER-AUT

BODY SLIDE THROW

STICKS TO

BLACK CAT

CONTACT LENSES DETECT

MYSTERIO

ILLUSION SUIT PRANKS

ANT-MAN

CYCLOPS

WHO HAS NOTHING I CAN TAKE

HOBGOBLIN

RUNS INTO

SHRINKS AND PUTS IN A JAR

GOBLIN BOMB KNOCKS OUT

THING

PURPLE MAN

STAR-LO

DROPPED

MIND CONTROL GASSES

DY OCTOPUS

DOCTOR STRANGE

ELEMENT FIRES A EASILY T

JEA GRE

AGNETO

HELMET PROTECTS AGAINST

ALSO BLASTS

EYE OF AGAM DEF

ACK NTHER

CLAWS

CHOOM CHOOM CHOOM

Wait. "Choom choom choom"?

Hah hah hah! *Yes.*

Yes friggin' *please.*

This page firmly establishes in canon that the sound a knocked-out Deadpool makes when landing on a pile of other knocked-out heroes is "plopp." Three P's. It's sort of a gross sound. Deadpool, man, why you gotta make such gross-nasty noises??

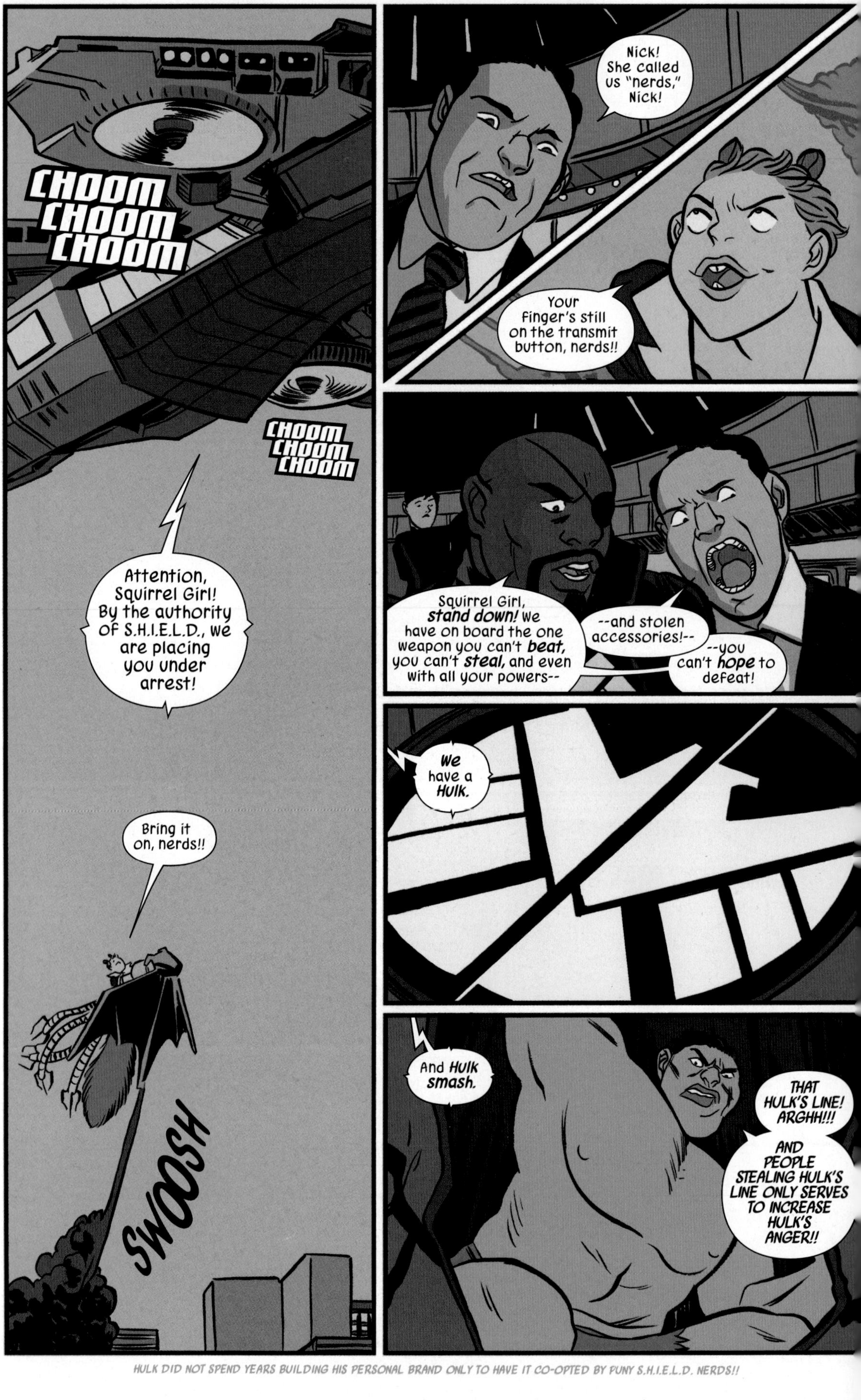
CHOOM CHOOM CHOOM
CHOOM CHOOM CHOOM
Attention, Squirrel Girl! By the authority of S.H.I.E.L.D., we are placing you under arrest!
Bring it on, nerds!!
SWOOSH
Nick! She called us "nerds," Nick!
Your finger's still on the transmit button, nerds!!
Squirrel Girl, stand down! We have on board the one weapon you can't beat, you can't steal, and even with all your powers--
--and stolen accessories!--
--you can't hope to defeat!
We have a Hulk.
And Hulk smash.
THAT HULK'S LINE! ARGHH!!!
AND PEOPLE STEALING HULK'S LINE ONLY SERVES TO INCREASE HULK'S ANGER!!

HULK DID NOT SPEND YEARS BUILDING HIS PERSONAL BRAND ONLY TO HAVE IT CO-OPTED BY PUNY S.H.I.E.L.D. NERDS!!

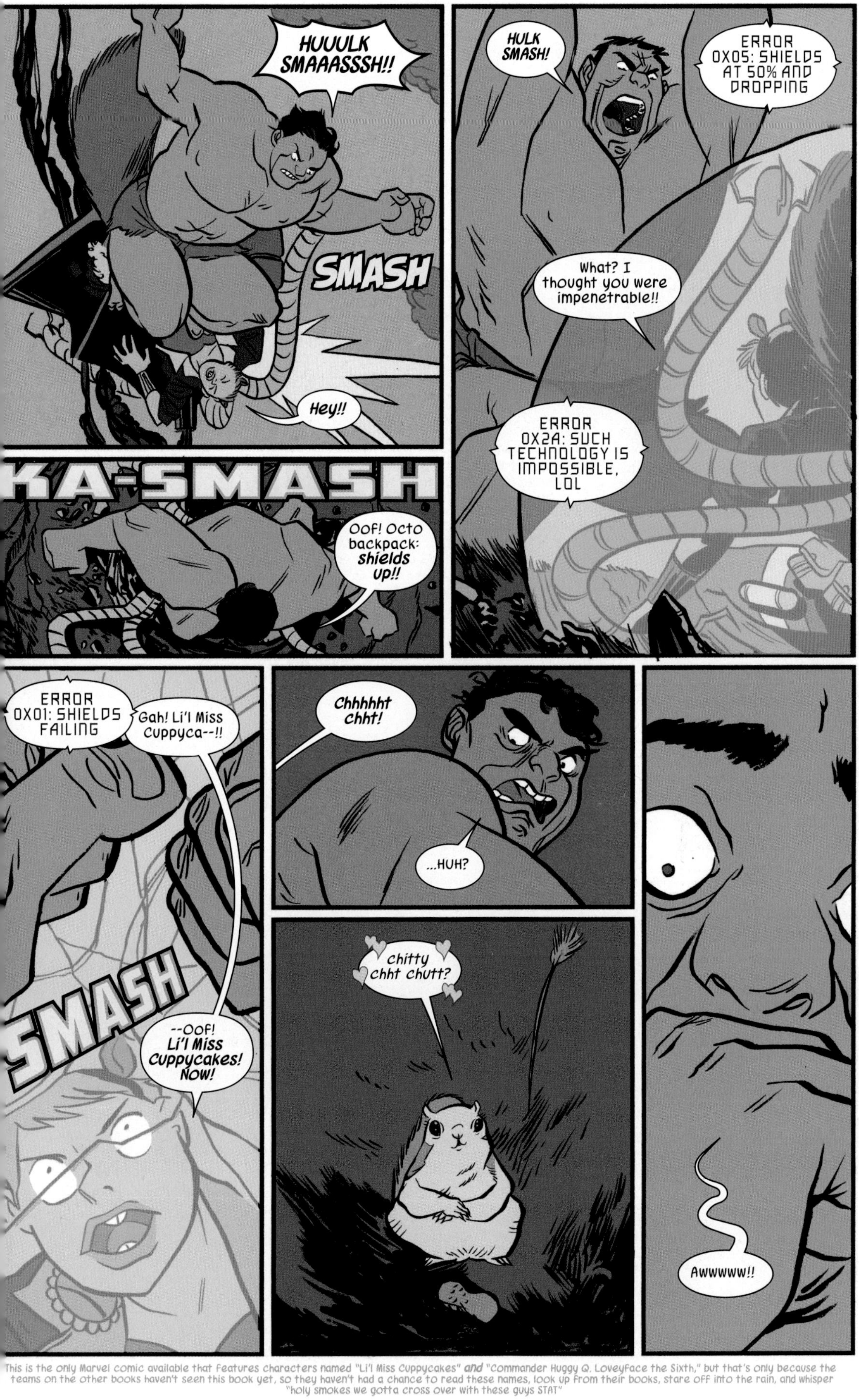
HUUULK SMAAASSSH!!
SMASH
Hey!!
KA-SMASH
Oof! Octo backpack: shields up!!
HULK SMASH!
ERROR 0X05: SHIELDS AT 50% AND DROPPING
What? I thought you were impenetrable!!
ERROR 0X2A: SUCH TECHNOLOGY IS IMPOSSIBLE, LOL
ERROR 0X01: SHIELDS FAILING
Gah! Li'l Miss Cuppyca--!!
SMASH
--OOF! Li'l Miss Cuppycakes! NOW!
Chhhhht chht!
...HUH?
chitty chht chutt?
AWWWWW!!

This is the only Marvel comic available that features characters named "Li'l Miss Cuppycakes" *and* "Commander Huggy Q. LoveyFace the Sixth," but that's only because the teams on the other books haven't seen this book yet, so they haven't had a chance to read these names, look up from their books, stare off into the rain, and whisper "holy smokes we gotta cross over with these guys STAT"

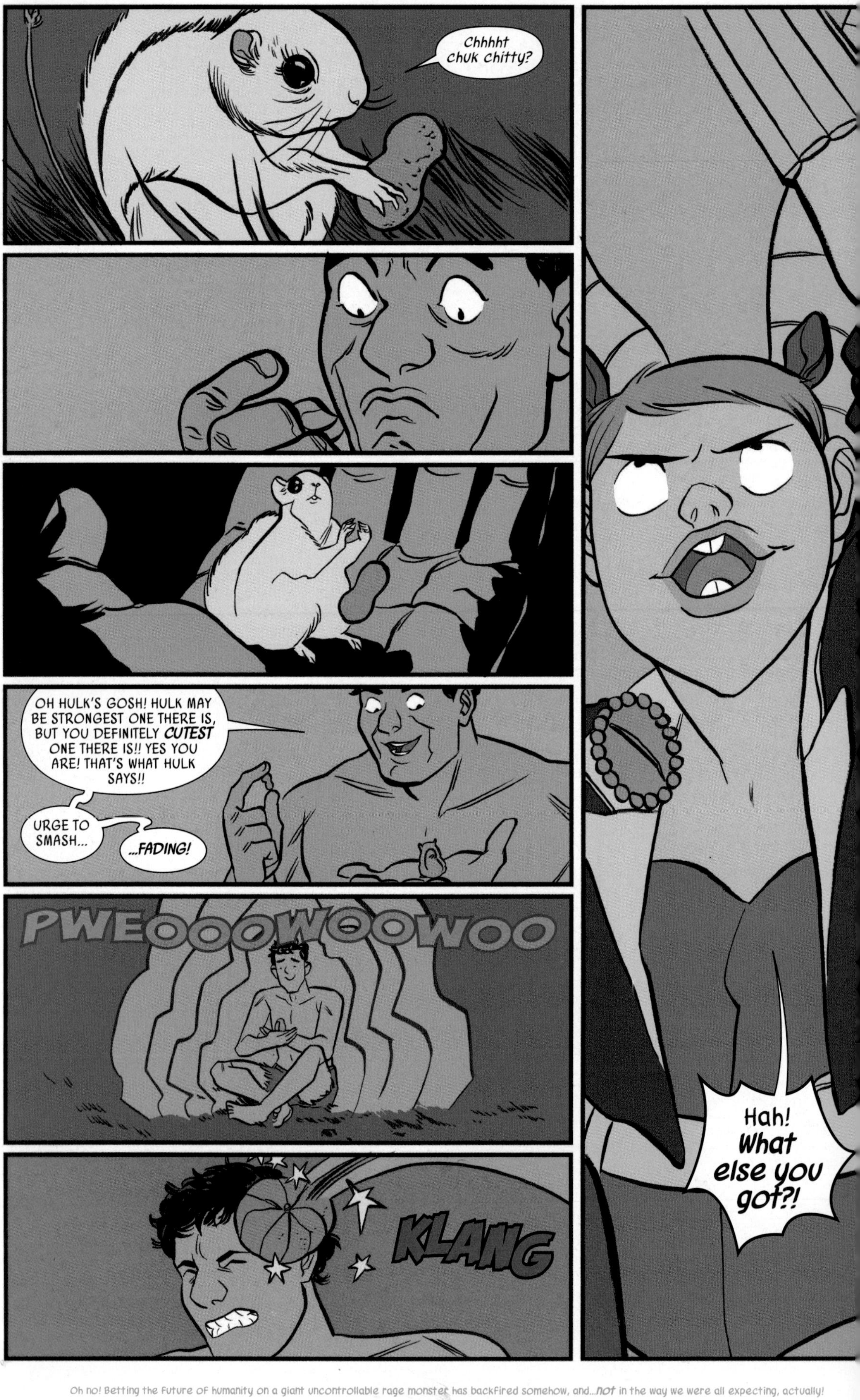
Chhhht chuk chitty?
OH HULK'S GOSH! HULK MAY BE STRONGEST ONE THERE IS, BUT YOU DEFINITELY CUTEST ONE THERE IS!! YES YOU ARE! THAT'S WHAT HULK SAYS!!
URGE TO SMASH...
...FADING!
PWEOOOWOOWOO
KLANG
Hah! What else you got?!

Oh no! Betting the future of humanity on a giant uncontrollable rage monster has backfired somehow, and...*not* in the way we were all expecting, actually!

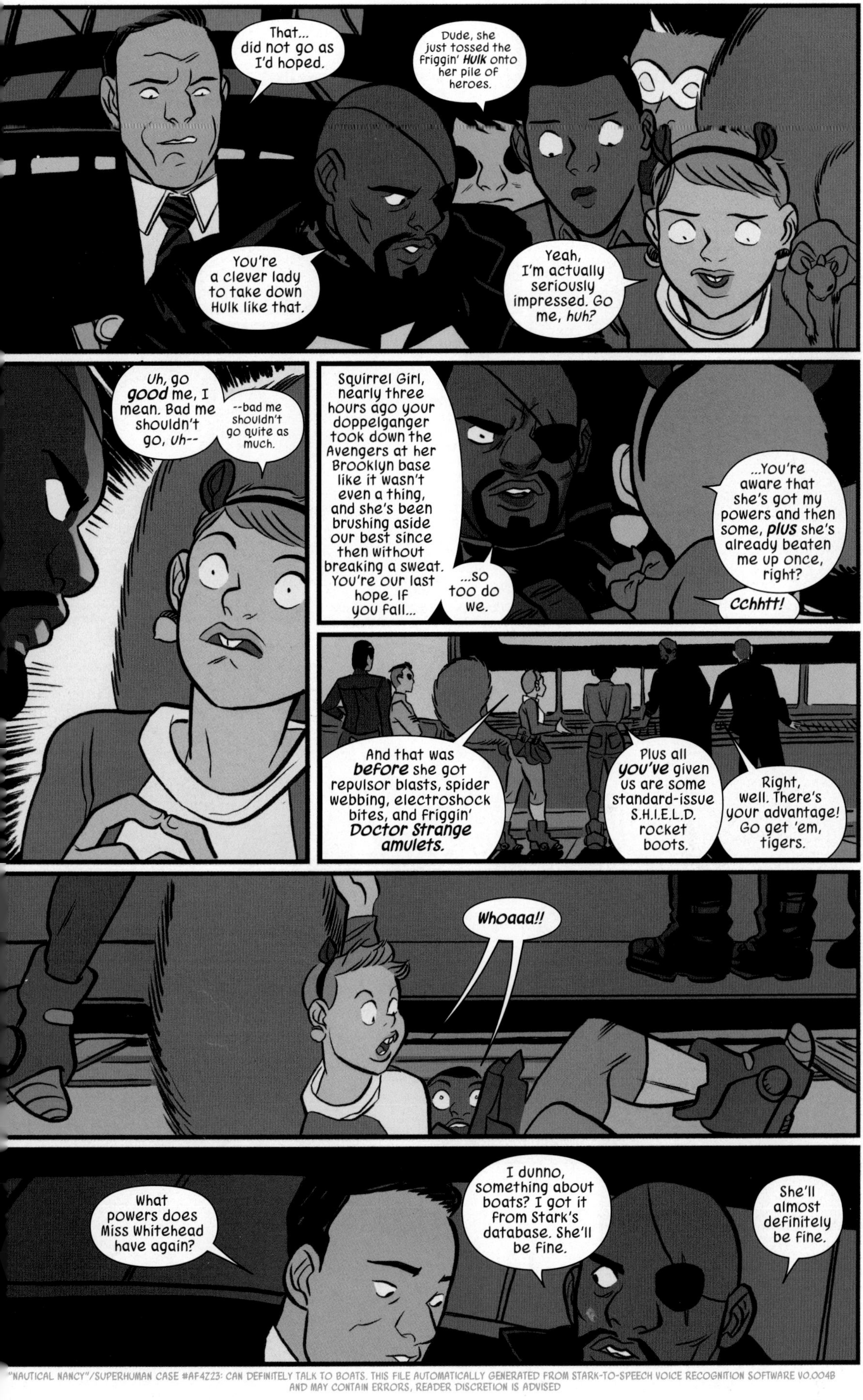
That... did not go as I'd hoped.
Dude, she just tossed the friggin' HULK onto her pile of heroes.
You're a clever lady to take down Hulk like that.
Yeah, I'm actually seriously impressed. Go me, huh?
Uh, go good me, I mean. Bad me shouldn't go, uh--
--bad me shouldn't go quite as much.
Squirrel Girl, nearly three hours ago your doppelganger took down the Avengers at her Brooklyn base like it wasn't even a thing, and she's been brushing aside our best since then without breaking a sweat. You're our last hope. If you fall...
...so too do we.
...You're aware that she's got my powers and then some, PLUS she's already beaten me up once, right?
Cchhtt!
And that was before she got repulsor blasts, spider webbing, electroshock bites, and friggin' Doctor Strange amulets.
Plus all you've given us are some standard-issue S.H.I.E.L.D. rocket boots.
Right, well. There's your advantage! Go get 'em, tigers.
Whoaaa!!
What powers does Miss Whitehead have again?
I dunno, something about boats? I got it from Stark's database. She'll be fine.
She'll almost definitely be fine.

"NAUTICAL NANCY"/SUPERHUMAN CASE #AF4Z23: CAN DEFINITELY TALK TO BOATS. THIS FILE AUTOMATICALLY GENERATED FROM STARK-TO-SPEECH VOICE RECOGNITION SOFTWARE V0.004B AND MAY CONTAIN ERRORS, READER DISCRETION IS ADVISED

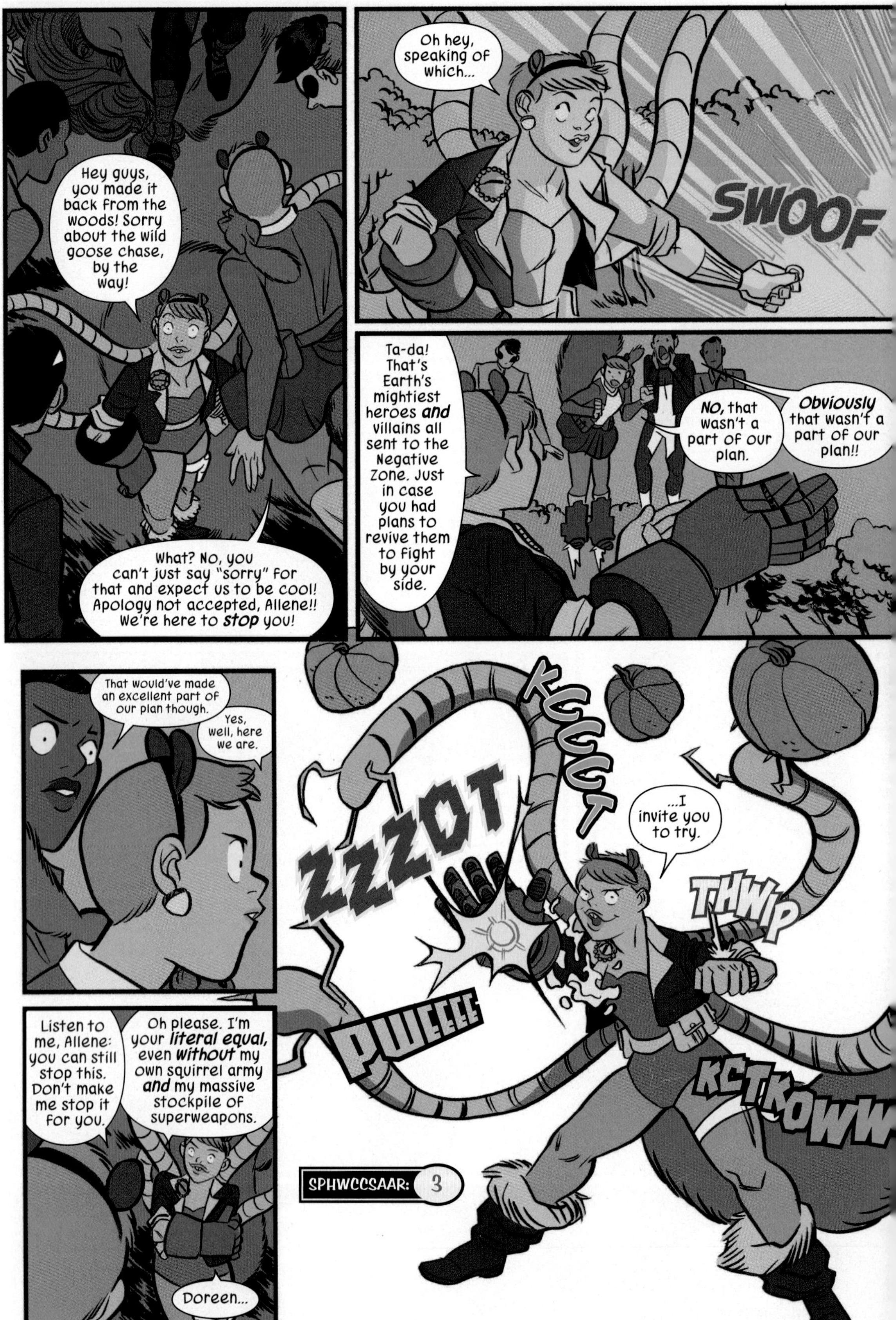
Hey guys, you made it back from the woods! Sorry about the wild goose chase, by the way!
What? No, you can't just say "sorry" for that and expect us to be cool! Apology not accepted, Allene!! We're here to *stop* you!
Oh hey, speaking of which...
SWOOF
Ta-da! That's Earth's mightiest heroes **and** villains all sent to the Negative Zone. Just in case you had plans to revive them to fight by your side.
NO, that wasn't a part of our plan.
Obviously that wasn't a part of our plan!!
That would've made an excellent part of our plan though.
Yes, well, here we are.
KCCCT
ZZZOT
...I invite you to try.
THWIP
PWEEEE
KCTKOWW
Listen to me, Allene: you can still stop this. Don't make me stop it for you.
Oh please. I'm your *literal equal,* even *without* my own squirrel army *and* my massive stockpile of superweapons.
Doreen...
SPHWCCSAAR: 3

On one hand, super amazing rocket boots. On the other hand, every super hero power ever. But back on the first hand...Friggin' super amazing rocket boots!!

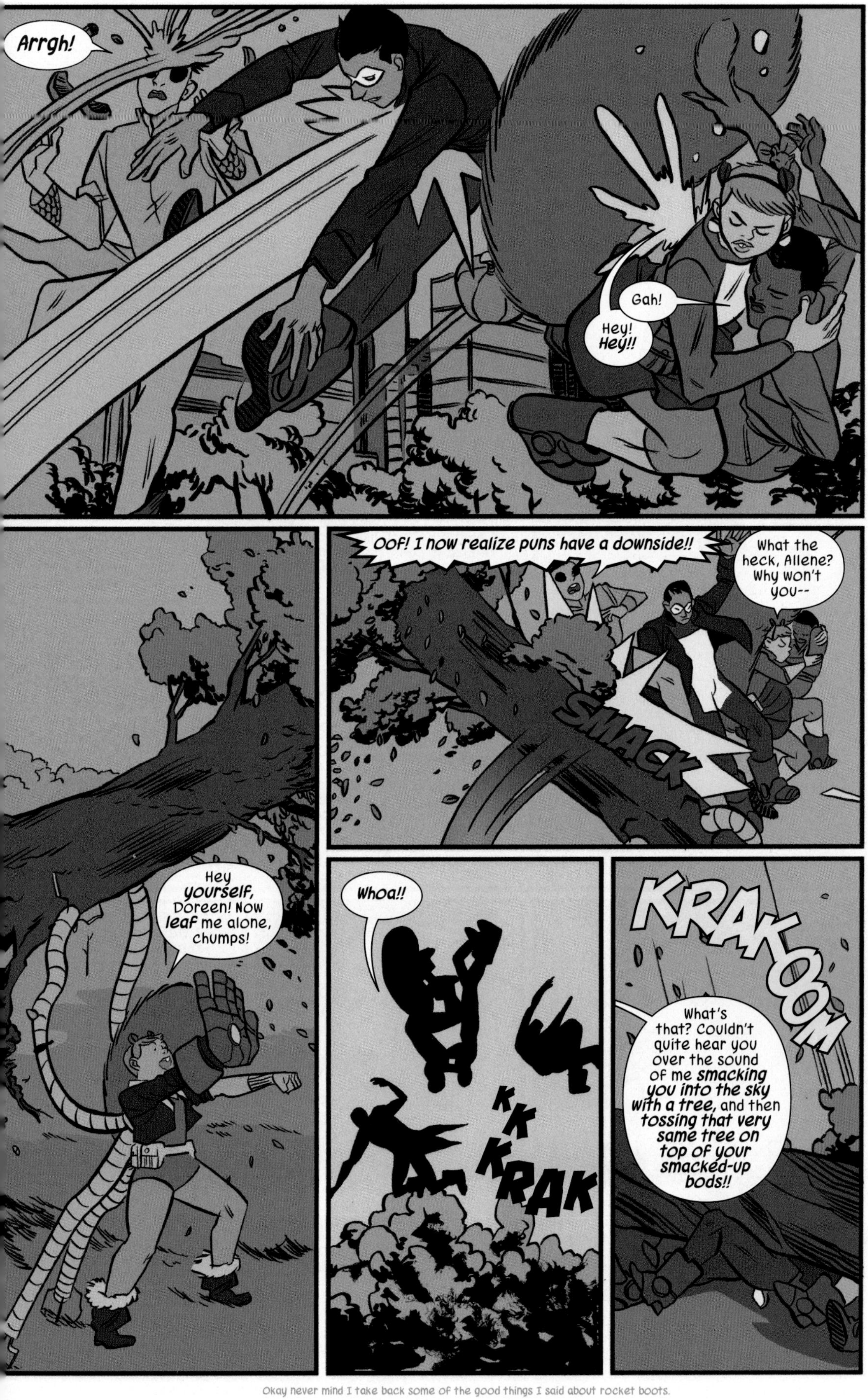

Arrgh!
Gah!
Hey! Hey!!
Oof! I now realize puns have a downside!!
What the heck, Allene? Why won't you--
SMACK
Hey yourself, Doreen! Now leaf me alone, chumps!
Whoa!!
KKKRAK
KRAKOOM
What's that? Couldn't quite hear you over the sound of me smacking you into the sky with a tree, and then tossing that very same tree on top of your smacked-up bods!!

Okay never mind I take back some of the good things I said about rocket boots.

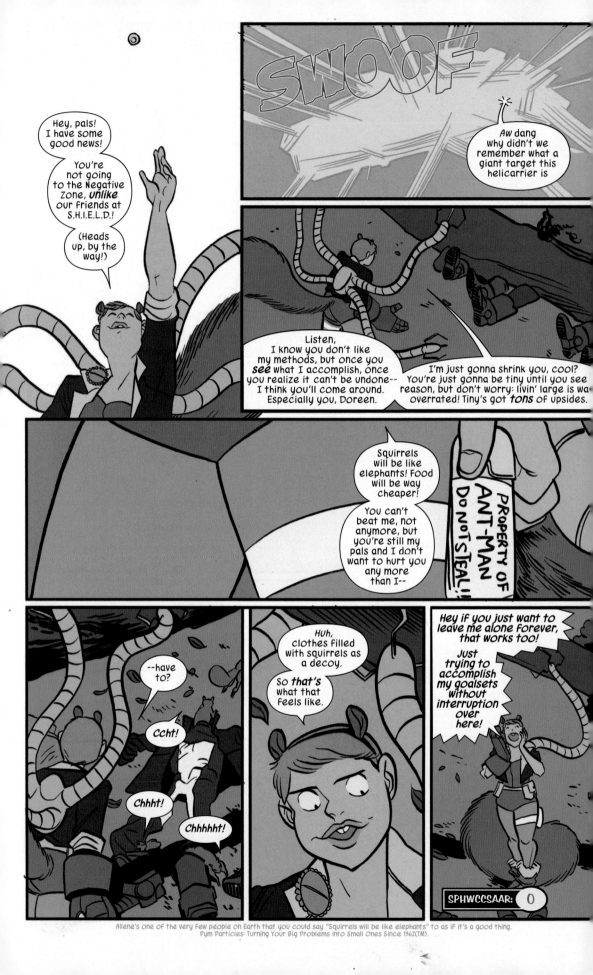

SWOOF

Hey, pals! I have some good news!

You're not going to the Negative Zone, *unlike* our friends at S.H.I.E.L.D.!

(Heads up, by the way!)

Aw dang why didn't we remember what a giant target this helicarrier is

Listen, I know you don't like my methods, but once you *see* what I accomplish, once you realize it can't be undone-- I think you'll come around. Especially you, Doreen.

I'm just gonna shrink you, cool? You're just gonna be tiny until you see reason, but don't worry: livin' large is *way* overrated! Tiny's got *tons* of upsides.

Squirrels will be like elephants! Food will be way cheaper!

You can't beat me, not anymore, but you're still my pals and I don't want to hurt you any more than I--

PROPERTY OF ANT-MAN DO NOT STEAL!!

--have to?

Ccht!

Chhht!

Chhhht!

Huh, clothes filled with squirrels as a decoy.

So *that's* what that feels like.

Hey if you just want to leave me alone forever, that works too!

Just trying to accomplish my goalsets without interruption over here!

SPHWCCSAAR: 0

Allene's one of the very few people on Earth that you could say "Squirrels will be like elephants" to as if it's a good thing.
Pym Particles: Turning Your Big Problems Into Small Ones Since 1962(TM).

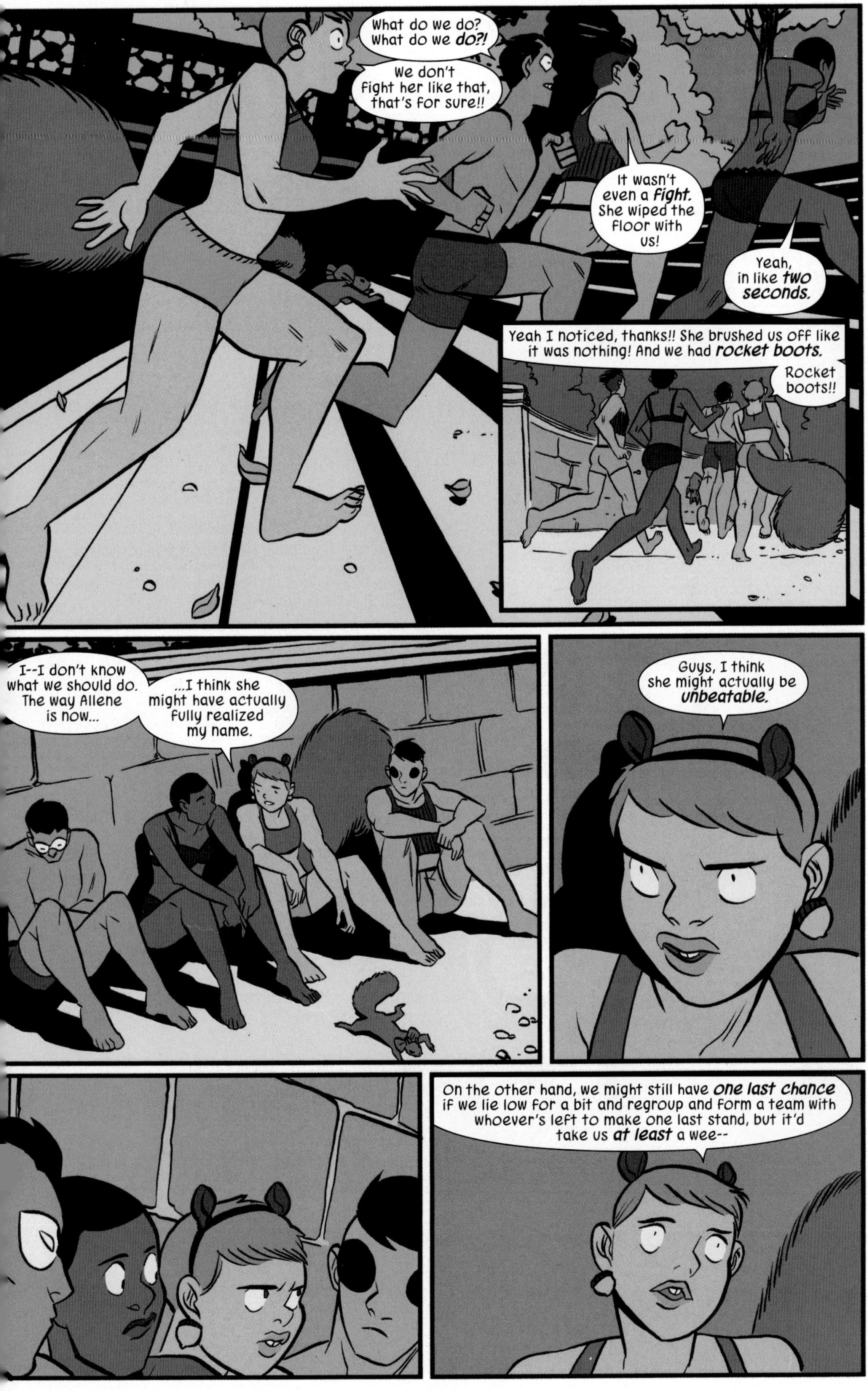
What do we do? What do we do?!
We don't fight her like that, that's for sure!!
It wasn't even a fight. She wiped the floor with us!
Yeah, in like two seconds.
Yeah I noticed, thanks!! She brushed us off like it was nothing! And we had rocket boots.
Rocket boots!!
I--I don't know what we should do. The way Allene is now...
...I think she might have actually fully realized my name.
Guys, I think she might actually be unbeatable.
On the other hand, we might still have one last chance if we lie low for a bit and regroup and form a team with whoever's left to make one last stand, but it'd take us at least a wee--

ONE WEEK LATER

THE NEW YORK BULLETIN 5¢

SQUIRREL GIRL'S ATTACKS NOW WORLDWIDE

FOR FIRST TIME SINCE 1800s, ENTIRE PLANET NOW WITHOUT ELECTRICITY

· GLOBAL POWER GRIDS STILL DOWN, TRANSFORMER STATIONS DESTROYED, SQUIRRELS DISRUPTING ANY ATTEMPT AT REPAIR
· IT'S NOT THAT BAD THOUGH, IT'S KINDA NICE, EVERYTHING'S REAL QUIET AND PEACEFUL AND WE ALL GET TO GO TO BED AS SOON AS IT'S DARK OUT

Lorem ipsum dolor sit amet, consectetur adipiscing elit. Proin quam massa, gravida consequat eros nec, condimentum imperdiet massa. Mauris fringilla dolor a sapien malesuada, sit amet consectetur eros fermentum. Phasellus justo tortor, mattis vitae eros vitae, mollis auctor nisl. Fusce sit amet malesuada tortor, sit amet maximus augue. Vestibulum dapibus convallis leo quis posuere. Donec quis ornare nisi. Nam rutrum ante feugiat, sollicitudin neque eu, rhoncus tortor. Quisque non magna id eros viverra tempus. Suspendisse ac ornare eros. Nullam at vehicula purus, eu convallis dolor. Vivamus vel rutrum odio. Etiam in mi elit.

In porttitor efficitur ligula at auctor. Nam ligula justo, pharetra quis luctus non, consequat sagittis ligula. Aenean porta vulputate quam, non fermentum magna. Cras massa arcu, tincidunt in odio in, consequat dapibus elit. Nullam nec neque commodo, bibendum mauris sed, lobortis orci. Suspendisse laoreet vitae leo ut bibendum. Morbi tristique gravida nulla, eget volutpat eros tempus eu. Sed a malesuada eros. Etiam vitae efficitur ante. Mauris dignissim cursus nisl nec dignissim. Donec porttitor magna id tortor pharetra, id semper lectus semper. In tristique mauris sed nisl commodo dignissim. Phasellus hendrerit ex lacus, vitae fringilla est vulputate nec. Nunc eu euismod nulla, ac finibus mi. Etiam facilisis turpis mollis nunc vestibulum convallis. Vivamus posuere libero sed commodo ultrices.

Vestibulum at ullamcorper neque. Integer tortor risus, efficitur in bibendum non,

---

NO SUPER-POWERED INDIVIDUAL SPOTTED FOR THREE DAYS

IS SQUIRREL GIRL NOW TRULY UNSTOPPABLE??

Pilus tellus a nibh blandit tempor. Pellentesque a ex malesuada, mattis metus sit amet, dictum lorem. Suspendisse lacinia egestas enim non faucibus. Aenean erat velit, rhoncus et justo non, mollis consectetur tellus. Integer lacinia lacus elit, ac vestibulum nunc laoreet et. Proin finibus diam quis tortor dapibus, eget tempus nulla malesuada. Pellentesque habitant morbi tristique senectus et netus et malesuada fames ac turpis egestas. Sed at dui at dolor posuere suscipit. Fusce pharetra dapibus elit. Interdum et malesuada fames ac ante ipsum primis in faucibus. Donec ultrices nisl dolor, at ultrices ligula dapibus non.

Nunc egestas, mauris sit amet volutpat feugiat, urna tellus rhoncus dolor, et suscipit purus ligula eget lacus. Vivamus tinciLorem ipsum dolor sit amet, consectetur adipiscing elit. Proin quam massa, gravida consequat eros nec, condimentum imperdiet massa. Mauris fringilla dolor a sapien malesuada, sit amet consectetur eros fermentum. Phasellus justo tortor, mattis vitae eros vitae, mollis auctor nisl. Fusce sit amet malesuada tortor, sit amet maximus augue. Vestibulum dapibus convallis leo quis posuere. Donec quis ornare nisi. Nam rutrum ante feugiat, sollicitudin neque eu, rhoncus tortor. Quisque non magna id eros viverra tempus. Suspendisse ac ornare eros. Nullam at vehicula purus, eu convallis dolor. Vivamus vel rutrum odio. Etiam in mi ele.

In porttitor efficitur ligula at auctor. Nam ligula justo, pharetra quis luctus non, consequat sagittis ligula. Aenean porta vulputate quam, non fermentum magna. Cras massa arcu, tincidunt in odio in, consequat dapibus elit. Nullam nec neque commodo, bibendum mauris sed, lobortis orci. Suspendisse laoreet vitae leo ut bibendum. Morbi tristique gravida nulla, eget volutpat eros tempus eu. Sed a malesuada eros. Etiam

---

Integer faucibus ante ac enim auctor, eu sagittis leo finibus. Curabitur vestibulum ante massa, fringilla posuere venenatis dui hendrerit vel. Nullam posuere enim felis, facilisis aliquet enim fringilla vitae. Quisque sit amet ex sit amet lectus blandit pharetra. Sed auctor, elit at finibus tincidunt, erat sapien tristique lectus, nec elementum quam nibh vitae sem. In laoreet blandit purus, at dignissim nunc. Vivamus fringilla lacus nec pellentesque tincidunt.

continued on A3

AMMUNITION MISSING WORLDWIDE HUMANITY'S WEAPONS USELESS. SQUIRRELS BLAMED FOR THEFT.

STEAM ENGINE USED TO RESTORE NEW YORK BULLETIN'S VINTAGE PRINTING PRESS TO OPERATION.
CURATOR FROM THE MUSEUM OF STEAM ENGINES: "I TOLD YOU ALL THIS DAY WOULD COME"

MORE STARS NOW VISIBLE AT NIGHT DUE TO SUDDEN LACK OF LIGHT POLLUTION
ASTRONOMERS: "I'M JUST SAYING: IT'S AN UPSIDE"

Condimentum imperdiet massa. Mauris fringilla dolor a sapien malesuada, sit amet consectetur eros fermentum. Phasellus justo tortor, mattis vitae eros vitae, mollis auctor nisl. Fusce a amet malesuada tortor, sit amet maximus augue. Vestibulum dapibus convallis leo quis posuere. Donec

---

Ah. The last few stragglers. You guys rounded them up for me.

Perfect.

Hello?! That's obviously not what we're doing here!!

Yeah! We're here to eat nuts and kick butts!

Thank you, Tomas!

Hey, it's Rocket Raccoon! Did you know that in German, a raccoon is called a Waschbär? That means "wash bear": they're like little bears who wash their food! That is 100% adorable, which is very misleading because in real life washbears are screeching intelligent garbage monsters, so be warned.

Squirrels? *Sic 'em.*

Good guy squirrels: run interference!! Everyone else: it's like we practiced!!

New rhetorical angle, Allene! You're acting like a dictator, trying to impose your will on the world with no friends except the vast army of squirrel pals you've manufactured for yourself. You're alone! And *that's* why you're doomed!

Hah! *Explain.*

Me and my friends-- we're a *team*, squirrel *and* human. We've come *together* to oppose you, and *all* of us together are stronger than *any* of us alone! Even *squirrels* live together, yo!!

Uh, you know as well as I do that *most* squirrels actually live alone, with only a few species and prairie dog cousins living more communally.

You get my point.

Even solitary squirrels warn each other of predators! Teamwork beats totalitarianism, yo! Making friends, working together, finding compromises, *helping each other*-- that's the true source of our strength!

Adorable speech, Doreen.

But I dunno, it *kinda* seems like the true source of *my* strength might actually be all these incredible powers I've granted myself??

ZZOT

Dang it!!

OW OW OW!

KCKCHOW

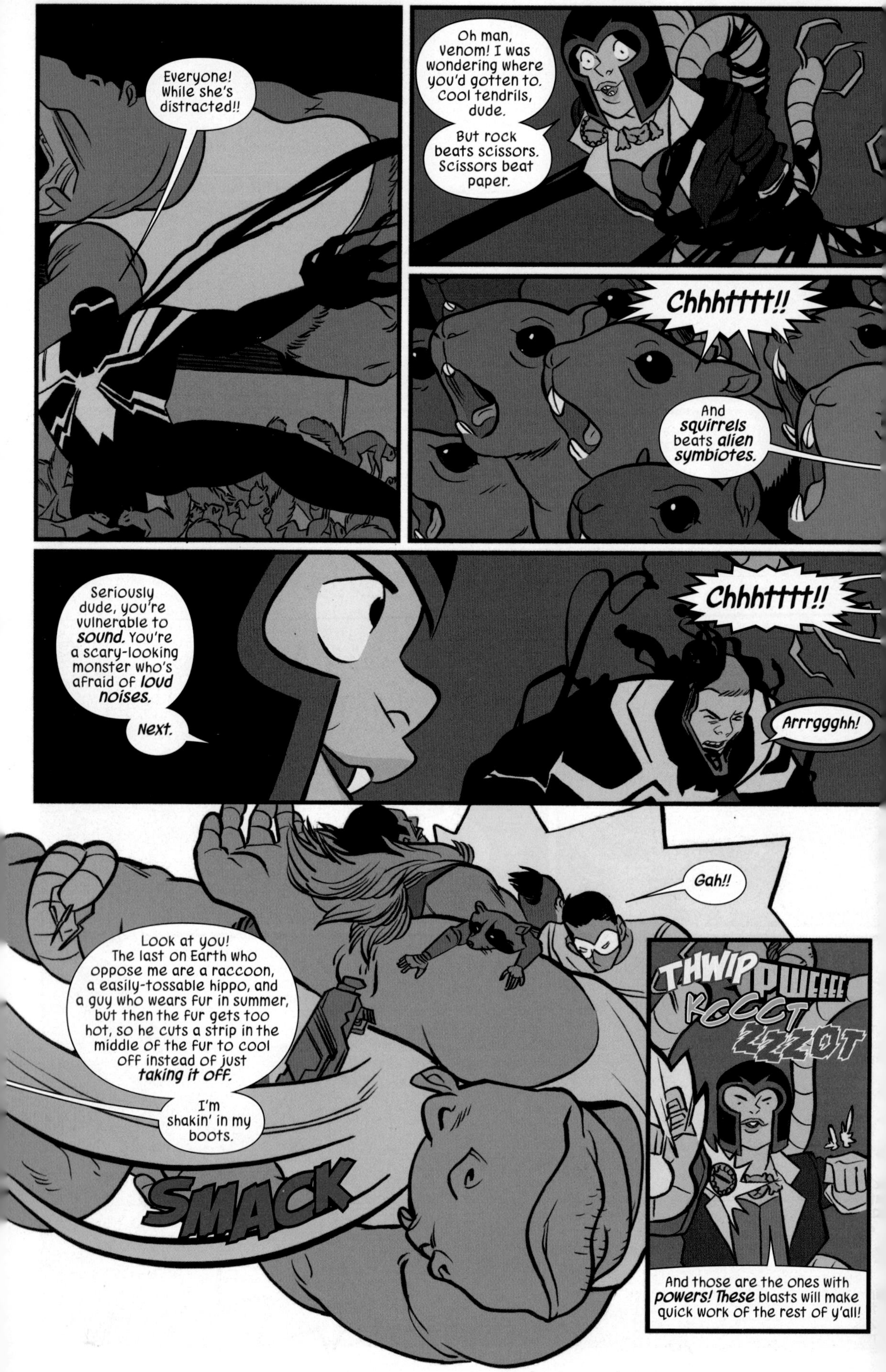

Everyone! While she's distracted!!
Oh man, Venom! I was wondering where you'd gotten to. Cool tendrils, dude.
But rock beats scissors. Scissors beat paper.
Chhhtttt!!
And squirrels beats alien symbiotes.
Seriously dude, you're vulnerable to sound. You're a scary-looking monster who's afraid of loud noises.
Next.
Chhhtttt!!
Arrrggghh!
Gah!!
Look at you! The last on Earth who oppose me are a raccoon, a easily-tossable hippo, and a guy who wears fur in summer, but then the fur gets too hot, so he cuts a strip in the middle of the fur to cool off instead of just taking it off.
I'm shakin' in my boots.
SMACK
THWIP PWEEEE KCCCT ZZZOT
And those are the ones with powers! These blasts will make quick work of the rest of y'all!

DID YOU KNOW: That way to beat Venom actually came to her in a dream? That's pretty nice, actually! I'd love to wake up and have my dreams be all "Okay, here's how you solve every one of your problems today." I--I'd actually really like that a lot.

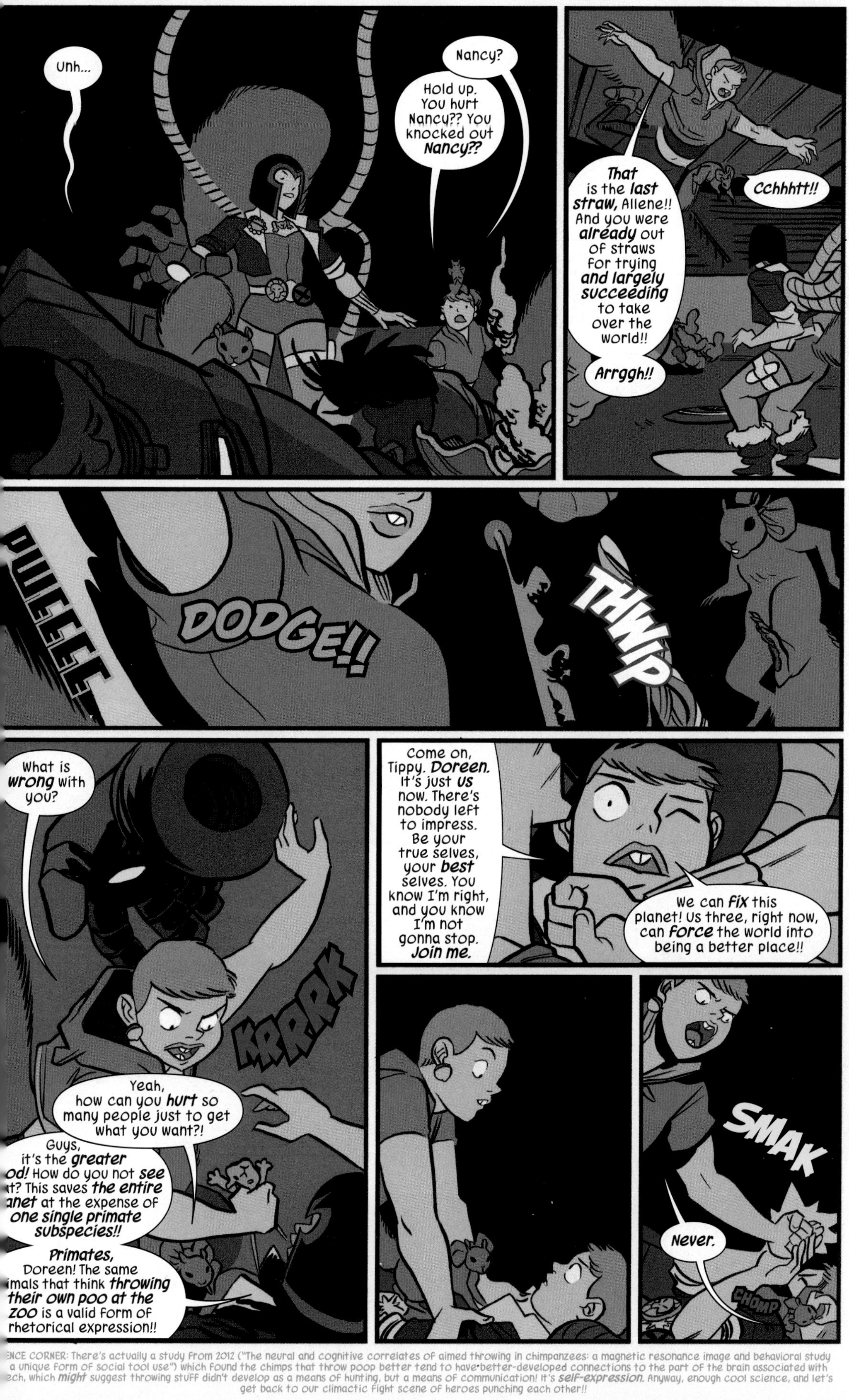
Unh...
Nancy?
Hold up. You hurt Nancy?? You knocked out Nancy??
That is the last straw, Allene!! And you were already out of straws for trying and largely succeeding to take over the world!!
Cchhhtt!!
Arrggh!!
DUFFFF
DODGE!!
THWIP
What is wrong with you?
KRRRK
Yeah, how can you hurt so many people just to get what you want?!
Guys, it's the greater od! How do you not see it? This saves the entire anet at the expense of one single primate subspecies!!
Primates, Doreen! The same imals that think throwing their own poo at the ZOO is a valid form of rhetorical expression!!
Come on, Tippy. Doreen. It's just us now. There's nobody left to impress. Be your true selves, your best selves. You know I'm right, and you know I'm not gonna stop. Join me.
We can fix this planet! Us three, right now, can force the world into being a better place!!
SMAK
Never.
CHOMP

ENCE CORNER: There's actually a study from 2012 ("The neural and cognitive correlates of aimed throwing in chimpanzees: a magnetic resonance image and behavioral study a unique form of social tool use") which found the chimps that throw poop better tend to have better-developed connections to the part of the brain associated with ech, which *might* suggest throwing stuff didn't develop as a means of hunting, but a means of communication! It's ***self-expression.*** Anyway, enough cool science, and let's get back to our climactic fight scene of heroes punching each other!!

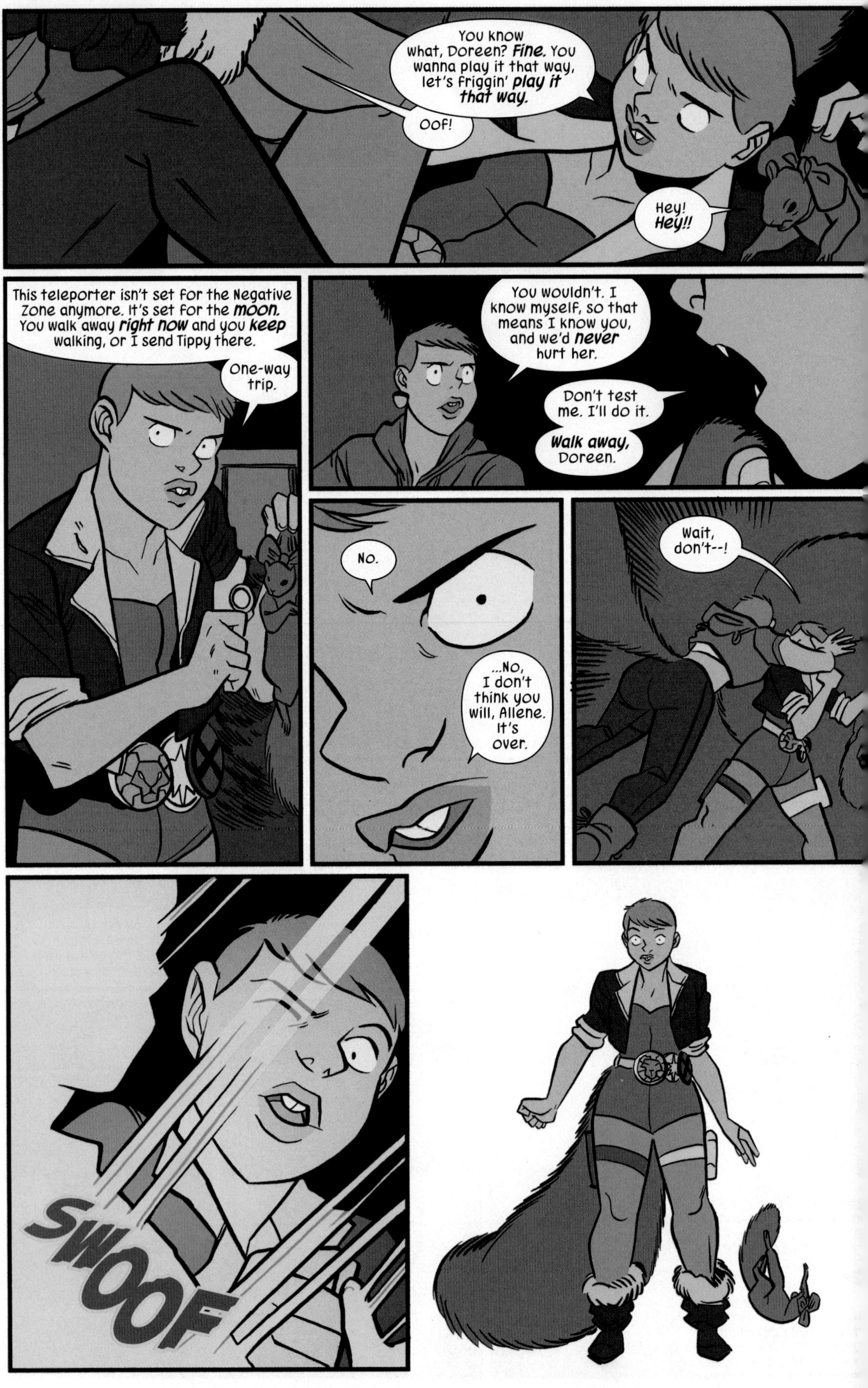
You know what, Doreen? *Fine.* You wanna play it that way, let's friggin' *play it that way.*
Oof!
Hey! *Hey!!*
This teleporter isn't set for the Negative Zone anymore. It's set for the *moon.* You walk away *right now* and you *keep* walking, or I send Tippy there.
One-way trip.
You wouldn't. I know myself, so that means I know you, and we'd *never* hurt her.
Don't test me. I'll do it.
Walk away, Doreen.
No.
...No, I don't think you will, Allene. It's over.
Wait, don't--!
SWOOF

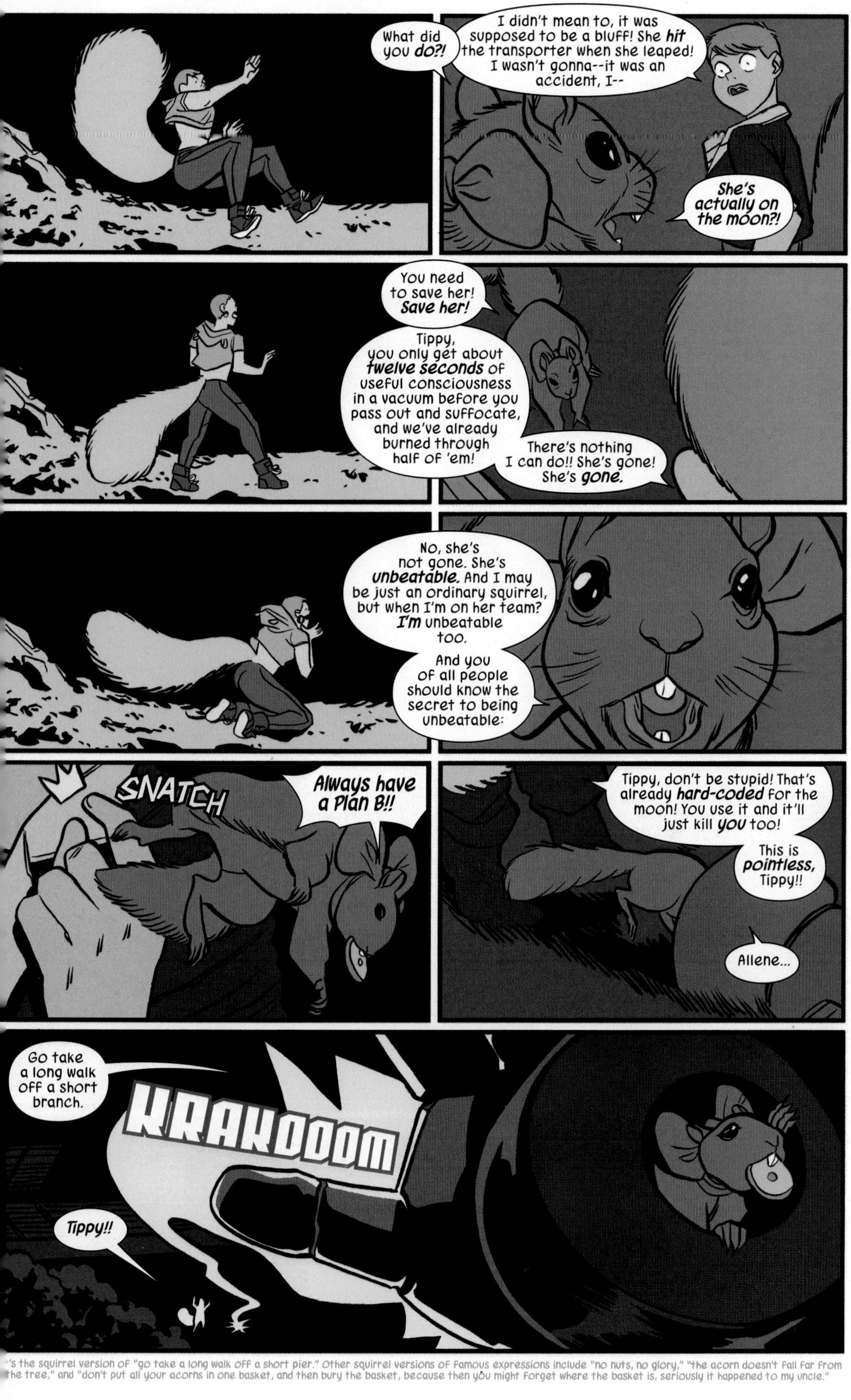
What did you do?!
I didn't mean to, it was supposed to be a bluff! She hit the transporter when she leaped! I wasn't gonna--it was an accident, I--
She's actually on the moon?!
You need to save her! Save her!
Tippy, you only get about twelve seconds of useful consciousness in a vacuum before you pass out and suffocate, and we've already burned through half of 'em!
There's nothing I can do!! She's gone! She's gone.
No, she's not gone. She's unbeatable. And I may be just an ordinary squirrel, but when I'm on her team? I'm unbeatable too.
And you of all people should know the secret to being unbeatable:
SNATCH
Always have a Plan B!!
Tippy, don't be stupid! That's already hard-coded for the moon! You use it and it'll just kill you too!
This is pointless, Tippy!!
Allene...
Go take a long walk off a short branch.
KRAKOOOM
Tippy!!

's the squirrel version of "go take a long walk off a short pier." Other squirrel versions of famous expressions include "no nuts, no glory," "the acorn doesn't fall far from the tree," and "don't put all your acorns in one basket, and then bury the basket, because then you might forget where the basket is, seriously it happened to my uncle."

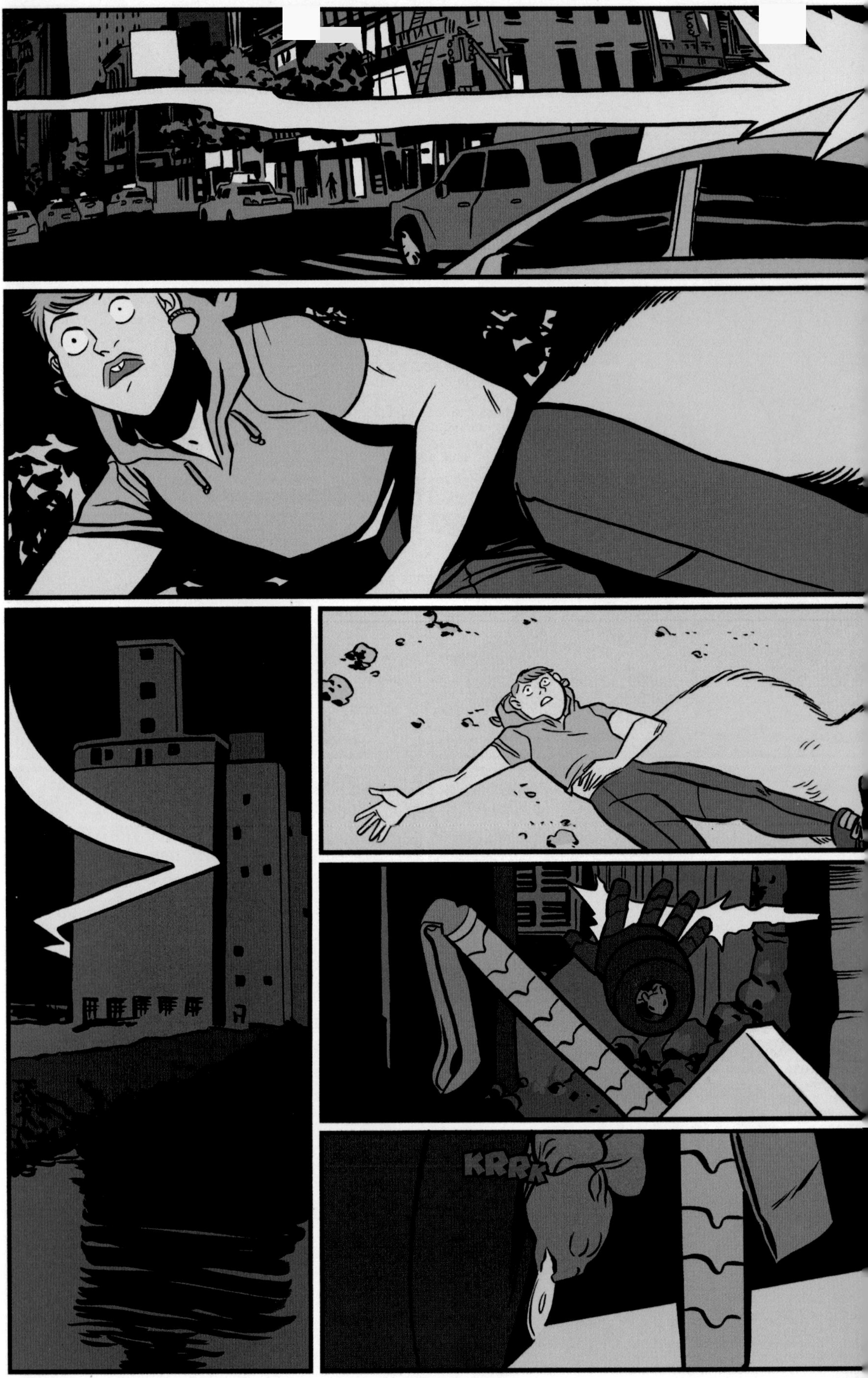
KRRK

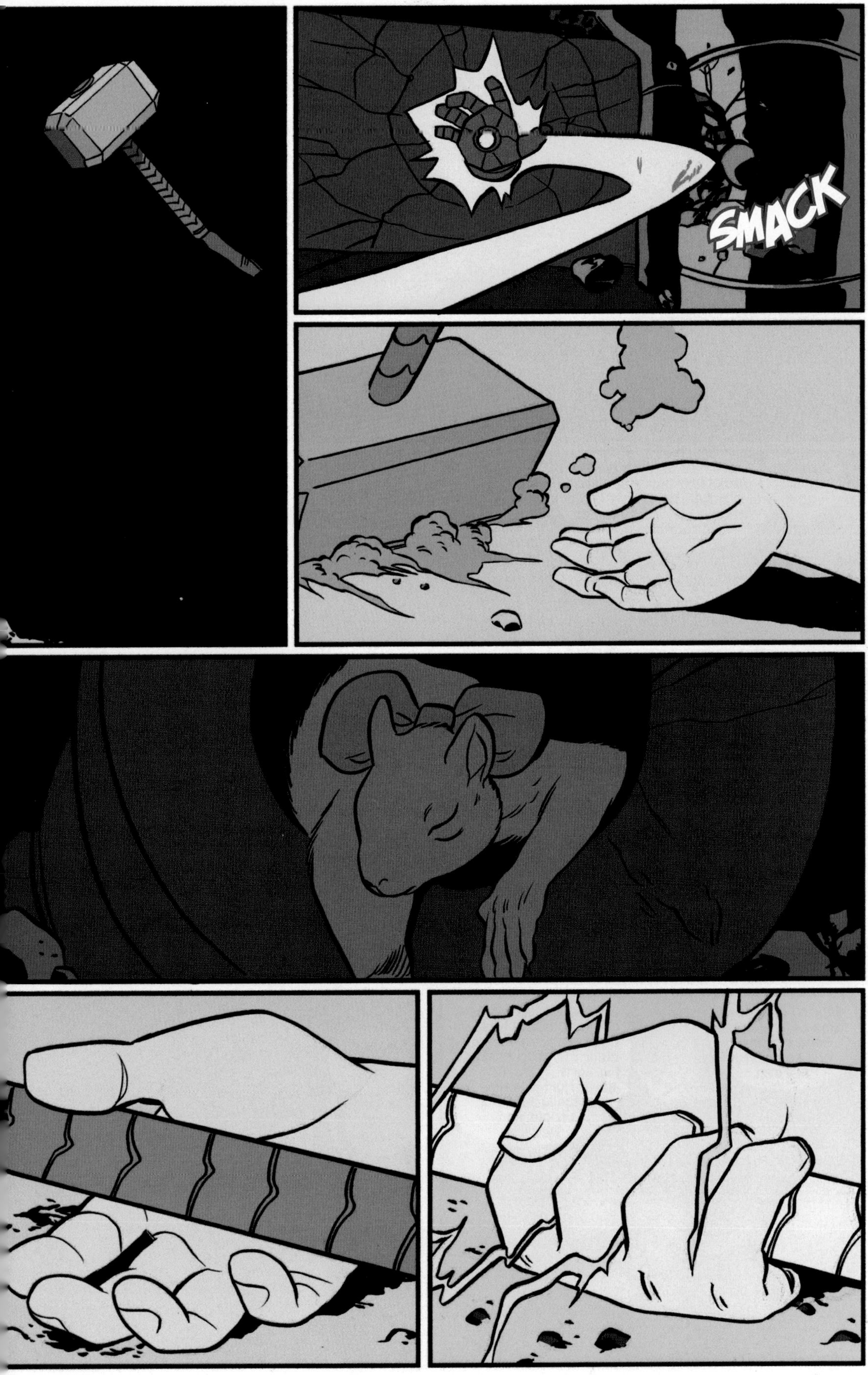
SMACK

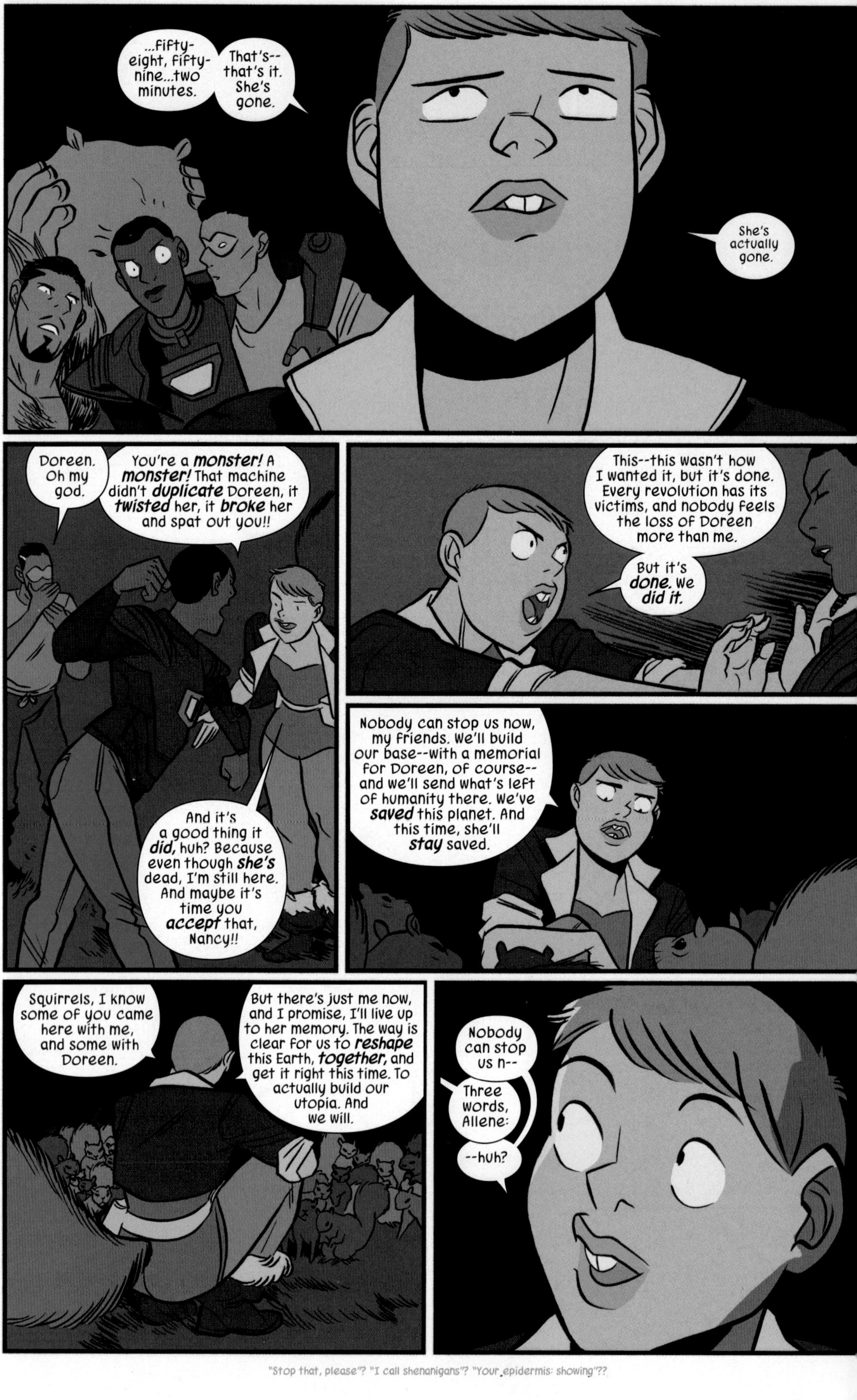
...fifty-eight, fifty-nine...two minutes.
That's--that's it. She's gone.
She's actually gone.
Doreen. Oh my god.
You're a monster! A monster! That machine didn't duplicate Doreen, it twisted her, it broke her and spat out you!!
And it's a good thing it did, huh? Because even though she's dead, I'm still here. And maybe it's time you accept that, Nancy!!
This--this wasn't how I wanted it, but it's done. Every revolution has its victims, and nobody feels the loss of Doreen more than me.
But it's done. We did it.
Nobody can stop us now, my friends. We'll build our base--with a memorial for Doreen, of course--and we'll send what's left of humanity there. We've saved this planet. And this time, she'll stay saved.
Squirrels, I know some of you came here with me, and some with Doreen.
But there's just me now, and I promise, I'll live up to her memory. The way is clear for us to reshape this Earth, together, and get it right this time. To actually build our utopia. And we will.
Nobody can stop us n--
Three words, Allene:
--huh?

"Stop that, please"? "I call shenanigans"? "Your epidermis: showing"??

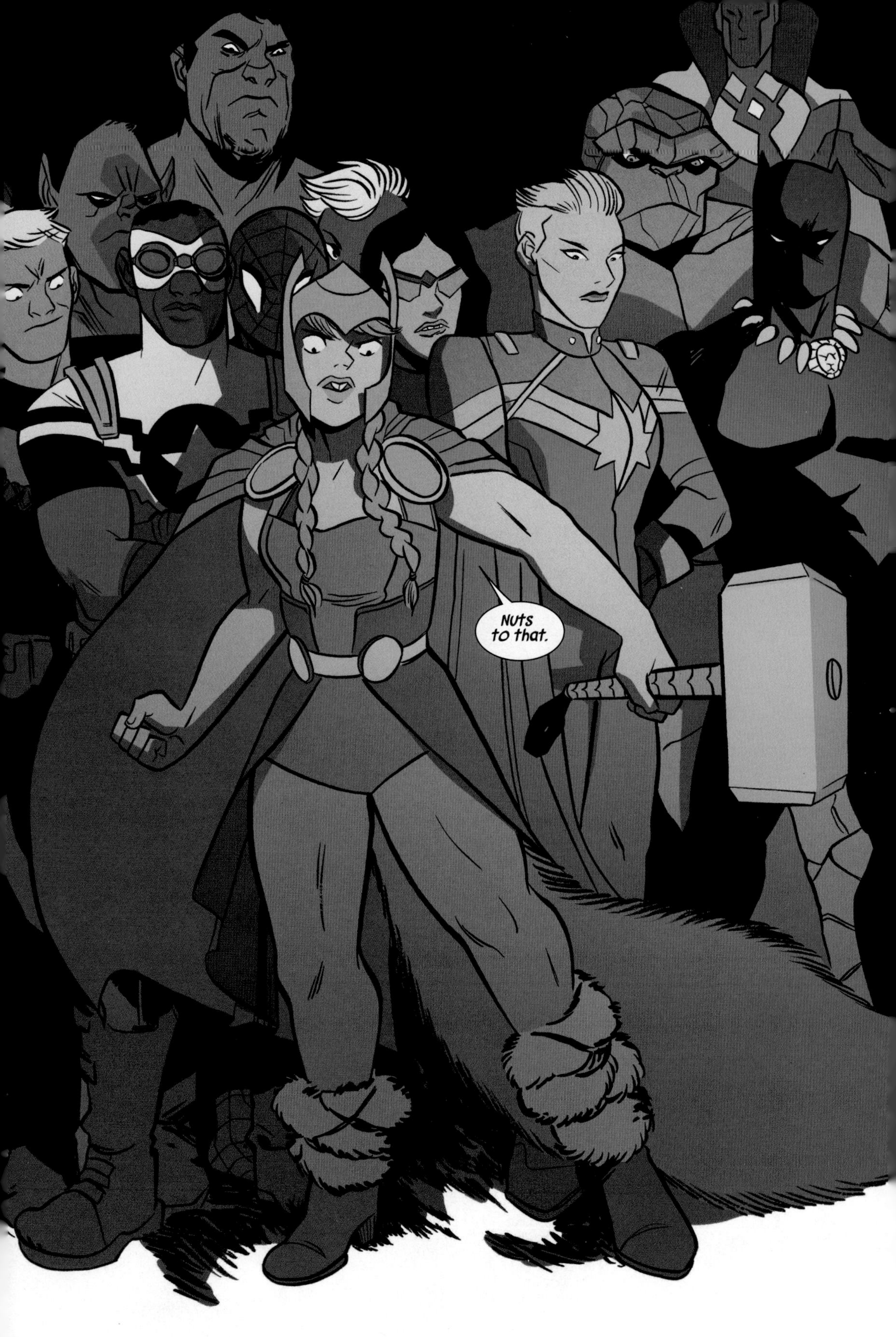
NUTS TO THAT.

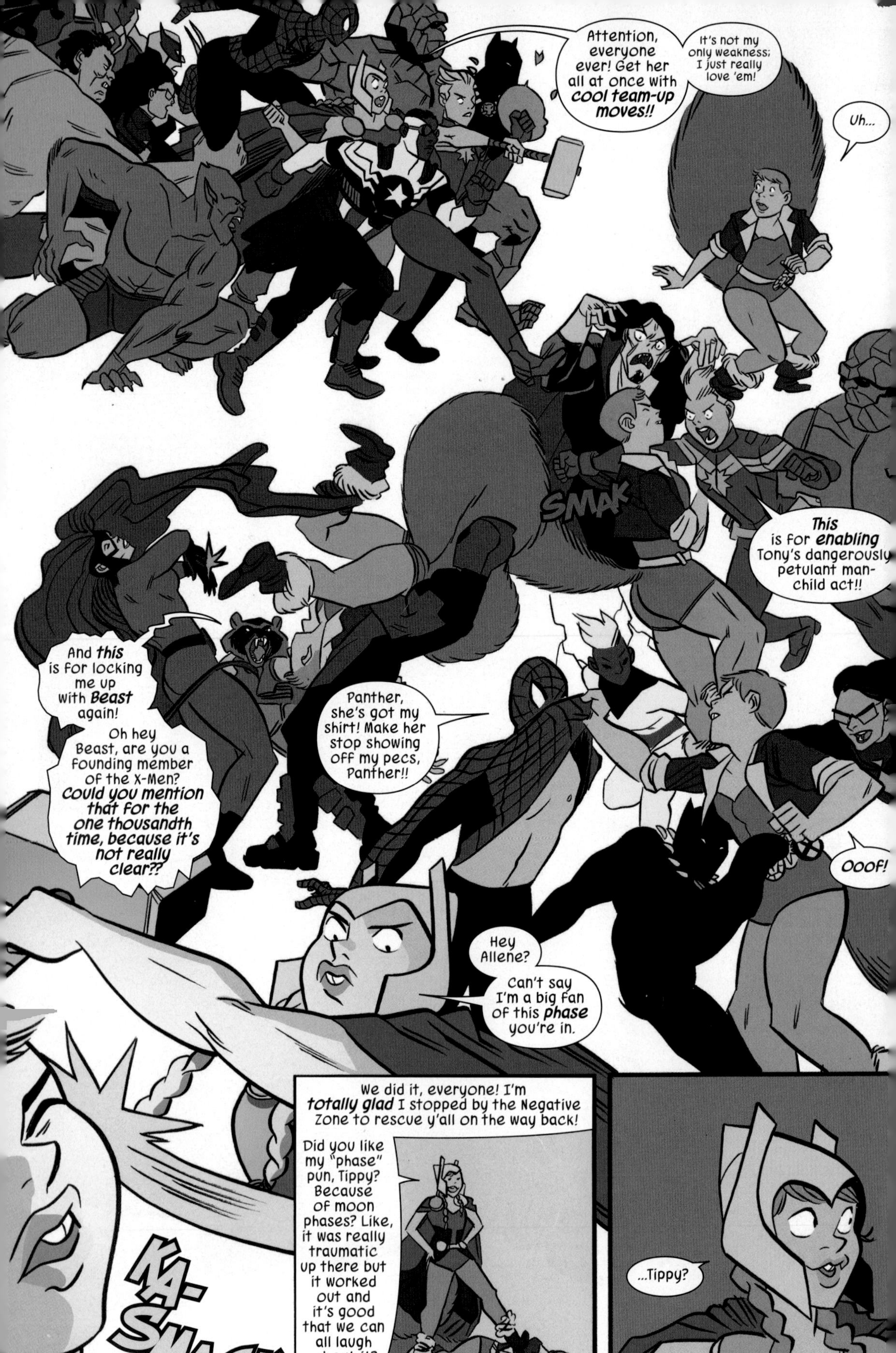
Attention, everyone ever! Get her all at once with cool team-up moves!!
It's not my only weakness; I just really love 'em!
Uh...
SMAK
This is for enabling Tony's dangerously petulant man-child act!!
And this is for locking me up with Beast again!
Oh hey Beast, are you a founding member of the X-Men? Could you mention that for the one thousandth time, because it's not really clear??
Panther, she's got my shirt! Make her stop showing off my pecs, Panther!!
OOOF!
Hey Allene?
Can't say I'm a big fan of this phase you're in.
KA-SMACK
We did it, everyone! I'm totally glad I stopped by the Negative Zone to rescue y'all on the way back!
Did you like my "phase" pun, Tippy? Because of moon phases? Like, it was really traumatic up there but it worked out and it's good that we can all laugh about it?
...Tippy?

Every Marvel character ever is here for this fight; we just didn't have room for them all on this page! You know what this means, right? This means ***every single "Squirrel Girl versus [your favorite character]" fight scene fan art you draw is now canon.*** Thank me later!!

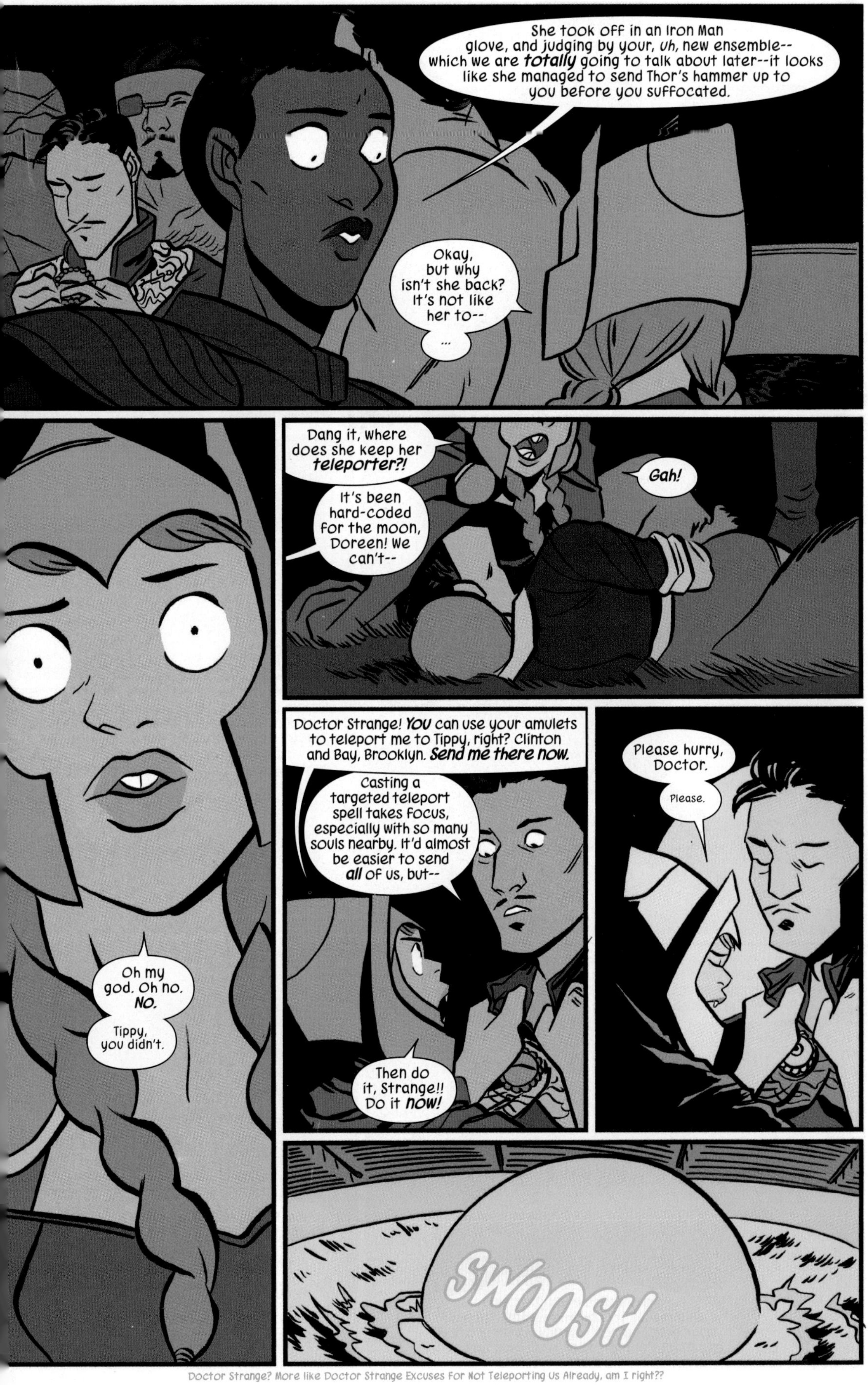
She took off in an Iron Man glove, and judging by your, uh, new ensemble-- which we are totally going to talk about later--it looks like she managed to send Thor's hammer up to you before you suffocated.
Okay, but why isn't she back? It's not like her to--
...
Dang it, where does she keep her teleporter?!
It's been hard-coded for the moon, Doreen! We can't--
Gah!
Oh my god. Oh no. NO.
Tippy, you didn't.
Doctor Strange! YOU can use your amulets to teleport me to Tippy, right? Clinton and Bay, Brooklyn. Send me there now.
Casting a targeted teleport spell takes focus, especially with so many souls nearby. It'd almost be easier to send all of us, but--
Then do it, Strange!! Do it NOW!
Please hurry, Doctor.
Please.
SWOOSH

Doctor Strange? More like Doctor Strange Excuses For Not Teleporting Us Already, am I right??

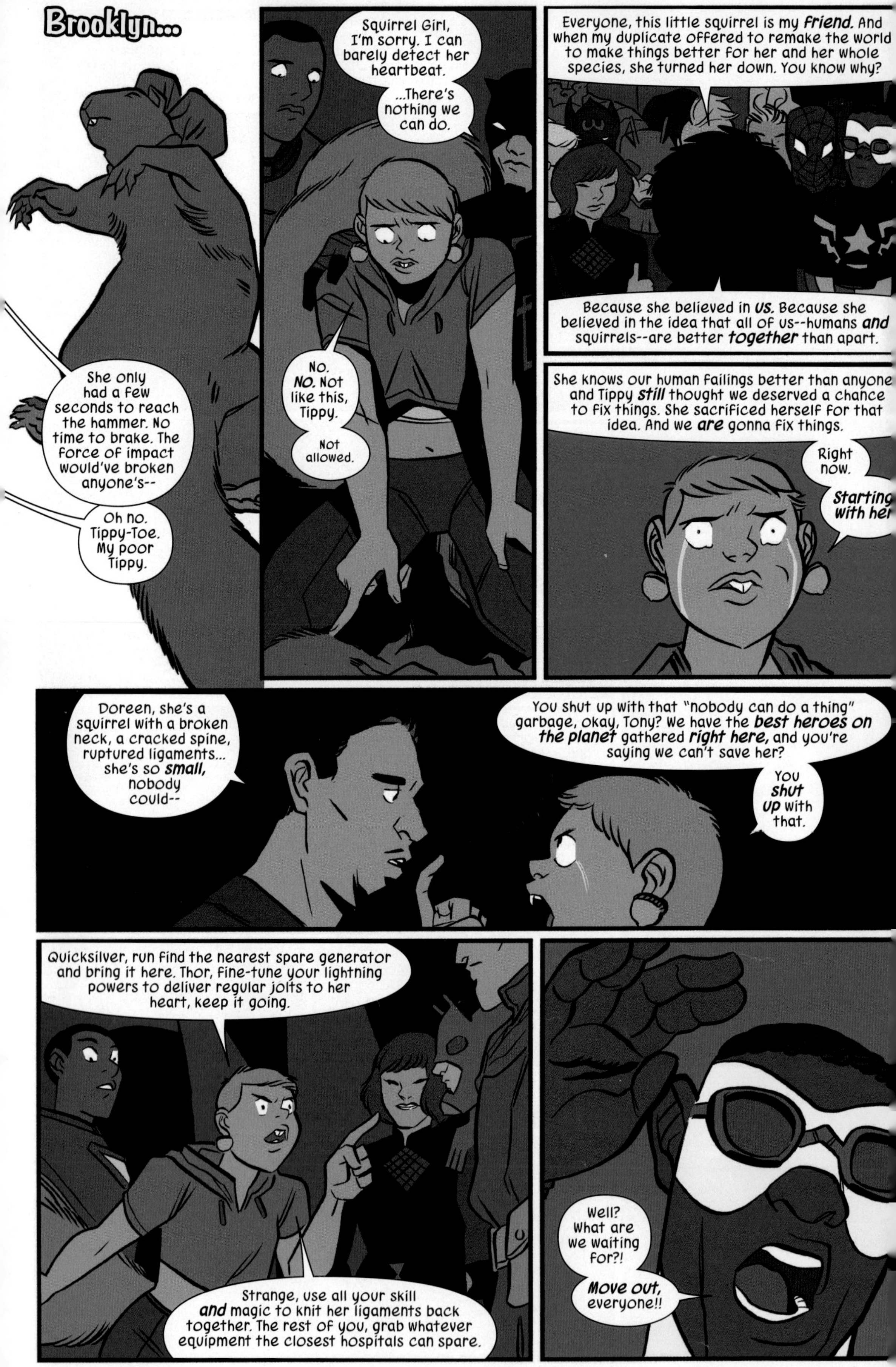
Brooklyn...
She only had a few seconds to reach the hammer. No time to brake. The force of impact would've broken anyone's--
Oh no. Tippy-Toe. My poor Tippy.
Squirrel Girl, I'm sorry. I can barely detect her heartbeat.
...There's nothing we can do.
No. NO. Not like this, Tippy.
Not allowed.
Everyone, this little squirrel is my friend. And when my duplicate offered to remake the world to make things better for her and her whole species, she turned her down. You know why?
Because she believed in US. Because she believed in the idea that all of us--humans and squirrels--are better together than apart.
She knows our human failings better than anyone and Tippy still thought we deserved a chance to fix things. She sacrificed herself for that idea. And we are gonna fix things.
Right now.
Starting with her
Doreen, she's a squirrel with a broken neck, a cracked spine, ruptured ligaments... she's so small, nobody could--
You shut up with that "nobody can do a thing" garbage, okay, Tony? We have the best heroes on the planet gathered right here, and you're saying we can't save her?
You shut up with that.
Quicksilver, run find the nearest spare generator and bring it here. Thor, fine-tune your lightning powers to deliver regular jolts to her heart, keep it going.
Strange, use all your skill and magic to knit her ligaments back together. The rest of you, grab whatever equipment the closest hospitals can spare.
Well? What are we waiting for?!
Move out, everyone!!

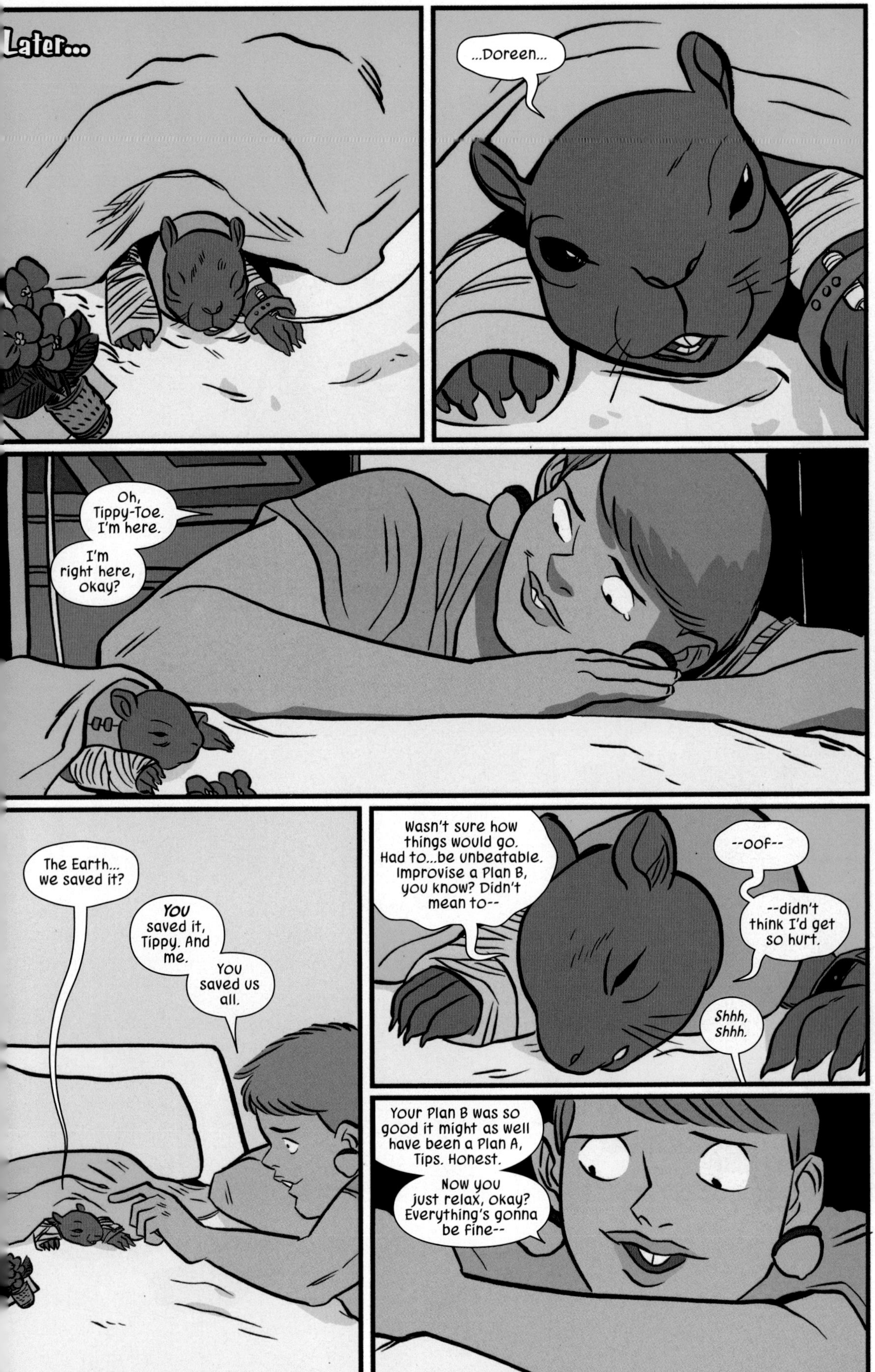
Later...
...Doreen...
Oh, Tippy-Toe. I'm here.
I'm right here, okay?
The Earth... we saved it?
YOU saved it, Tippy. And me.
You saved us all.
Wasn't sure how things would go. Had to...be unbeatable. Improvise a Plan B, you know? Didn't mean to--
--oof--
--didn't think I'd get so hurt.
Shhh, shhh.
Your Plan B was so good it might as well have been a Plan A, Tips. Honest.
Now you just relax, okay? Everything's gonna be fine--

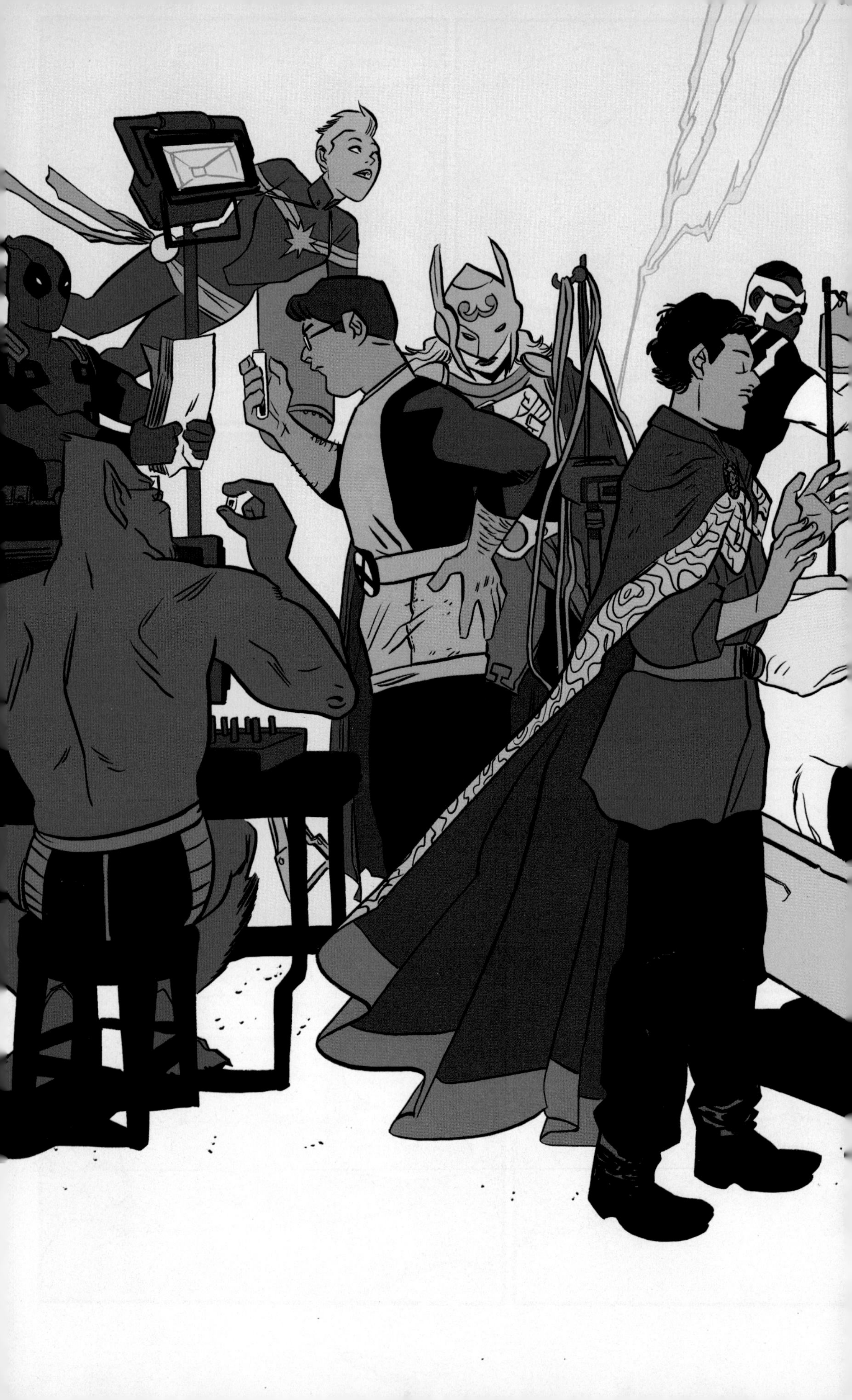

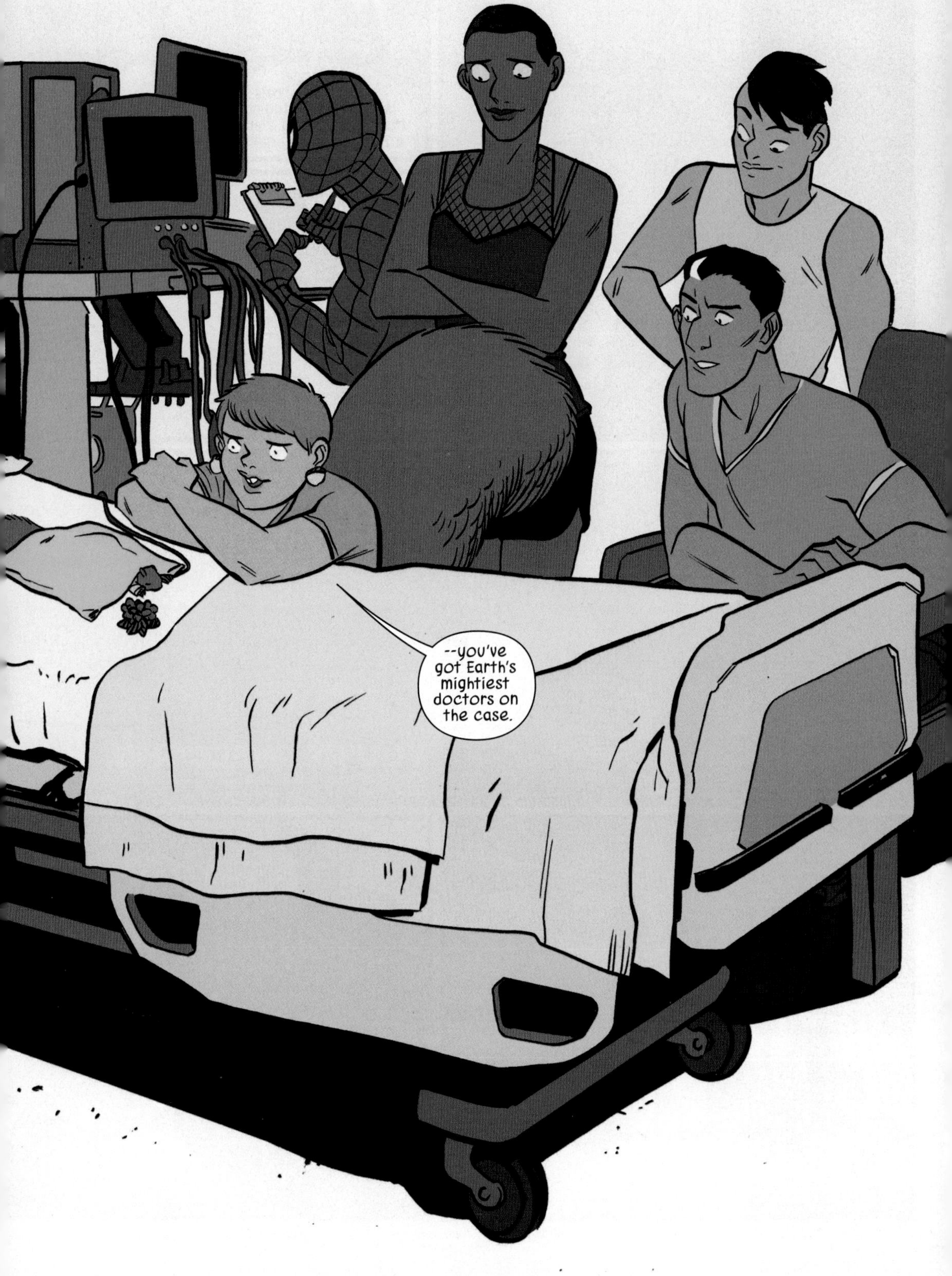
--you've got Earth's mightiest doctors on the case.

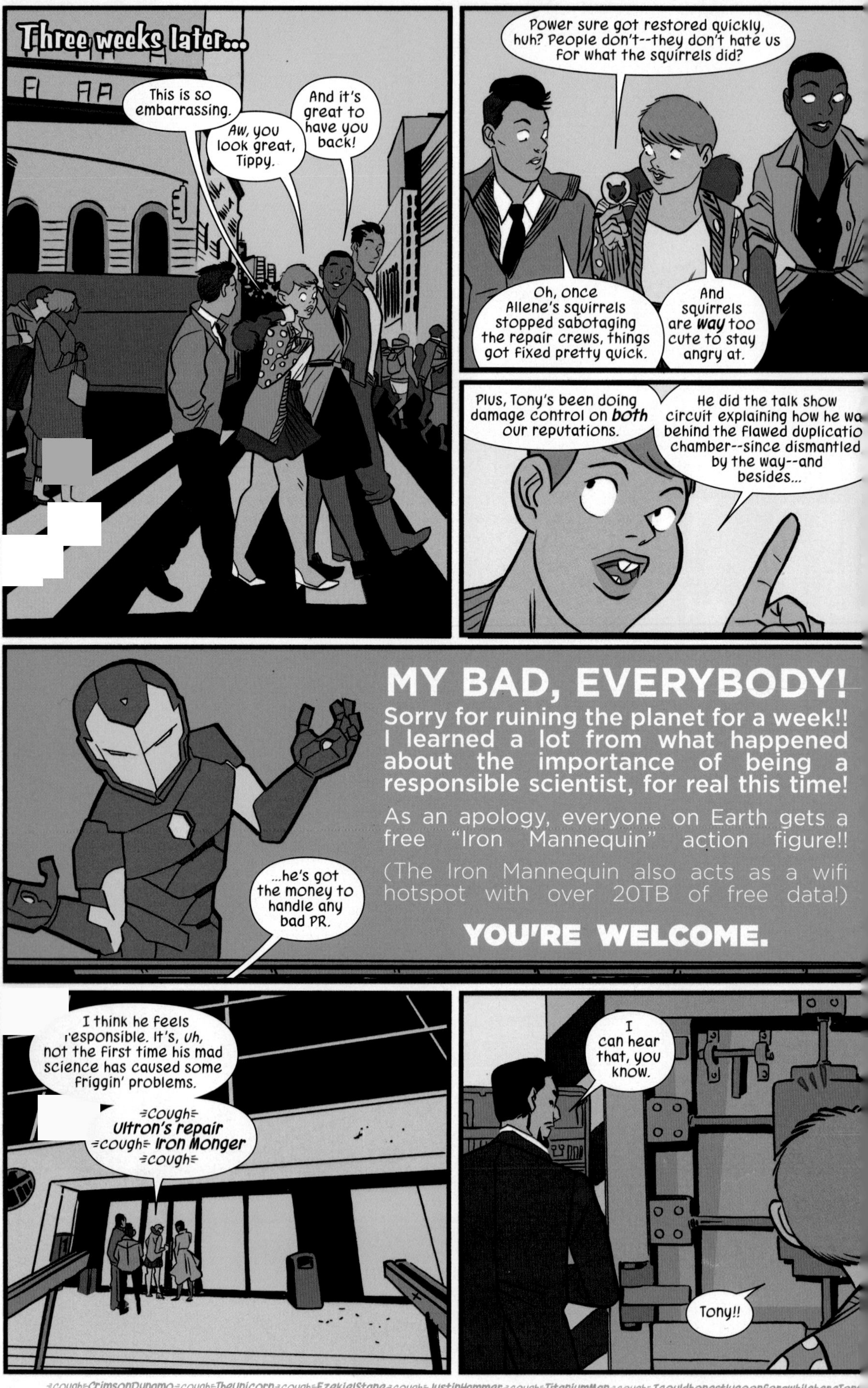
Three weeks later...
This is so embarrassing.
Aw, you look great, Tippy.
And it's great to have you back!
Power sure got restored quickly, huh? People don't--they don't hate us for what the squirrels did?
Oh, once Allene's squirrels stopped sabotaging the repair crews, things got fixed pretty quick.
And squirrels are **way** too cute to stay angry at.
Plus, Tony's been doing damage control on **both** our reputations.
He did the talk show circuit explaining how he wa behind the flawed duplicatio chamber--since dismantled by the way--and besides...
MY BAD, EVERYBODY!
Sorry for ruining the planet for a week!! I learned a lot from what happened about the importance of being a responsible scientist, for real this time!
As an apology, everyone on Earth gets a free "Iron Mannequin" action figure!!
(The Iron Mannequin also acts as a wifi hotspot with over 20TB of free data!)
YOU'RE WELCOME.
...he's got the money to handle any bad PR.
I think he feels responsible. It's, uh, not the first time his mad science has caused some friggin' problems.
=cough= Ultron's repair =cough= Iron Monger =cough=
I can hear that, you know.
Tony!!

=cough=CrimsonDynamo=cough=TheUnicorn=cough=EzekielStane=cough=JustinHammer=cough=TitaniumMan=cough=IcouldhonestlygoonForawhilehereTon
=cough==cough=

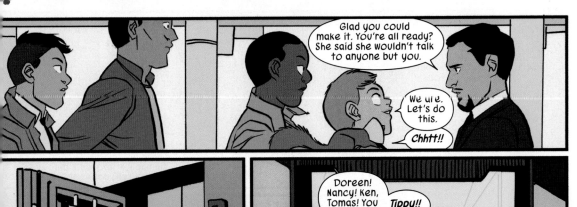

Glad you could make it. You're all ready? She said she wouldn't talk to anyone but you.

We are. Let's do this.

Chhtt!!

Doreen! Nancy! Ken, Tomas! You came!!

Tippy!!

How are things, Allene?

Dude, I'm locked in a cage with no squirrels to keep me company. Plus, **plus,** the squirrels I duplicated are all kept in a different cage off-site. Could you **please** tell them we don't control squirrels telepathically??

This hat itches like crazy. No **wonder** Magneto's so testy all the time.

Listen, Doreen...I know how this goes. I'm supposed to say I made a mistake, that I was wrong. But I can't. It's not true.

I still think I have the best way forward for everyone. I still think my path causes the most happiness, planet-wide.

But after what Tippy did, and after what you said when you saved her, about the power of working together...it made me think.

And, well...

...I want to suggest a compromise.

Plus I'm pretty sure if Magneto finds out I'm biting his style on the regular, he's gonna be even more irritable than he normally is, which is to say: *quite a bit??*

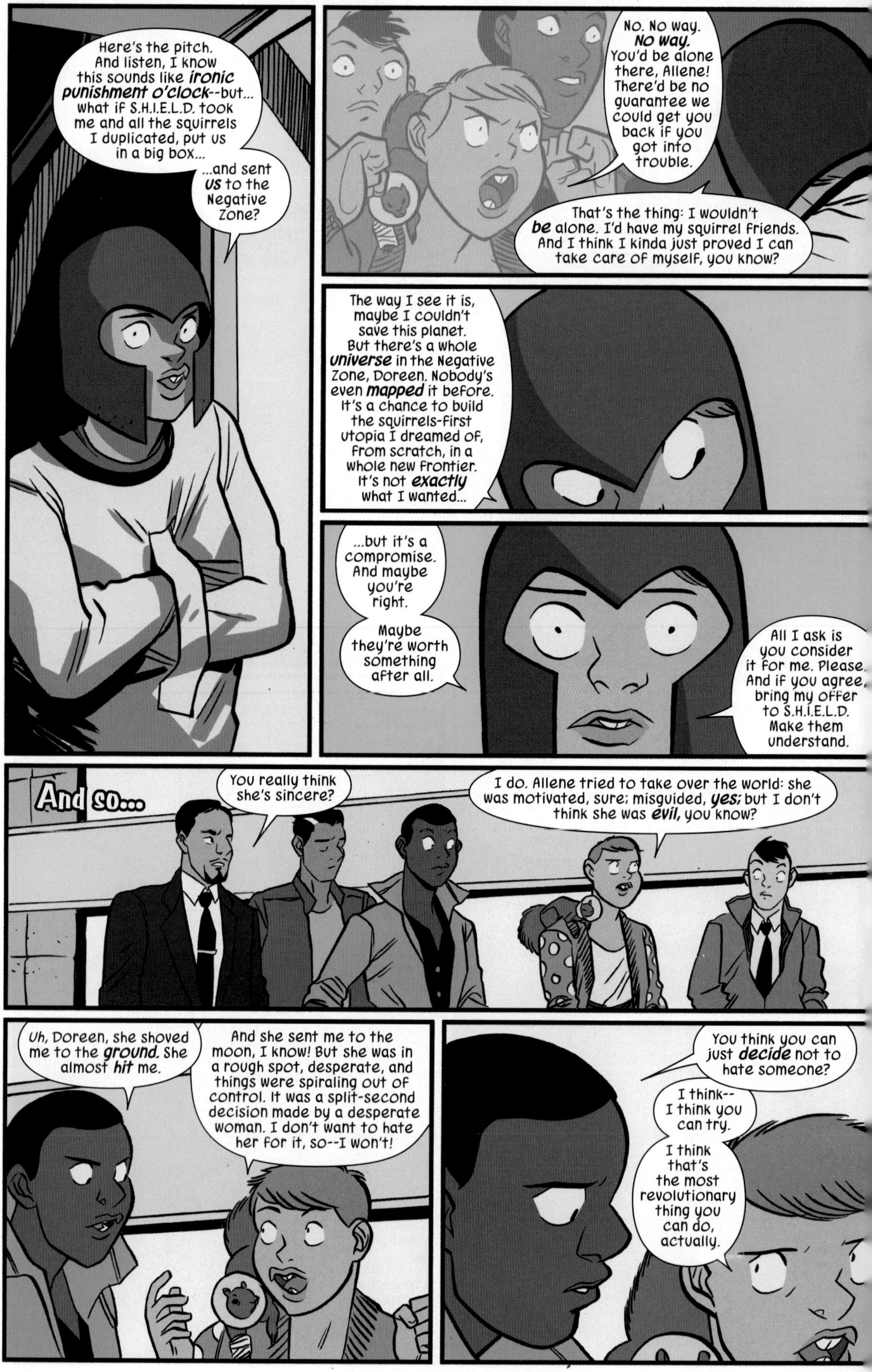
Here's the pitch. And listen, I know this sounds like ironic punishment o'clock--but... what if S.H.I.E.L.D. took me and all the squirrels I duplicated, put us in a big box...
...and sent US to the Negative Zone?
No. No way. NO WAY. You'd be alone there, Allene! There'd be no guarantee we could get you back if you got into trouble.
That's the thing: I wouldn't be alone. I'd have my squirrel friends. And I think I kinda just proved I can take care of myself, you know?
The way I see it is, maybe I couldn't save this planet. But there's a whole universe in the Negative Zone, Doreen. Nobody's even mapped it before. It's a chance to build the squirrels-first utopia I dreamed of, from scratch, in a whole new frontier. It's not exactly what I wanted...
...but it's a compromise. And maybe you're right.
Maybe they're worth something after all.
All I ask is you consider it for me. Please. And if you agree, bring my offer to S.H.I.E.L.D. Make them understand.
And so...
You really think she's sincere?
I do. Allene tried to take over the world: she was motivated, sure; misguided, yes; but I don't think she was evil, you know?
Uh, Doreen, she shoved me to the ground. She almost hit me.
And she sent me to the moon, I know! But she was in a rough spot, desperate, and things were spiraling out of control. It was a split-second decision made by a desperate woman. I don't want to hate her for it, so--I won't!
You think you can just decide not to hate someone?
I think-- I think you can try.
I think that's the most revolutionary thing you can do, actually.

Look, Allene's not me, but she's got parts of me. And when I imagine her staying in that cage forever...

...she won't be happy. We're not helping anyone by keeping her there. Or **here**, on Earth.

But to give her a whole dimension to explore, to build in...

It gives her purpose. And with so many uninhabited worlds there, she gets her squirrel utopia planet without messing with ours. We can **all** get what we want.

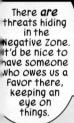

There **are** threats hiding in the Negative Zone. It'd be nice to have someone who owes us a favor there, keeping an eye on things.

...I'm gonna recommend S.H.I.E.L.D. go for it.

Thank you, Tony. I don't think she's a bad person. And her ideas weren't **all** bad, right?

Ha ha, not the **take over the world** ideas, obviously! But the Squirrels Avengers Initiative, Mark 1! We could **do** that.

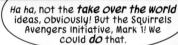

Plant trees, do a neighborhood watch. It'll take some time before people **fully** trust squirrels again, but we can still **help** people. Save the world, you know?

Her legacy could actually be one of making the Earth a better place.

Right? I'd like that.

Doreen, look. Nothing's gonna happen overnight. But... I'll put a good word in with S.H.I.E.L.D.

It's something to think about, anyway. Just a girl, her squirrels, and all the time in the world...

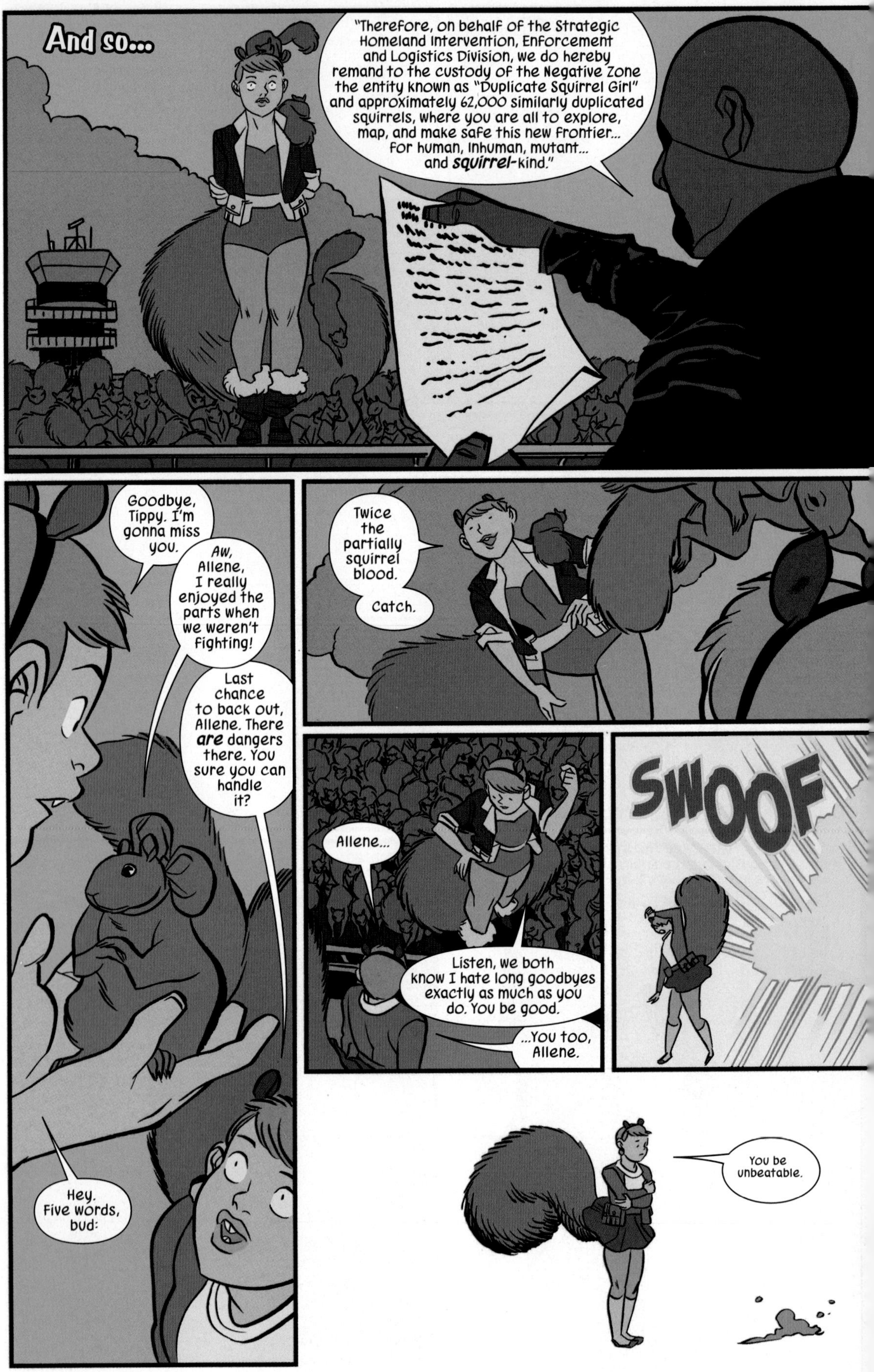
And so...
"Therefore, on behalf of the Strategic Homeland Intervention, Enforcement and Logistics Division, we do hereby remand to the custody of the Negative Zone the entity known as "Duplicate Squirrel Girl" and approximately 62,000 similarly duplicated squirrels, where you are all to explore, map, and make safe this new frontier... for human, inhuman, mutant... and squirrel-kind."
Goodbye, Tippy. I'm gonna miss you.
Aw, Allene, I really enjoyed the parts when we weren't fighting!
Last chance to back out, Allene. There are dangers there. You sure you can handle it?
Hey. Five words, bud:
Twice the partially squirrel blood.
Catch.
Allene...
Listen, we both know I hate long goodbyes exactly as much as you do. You be good.
...You too, Allene.
SWOOF
You be unbeatable.

Tony Stark @starkmantony
@unbeatablesg Heck of a week, huh?

Squirrel Girl @unbeatablesg
@starkmantony YEP. Heck of a -- wait, ALLENE POSTED TO MY ACCOUNT WHILE SHE WAS HERE?? Aw geez one sec I gotta do some damage control!!

Squirrel Girl @unbeatablesg
SQUIRRELS RULE HUMANS DROOL

Squirrel Girl @unbeatablesg
I CAN NEVER TAKE THIS BACK

Squirrel Girl @unbeatablesg
@unbeatablesg Hi everyone! Please disregard these messages! Please disregard all msgs I posted earlier this week actually, haha whoooops

Squirrel Girl @unbeatablesg
@unbeatablesg Also it wasn't me who changed my bio to "RULER OF PLANET EARTH, LOL" k thx!! don't @ me

Nancy Whitehead @sewwiththeflo
@unbeatablesg Hey, question

Squirrel Girl @unbeatablesg
@sewwiththeflo shoot

Nancy Whitehead @sewwiththeflo
@unbeatablesg How is it that as Squirrel Thor you could teleport to the Negative Zone to rescue everyone, but not to a Brooklyn warehouse??

Squirrel Girl @unbeatablesg
@sewwiththeflo haha I was hoping someone would ask this! THANK YOU NANCY, YOU ARE THE BEST FOREVER

Squirrel Girl @unbeatablesg
@imduderadtude okay so

Squirrel Girl @unbeatablesg
@sewwiththeflo using my CS skills I figured out how to get the hammer to manipulate electricity in the same way the transporters did

Squirrel Girl @unbeatablesg
@sewwiththeflo which allowed me to duplicate their basic transporter functionality!! but unfortunately with SIGNIFICANTLY less precision

Squirrel Girl @unbeatablesg
@sewwiththeflo so that was fine for INTER-dimensional travel (big target), but INTRA-dimensional travel is a much more delicate thing :(

Squirrel Girl @unbeatablesg
@sewwiththeflo and since i didn't want us to end up inside a wall, I needed Strange to teleport us! The end

Nancy Whitehead @sewwiththeflo
@unbeatablesg It is a perfectly reasonable explanation and I'm glad I asked!

Squirrel Girl @unbeatablesg
@sewwiththeflo The moral is BASIC COMPUTER SCIENCE KNOWLEDGE HELPED ME SAVE THE DAY, everyone should program at least a little!! It's fun

Squirrel Girl @unbeatablesg
@sewwiththeflo PLUS it can help you if you're trapped on the moon. Computers y'all!!

Nancy Whitehead @sewwiththeflo
@unbeatablesg Preaching to the choir here, SG. Hey uh Koi Boi says we're all going out for nachos tonight, so heads up on that.

Nancy Whitehead @sewwiththeflo
@unbeatablesg SQUIRREL GIRL THIS IS KOI BOI. YOUR PRESENCE IS REQUIRED AT THE NACHO EMPORIUM. WE WILL DEFEAT ALL NACHOS WITH OUR MOUTHS.

Squirrel Girl @unbeatablesg
@sewwiththeflo aw you guys!! YOU GUYS.

Squirrel Girl @unbeatablesg
@sewwiththeflo wouldn't miss it <3 <3 <3

search!

#squirrelgirls

#fivewordsbud

#SQUIRRELTHOR

#nuclearvolcano

#theavengersneedme

The End.

COVER PROCESS!

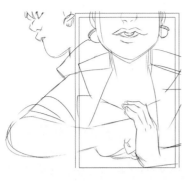

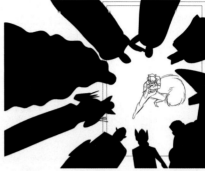

HERE ARE ERICA HENDERSON'S INITIAL COVER SKETCHES FOR THIS GRAPHIC NOVEL: ONE WITH SUPER-COOL DOREEN AND SHADE-THROWING ALLENE, AND ANOTHER WITH SQUIRREL GIRL GETTING READY TO BEAT UP THE MARVEL UNIVERSE! ISN'T ERICA GREAT?

MARVEL
ONE-SHOT
1
THE PUNISHER
ENNIS
BRAITHWAITE
KILLS THE MARVEL UNIVERSE

the unbeatable Squirrel Girl
BEATS UP THE MARVEL UNIVERSE!

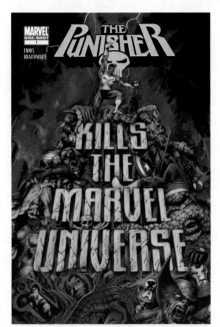

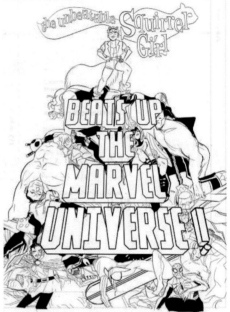

ULTIMATELY, ERICA COOKED UP AN AWESOME HOMAGE TO NICK PERCIVAL'S ICONIC COVER OF *PUNISHER KILLS THE MARVEL UNIVERSE*, A FUN ONE-SHOT FROM A WHILE BACK BY GARTH ENNIS & DOUG BRAITHWAITE.

(DEFINITELY NOT AN ALL-AGES COMIC, THOUGH!)

the unbeatable Squirrel Girl
BEATS UP THE MARVEL UNIVERSE!

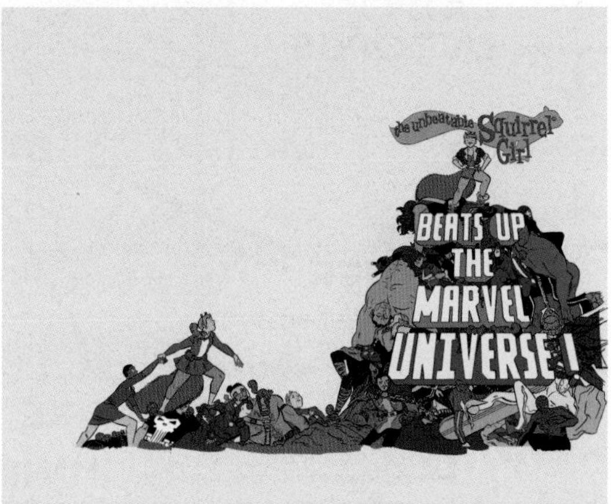

WHAT'S BETTER THAN SQUIRREL GIRL STANDING VICTORIOUS ATOP A PILE OF HER FALLEN FOES? NOTHING. NOTHING IS BETTER.

FIGHT CHART!

YOU MAY HAVE NOTICED A RAD (AND PERHAPS SLIGHTLY INTIMIDATING) "FIGHT CHART" ON ALLENE'S PHONE RIGHT BEFORE SHE TOOK ON THE HELICARRIER. WELL, HERE'S A LOOK AT ALMOST THE FULL THING! RYAN NORTH WANTED THIS CHART TO BE REALLY SPECIAL SO HE PUT IT TOGETHER HIMSELF. FUN FACT: RYAN LOVES CHARTS — FLOW CHARTS, PIE CHARTS, NAUTICAL CHARTS, SEATING CHARTS, YOU NAME IT.

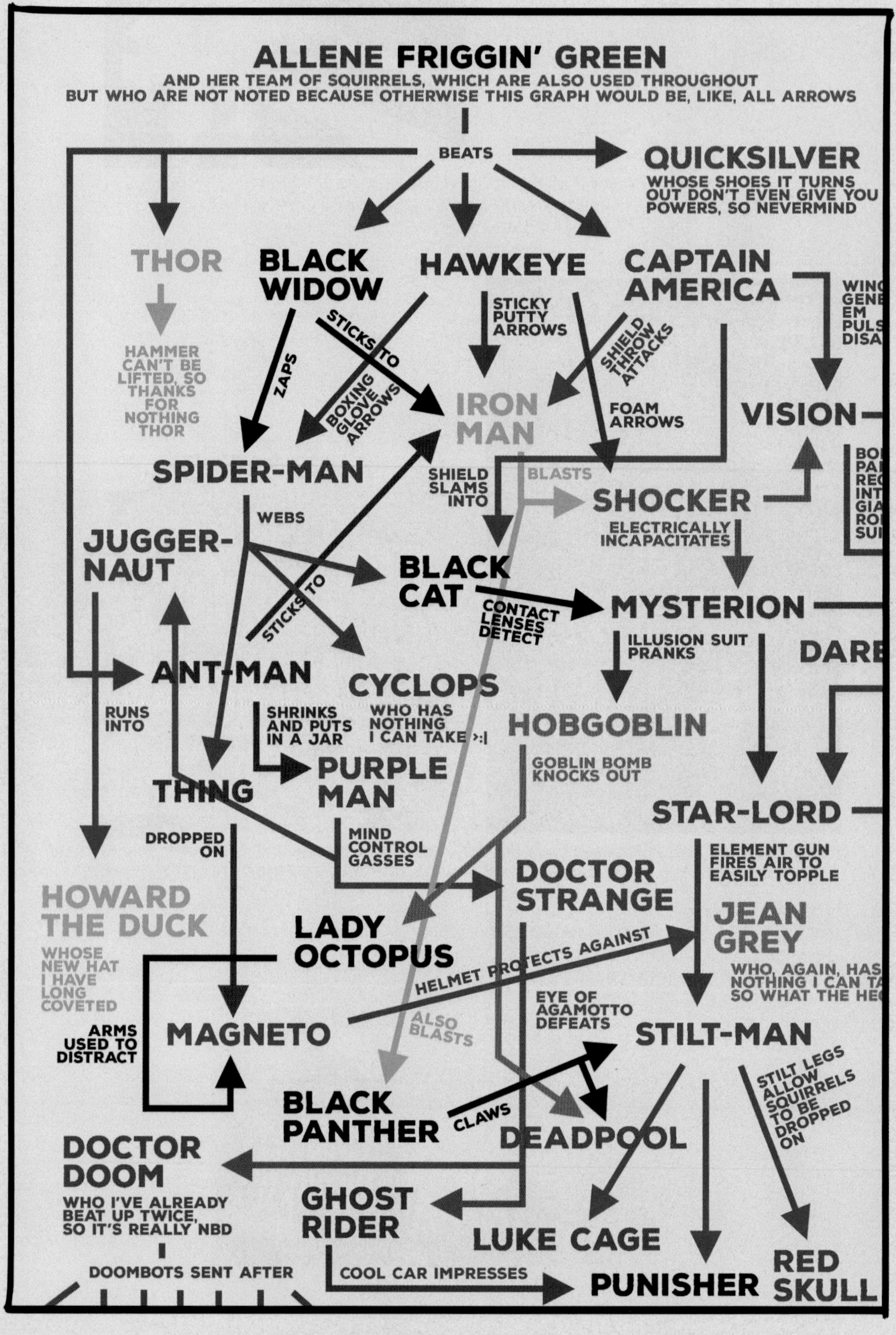

ALLENE FRIGGIN' GREEN
AND HER TEAM OF SQUIRRELS, WHICH ARE ALSO USED THROUGHOUT BUT WHO ARE NOT NOTED BECAUSE OTHERWISE THIS GRAPH WOULD BE, LIKE, ALL ARROWS
BEATS
QUICKSILVER
WHOSE SHOES IT TURNS OUT DON'T EVEN GIVE YOU POWERS, SO NEVERMIND
THOR
HAMMER CAN'T BE LIFTED, SO THANKS FOR NOTHING THOR
BLACK WIDOW
HAWKEYE
CAPTAIN AMERICA
ZAPS
STICKS TO
BOXING GLOVE ARROWS
STICKY PUTTY ARROWS
SHIELD THROW ATTACKS
FOAM ARROWS
IRON MAN
VISION
SPIDER-MAN
SHIELD SLAMS INTO
BLASTS
SHOCKER
ELECTRICALLY INCAPACITATES
WEBS
JUGGER-NAUT
BLACK CAT
STICKS TO
CONTACT LENSES DETECT
MYSTERION
ILLUSION SUIT PRANKS
ANT-MAN
CYCLOPS
WHO HAS NOTHING I CAN TAKE >:|
HOBGOBLIN
RUNS INTO
SHRINKS AND PUTS IN A JAR
PURPLE MAN
THING
GOBLIN BOMB KNOCKS OUT
STAR-LORD
DROPPED ON
MIND CONTROL GASSES
DOCTOR STRANGE
ELEMENT GUN FIRES AIR TO EASILY TOPPLE
HOWARD THE DUCK
WHOSE NEW HAT I HAVE LONG COVETED
LADY OCTOPUS
JEAN GREY
HELMET PROTECTS AGAINST
EYE OF AGAMOTTO DEFEATS
ARMS USED TO DISTRACT
MAGNETO
ALSO BLASTS
STILT-MAN
STILT LEGS ALLOW SQUIRRELS TO BE DROPPED ON
BLACK PANTHER
CLAWS
DEADPOOL
DOCTOR DOOM
WHO I'VE ALREADY BEAT UP TWICE, SO IT'S REALLY NBD
GHOST RIDER
LUKE CAGE
DOOMBOTS SENT AFTER
COOL CAR IMPRESSES
PUNISHER
RED SKULL

CHARACTER DESIGNS!

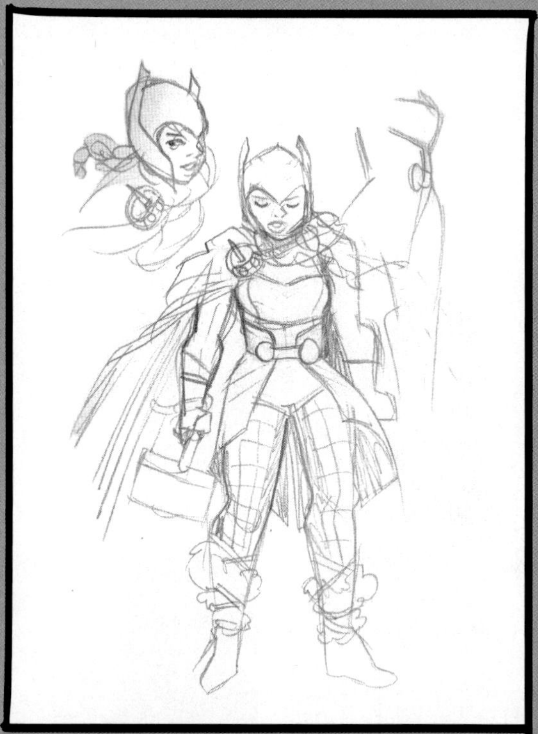

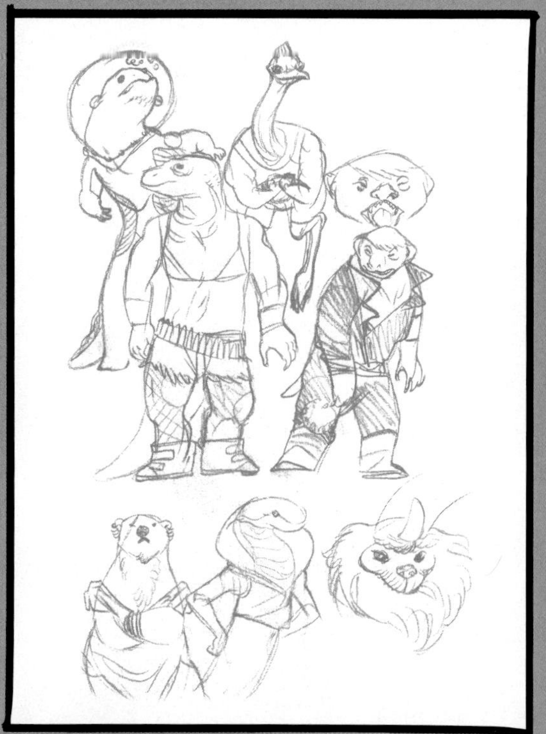

ERICA GOES A LITTLE NUTS (SORRY!) WHEN IT COMES TO CHARACTER DESIGNS. DOREEN WEARS AT LEAST ONE NEW OUTFIT IN EVERY ISSUE OF *UNBEATABLE SQUIRREL GIRL*. SO OF COURSE ERICA GAVE HER SOME NEW DUDS FOR HER FIRST OGN! HERE'S A LOOK AT ERICA'S DESIGN SKETCH FOR **SQUIRREL THOR**, DOREEN'S ALTER EGO WHEN SHE BRIEFLY WIELDS THOR'S HAMMER AND SAVES THE DAY!

AND THE WHOLE POINT OF THIS STORY WAS FOR SQUIRREL GIRL TO BEAT UP THE ENTIRE MARVEL UNIVERSE, SO RYAN THOUGHT IT WAS ONLY RIGHT THAT SHE FACE OFF AGAINST SOME **ANTHROPOMORPHIC GOONS** COURTESY OF MAD SCIENTIST BADDIE THE HIGH EVOLUTIONARY. IN RYAN'S OWN WORDS: "THEY'RE ALL APEX PREDATORS WITH HUMAN BODIES: LION-MEN, SHARK-MEN, KILLER-WHALE-MEN, ELECTRIC-EEL-MEN AND DINOSAUR-MEN. NAILED IT, ERICA. NAILED IT."

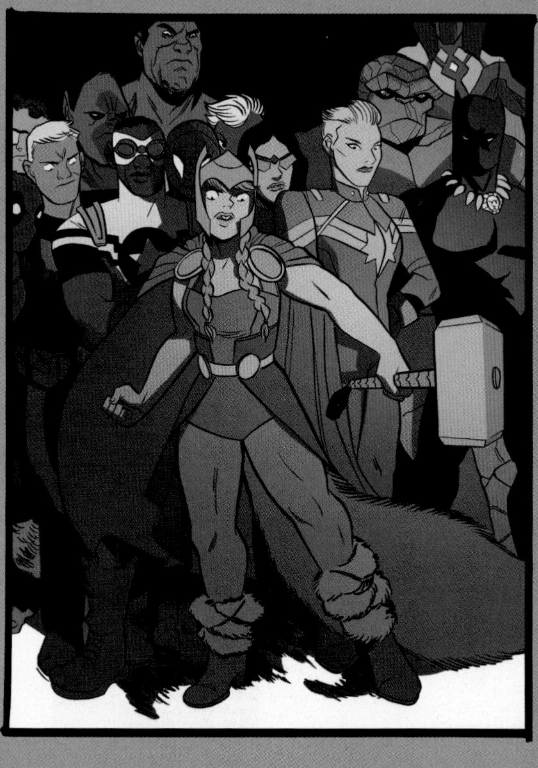

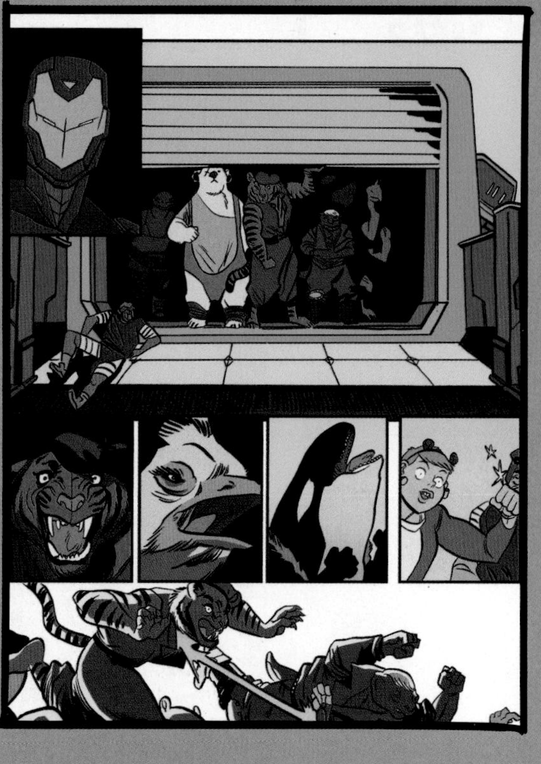

ART PROCESS!

ON A TYPICAL ISSUE OF SQUIRREL GIRL, ERICA HANDLES THE PENCILS AND INKS, AND THE STELLAR RICO RENZI (ARTIST OF THE AMAZING DEADPOOL CARDS IN THIS STORY!) HANDLES THE COLORS. FOR THIS OGN, THOUGH, ERICA WANTED TO TRY HER HAND AT ALL THREE DISCIPLINES. HERE'S A LOOK AT EACH STEP OF HER PROCESS!

PAGE 1

THUMBNAIL SKETCH

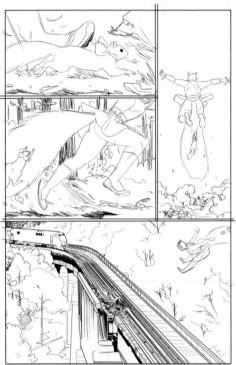

PENCILS

INKS

COLORS

PAGE 2

THUMBNAIL SKETCH

PENCILS

INKS

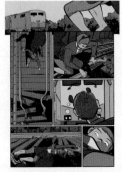

COLORS

DEADPOOL'S GUIDE TO SUPER VILLAINS CARDS!

HERE'S A SAMPLING OF SOME OF THE CARDS FROM PAST ISSUES OF *THE UNBEATABLE SQUIRREL GIRL* THAT HAVE HELPED DOREEN REMAIN UNBEATABLE! [CARD TEXT BY RYAN NORTH!]

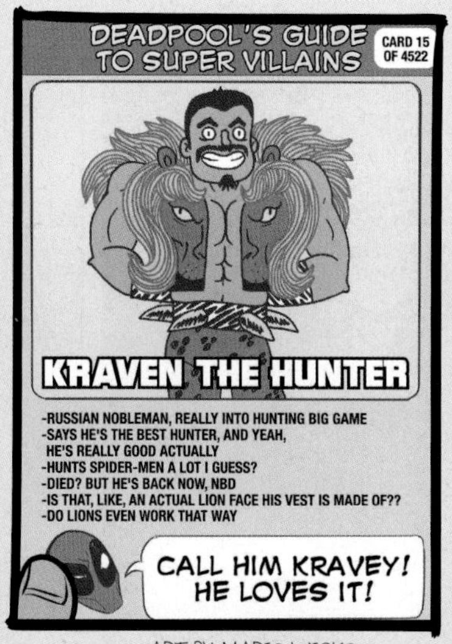
DEADPOOL'S GUIDE TO SUPER VILLAINS
CARD 15 OF 4522
KRAVEN THE HUNTER
-RUSSIAN NOBLEMAN, REALLY INTO HUNTING BIG GAME
-SAYS HE'S THE BEST HUNTER, AND YEAH, HE'S REALLY GOOD ACTUALLY
-HUNTS SPIDER-MEN A LOT I GUESS?
-DIED? BUT HE'S BACK NOW, NBD
-IS THAT, LIKE, AN ACTUAL LION FACE HIS VEST IS MADE OF??
-DO LIONS EVEN WORK THAT WAY
CALL HIM KRAVEY! HE LOVES IT!

ART BY MARIS WICKS

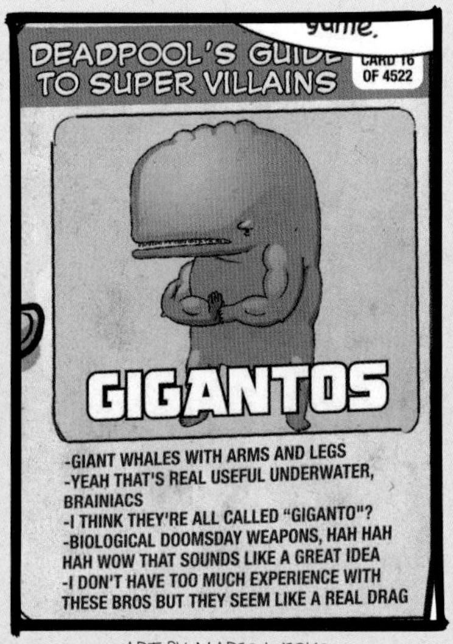
DEADPOOL'S GUIDE TO SUPER VILLAINS
OF 4522
GIGANTOS
-GIANT WHALES WITH ARMS AND LEGS
-YEAH THAT'S REAL USEFUL UNDERWATER, BRAINIACS
-I THINK THEY'RE ALL CALLED "GIGANTO"?
-BIOLOGICAL DOOMSDAY WEAPONS, HAH HAH HAH WOW THAT SOUNDS LIKE A GREAT IDEA
-I DON'T HAVE TOO MUCH EXPERIENCE WITH THESE BROS BUT THEY SEEM LIKE A REAL DRAG

ART BY MARIS WICKS

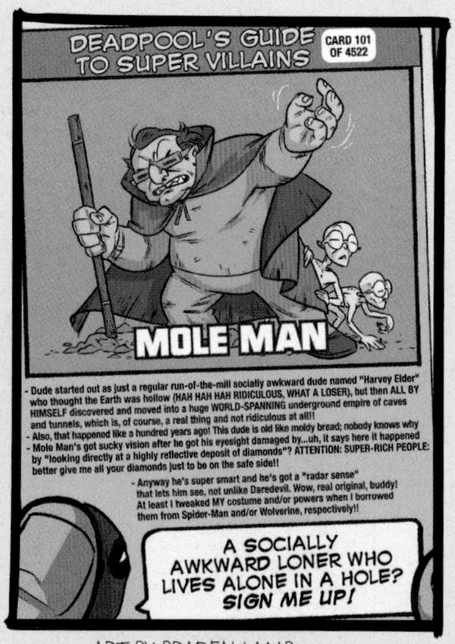
DEADPOOL'S GUIDE TO SUPER VILLAINS
CARD 101 OF 4522
MOLE MAN
- Dude started out as just a regular run-of-the-mill socially awkward dude named "Harvey Elder" who thought the Earth was hollow (HAH HAH HAH RIDICULOUS, WHAT A LOSER), but then ALL BY HIMSELF discovered and moved into a huge WORLD-SPANNING underground empire of caves and tunnels, which is, of course, a real thing and not ridiculous at all!!
- Also, that happened like a hundred years ago! This dude is old like moldy bread; nobody knows why
- Mole Man's got sucky vision after he got his eyesight damaged by...uh, it says here it happened by "looking directly at a highly reflective deposit of diamonds"? ATTENTION: SUPER-RICH PEOPLE: better give me all your diamonds just to be on the safe side!!
- Anyway he's super smart and he's got a "radar sense" that lets him see, not unlike Daredevil. Wow, real original, buddy! At least I tweaked MY costume and/or powers when I borrowed them from Spider-Man and/or Wolverine, respectively!!
A SOCIALLY AWKWARD LONER WHO LIVES ALONE IN A HOLE? SIGN ME UP!

ART BY BRADEN LAMB

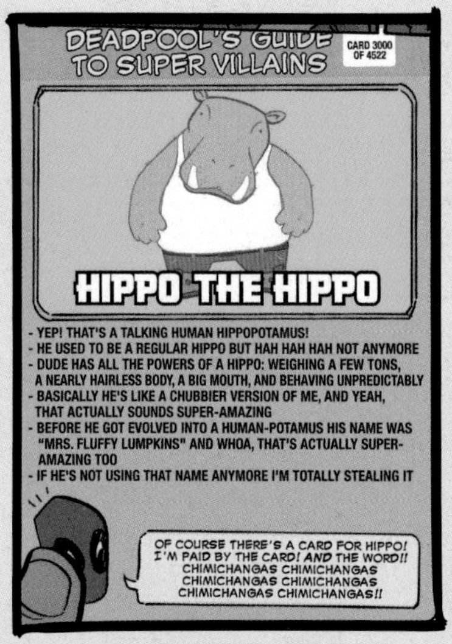
DEADPOOL'S GUIDE TO SUPER VILLAINS
CARD 3000 OF 4522
HIPPO THE HIPPO
- YEP! THAT'S A TALKING HUMAN HIPPOPOTAMUS!
- HE USED TO BE A REGULAR HIPPO BUT HAH HAH HAH NOT ANYMORE
- DUDE HAS ALL THE POWERS OF A HIPPO: WEIGHING A FEW TONS, A NEARLY HAIRLESS BODY, A BIG MOUTH, AND BEHAVING UNPREDICTABLY
- BASICALLY HE'S LIKE A CHUBBIER VERSION OF ME, AND YEAH, THAT ACTUALLY SOUNDS SUPER-AMAZING
- BEFORE HE GOT EVOLVED INTO A HUMAN-POTAMUS HIS NAME WAS "MRS. FLUFFY LUMPKINS" AND WHOA, THAT'S ACTUALLY SUPER-AMAZING TOO
- IF HE'S NOT USING THAT NAME ANYMORE I'M TOTALLY STEALING IT
OF COURSE THERE'S A CARD FOR HIPPO! I'M PAID BY THE CARD! AND THE WORD!! CHIMICHANGAS CHIMICHANGAS CHIMICHANGAS CHIMICHANGAS CHIMICHANGAS CHIMICHANGAS!!

ART BY ELOISE NARRINGTON

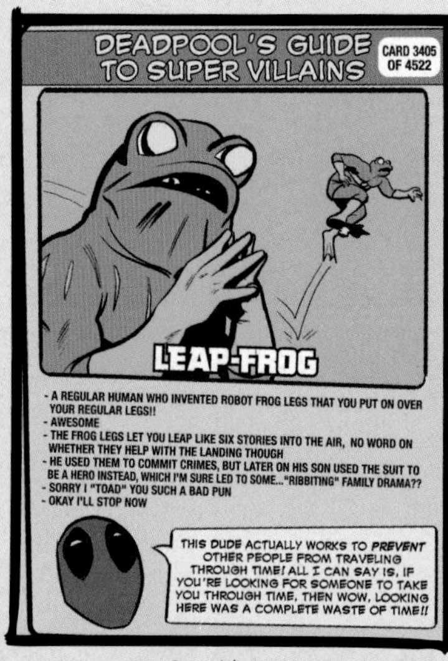
DEADPOOL'S GUIDE TO SUPER VILLAINS
CARD 3405 OF 4522
LEAP-FROG
- A REGULAR HUMAN WHO INVENTED ROBOT FROG LEGS THAT YOU PUT ON OVER YOUR REGULAR LEGS!!
- AWESOME
- THE FROG LEGS LET YOU LEAP LIKE SIX STORIES INTO THE AIR, NO WORD ON WHETHER THEY HELP WITH THE LANDING THOUGH
- HE USED THEM TO COMMIT CRIMES, BUT LATER ON HIS SON USED THE SUIT TO BE A HERO INSTEAD, WHICH I'M SURE LED TO SOME..."RIBBITING" FAMILY DRAMA??
- SORRY I "TOAD" YOU SUCH A BAD PUN
- OKAY I'LL STOP NOW
THIS DUDE ACTUALLY WORKS TO PREVENT OTHER PEOPLE FROM TRAVELING THROUGH TIME! ALL I CAN SAY IS, IF YOU'RE LOOKING FOR SOMEONE TO TAKE YOU THROUGH TIME, THEN WOW, LOOKING HERE WAS A COMPLETE WASTE OF TIME!!

ART BY CHIP ZDARSKY

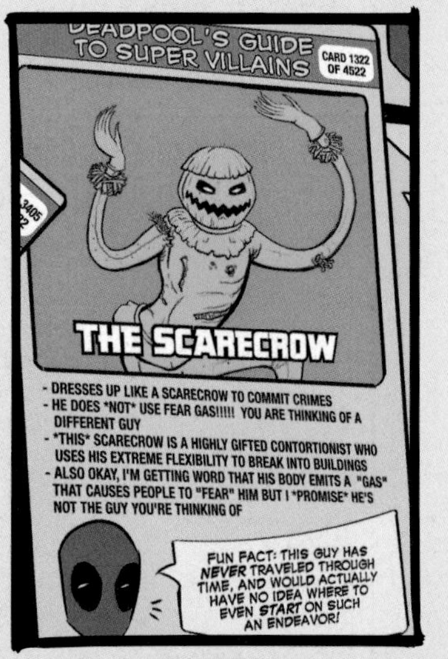
DEADPOOL'S GUIDE TO SUPER VILLAINS
CARD 1322 OF 4522
THE SCARECROW
- DRESSES UP LIKE A SCARECROW TO COMMIT CRIMES
- HE DOES *NOT* USE FEAR GAS!!!!! YOU ARE THINKING OF A DIFFERENT GUY
- *THIS* SCARECROW IS A HIGHLY GIFTED CONTORTIONIST WHO USES HIS EXTREME FLEXIBILITY TO BREAK INTO BUILDINGS
- ALSO OKAY, I'M GETTING WORD THAT HIS BODY EMITS A "GAS" THAT CAUSES PEOPLE TO "FEAR" HIM BUT I *PROMISE* HE'S NOT THE GUY YOU'RE THINKING OF
FUN FACT: THIS GUY HAS NEVER TRAVELED THROUGH TIME, AND WOULD ACTUALLY HAVE NO IDEA WHERE TO EVEN START ON SUCH AN ENDEAVOR!

ART BY DAVID ROBBINS

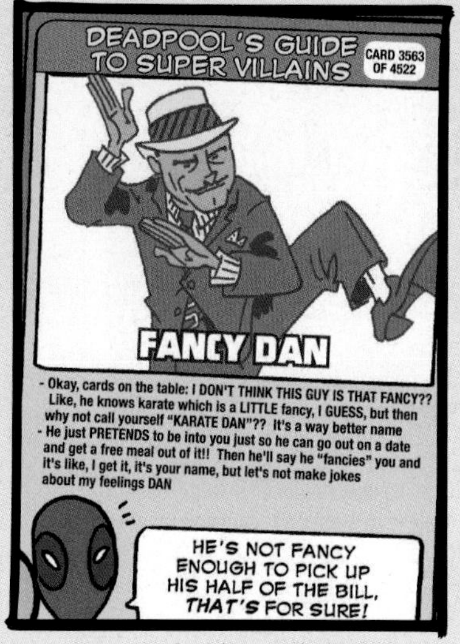
DEADPOOL'S GUIDE TO SUPER VILLAINS
CARD 3563 OF 4522
FANCY DAN
- Okay, cards on the table: I DON'T THINK THIS GUY IS THAT FANCY?? Like, he knows karate which is a LITTLE fancy, I GUESS, but then why not call yourself "KARATE DAN"?? It's a way better name
- He just PRETENDS to be into you just so he can go out on a date and get a free meal out of it!! Then he'll say he "fancies" you and it's like, I get it, it's your name, but let's not make jokes about my feelings DAN
HE'S NOT FANCY ENOUGH TO PICK UP HIS HALF OF THE BILL, THAT'S FOR SURE!

ART BY CHRIS SCHWEIZER

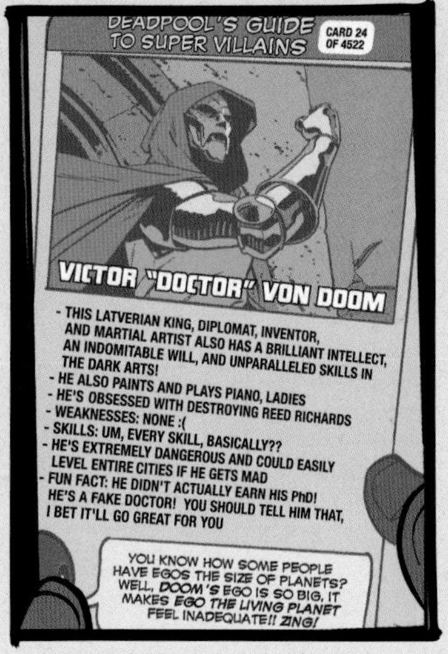
DEADPOOL'S GUIDE TO SUPER VILLAINS
CARD 24 OF 4522
VICTOR "DOCTOR" VON DOOM
- THIS LATVERIAN KING, DIPLOMAT, INVENTOR, AND MARTIAL ARTIST ALSO HAS A BRILLIANT INTELLECT, AN INDOMITABLE WILL, AND UNPARALLELED SKILLS IN THE DARK ARTS!
- HE ALSO PAINTS AND PLAYS PIANO, LADIES
- HE'S OBSESSED WITH DESTROYING REED RICHARDS
- WEAKNESSES: NONE :(
- SKILLS: UM, EVERY SKILL, BASICALLY??
- HE'S EXTREMELY DANGEROUS AND COULD EASILY LEVEL ENTIRE CITIES IF HE GETS MAD
- FUN FACT: HE DIDN'T ACTUALLY EARN HIS PhD! HE'S A FAKE DOCTOR! YOU SHOULD TELL HIM THAT, I BET IT'LL GO GREAT FOR YOU
YOU KNOW HOW SOME PEOPLE HAVE EGOS THE SIZE OF PLANETS? WELL, DOOM'S EGO IS SO BIG, IT MAKES EGO THE LIVING PLANET FEEL INADEQUATE!! ZING!

ART BY EVAN "DOC" SHANER

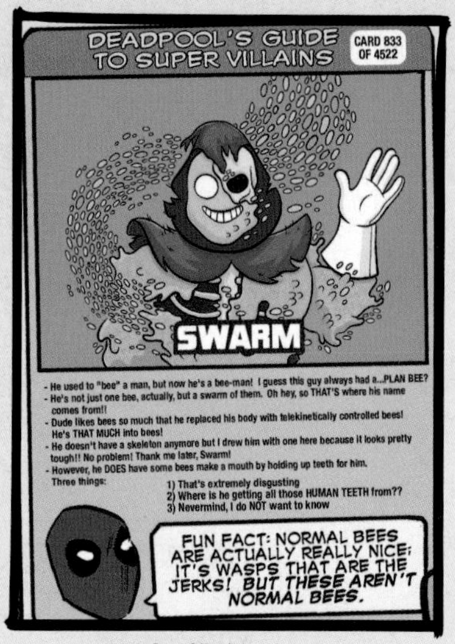
DEADPOOL'S GUIDE TO SUPER VILLAINS
CARD 833 OF 4522
SWARM
- He used to "bee" a man, but now he's a bee-man! I guess this guy always had a...PLAN BEE?
- He's not just one bee, actually, but a swarm of them. Oh hey, so THAT'S where his name comes from!!
- Dude likes bees so much that he replaced his body with telekinetically controlled bees! He's THAT MUCH into bees!
- He doesn't have a skeleton anymore but I drew him with one here because it looks pretty tough!! No problem! Thank me later, Swarm!
- However, he DOES have some bees make a mouth by holding up teeth for him.
Three things:
1) That's extremely disgusting
2) Where is he getting all those HUMAN TEETH from??
3) Nevermind, I do NOT want to know
FUN FACT: NORMAL BEES ARE ACTUALLY REALLY NICE; IT'S WASPS THAT ARE THE JERKS! BUT THESE AREN'T NORMAL BEES.

ART BY JOEY ELLIS

READ MORE ABOUT SQUIRREL GIRL IN THESE OTHER GREAT BOOKS!

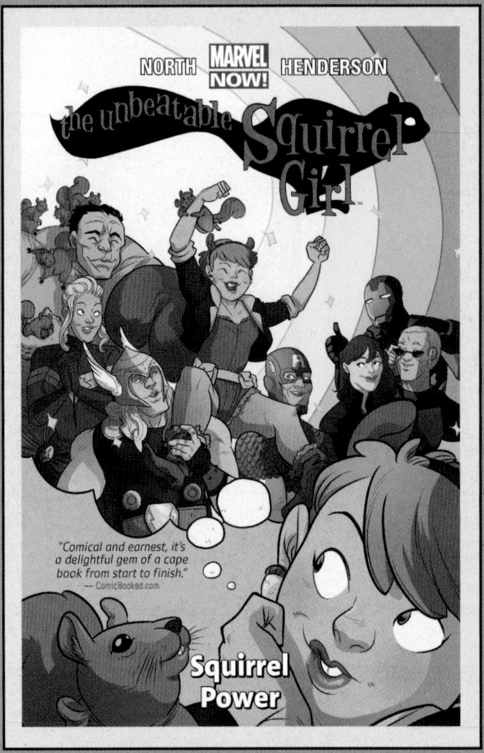
NORTH MARVEL NOW! HENDERSON
the unbeatable Squirrel Girl
"Comical and earnest, it's a delightful gem of a cape book from start to finish." — ComicBooked.com
Squirrel Power

THE UNBEATABLE SQUIRREL GIRL VOL. 1: SQUIRREL POWER

ISBN 978-0-7851-9702-7

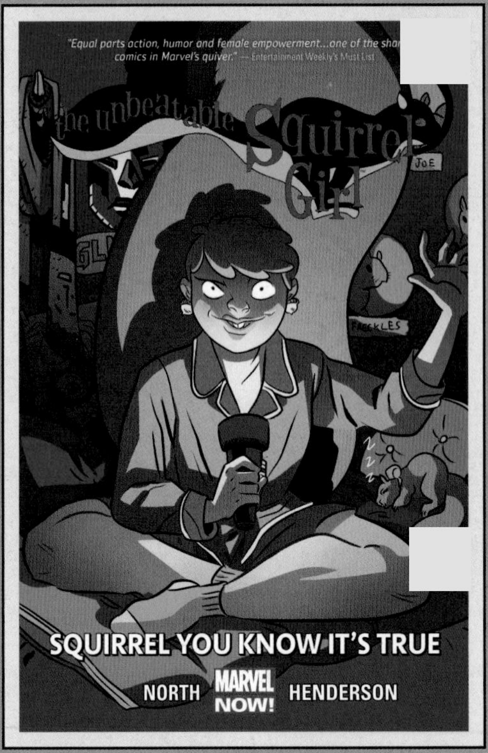
the unbeatable Squirrel Girl
SQUIRREL YOU KNOW IT'S TRUE
NORTH MARVEL NOW! HENDERSON

THE UNBEATABLE SQUIRREL GIRL VOL. 2: SQUIRREL YOU KNOW IT'S TRUE

ISBN 978-0-7851-9845-1

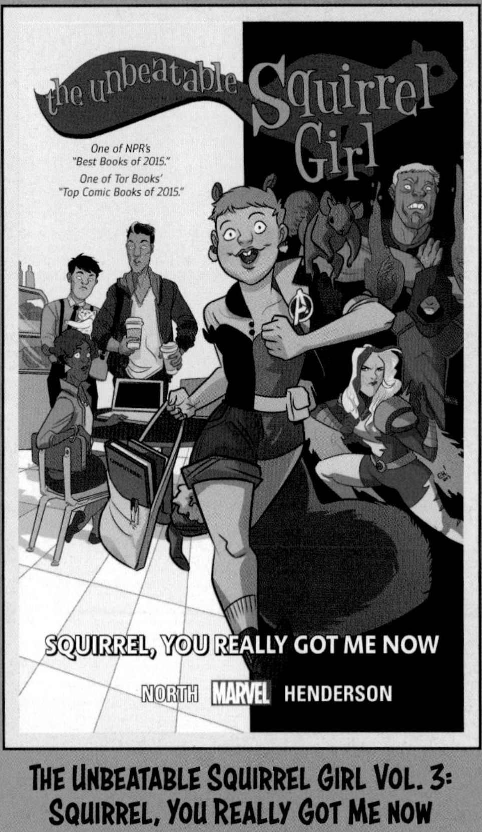
the unbeatable Squirrel Girl
One of NPR's "Best Books of 2015." One of Tor Books' "Top Comic Books of 2015."
SQUIRREL, YOU REALLY GOT ME NOW
NORTH MARVEL HENDERSON

THE UNBEATABLE SQUIRREL GIRL VOL. 3: SQUIRREL, YOU REALLY GOT ME NOW

ISBN 978-0-7851-9626-6

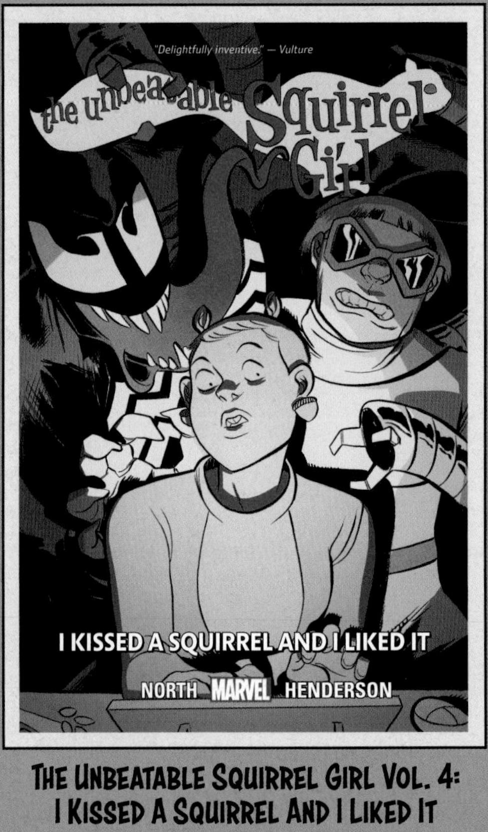
"Delightfully inventive." — Vulture
the unbeatable Squirrel Girl
I KISSED A SQUIRREL AND I LIKED IT
NORTH MARVEL HENDERSON

THE UNBEATABLE SQUIRREL GIRL VOL. 4: I KISSED A SQUIRREL AND I LIKED IT

ISBN 978-0-7851-9627-3

(ON SALE NOVEMBER 2016)

CHECK OUT THESE OTHER MARVEL COLLECTIONS!

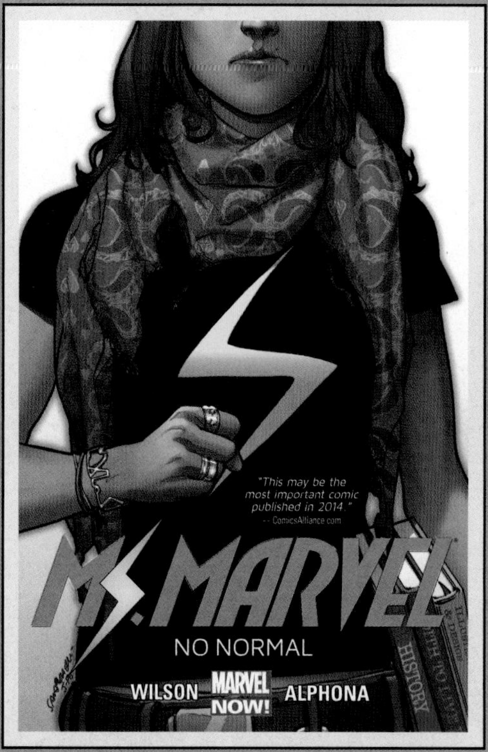
"This may be the most important comic published in 2014."
-- ComicsAlliance.com
MS. MARVEL
NO NORMAL
WILSON
MARVEL NOW!
ALPHONA

Ms. Marvel Vol. 1: No Normal

ISBN 978-0-7851-9021-9

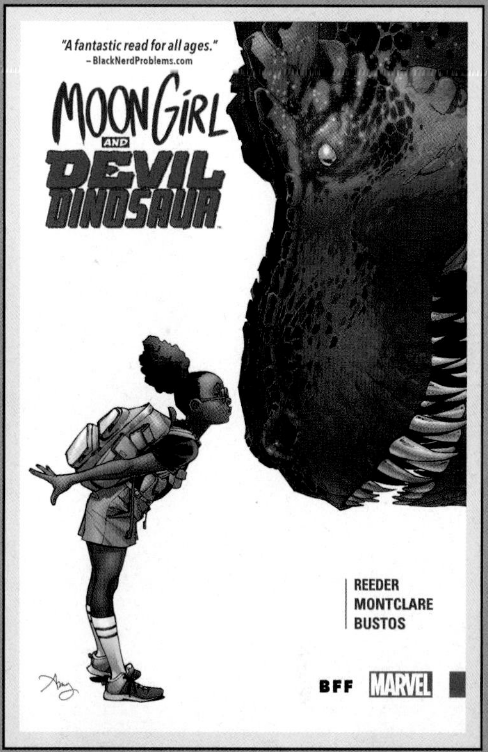
"A fantastic read for all ages."
– BlackNerdProblems.com
MOON GIRL AND DEVIL DINOSAUR
REEDER
MONTCLARE
BUSTOS
BFF
MARVEL

Moon Girl & Devil Dinosaur Vol. 1: BFF

ISBN 978-1-302-90005-2

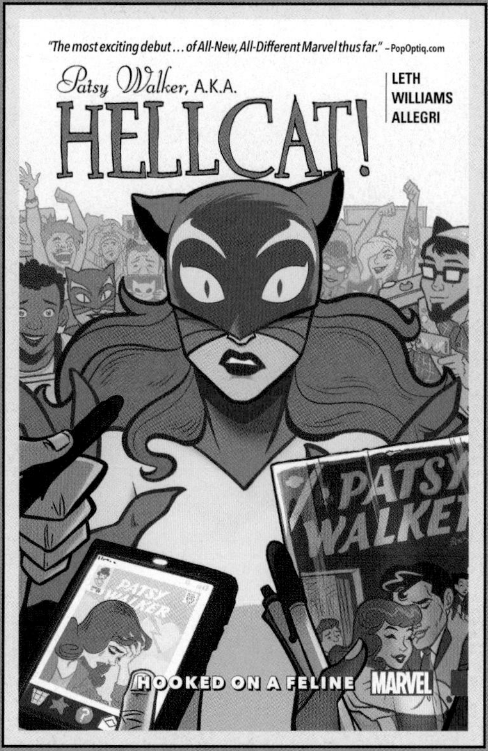
"The most exciting debut ... of All-New, All-Different Marvel thus far." –PopOptiq.com
Patsy Walker, A.K.A.
HELLCAT!
LETH
WILLIAMS
ALLEGRI
PATSY WALKER
HOOKED ON A FELINE
MARVEL

Patsy Walker, A.K.A. Hellcat! Vol. 1: Hooked on a Feline

ISBN 978-1-302-90035-9

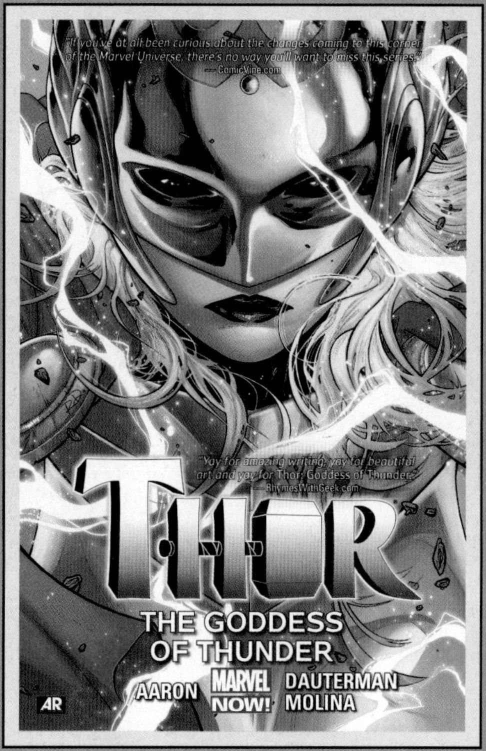
"If you've at all been curious about the changes coming to this corner of the Marvel Universe, there's no way you'll want to miss this series."
— ComicVine.com
"Yay for amazing writing, yay for beautiful art and yay for Thor, Goddess of Thunder."
— RhymesWithGeek.com
THOR
THE GODDESS OF THUNDER
AARON
MARVEL NOW!
DAUTERMAN
MOLINA
AR

Thor Vol. 1: The Goddess of Thunder

ISBN 978-0-7851-9239-8

Meanwhile, in the Negative Zone....

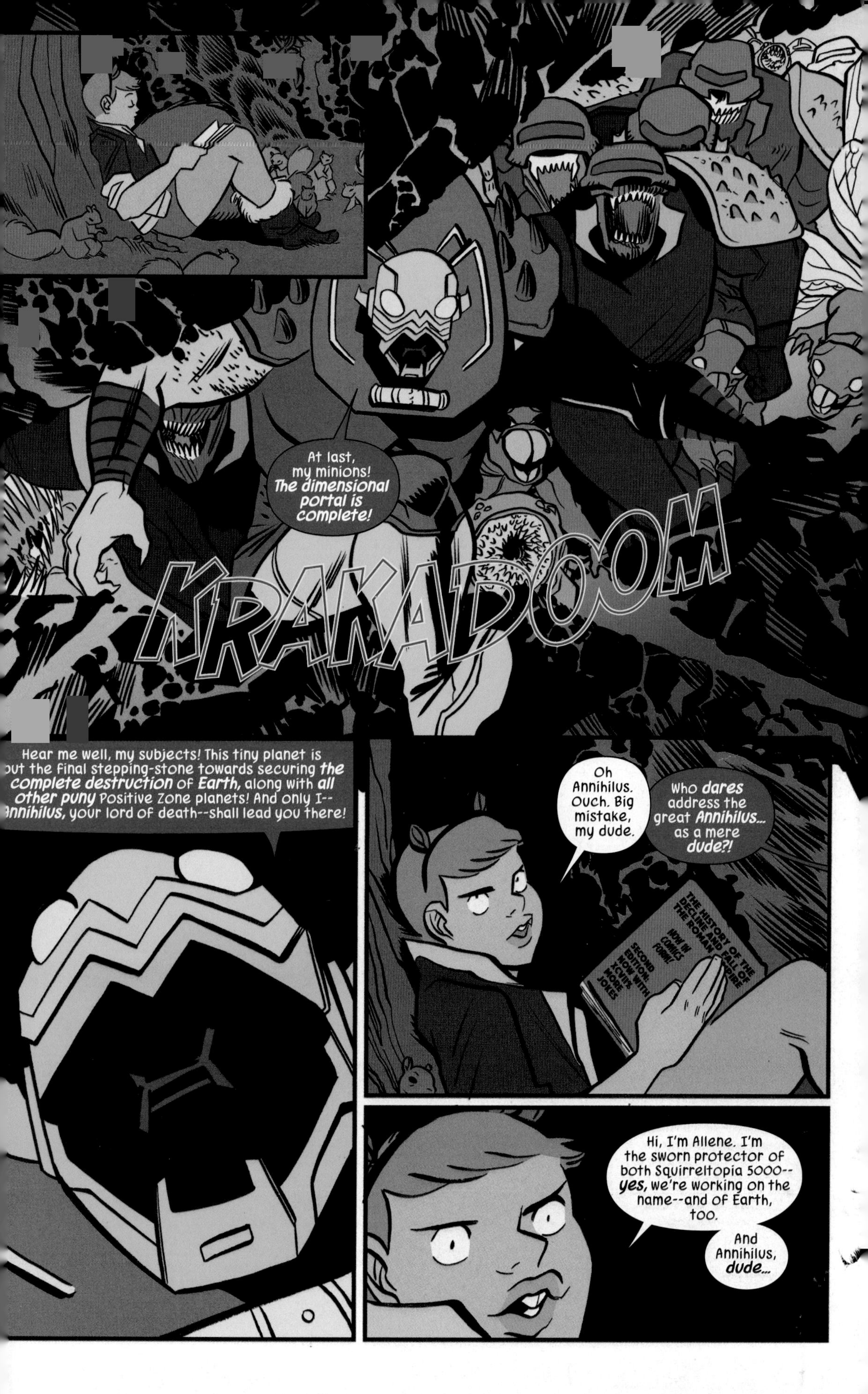
At last, my minions! The dimensional portal is complete!
KRAKADOOM
Hear me well, my subjects! This tiny planet is ut the final stepping-stone towards securing the complete destruction of Earth, along with all other puny Positive Zone planets! And only I-- nnihilus, your lord of death--shall lead you there!
Oh Annihilus. Ouch. Big mistake, my dude.
Who dares address the great Annihilus... as a mere dude?!
NOW IN COMICS FORM!
SECOND EDITION: NOW WITH XCVII% MORE JOKES
Hi, I'm Allene. I'm the sworn protector of both Squirreltopia 5000-- yes, we're working on the name--and of Earth, too.
And Annihilus, dude...

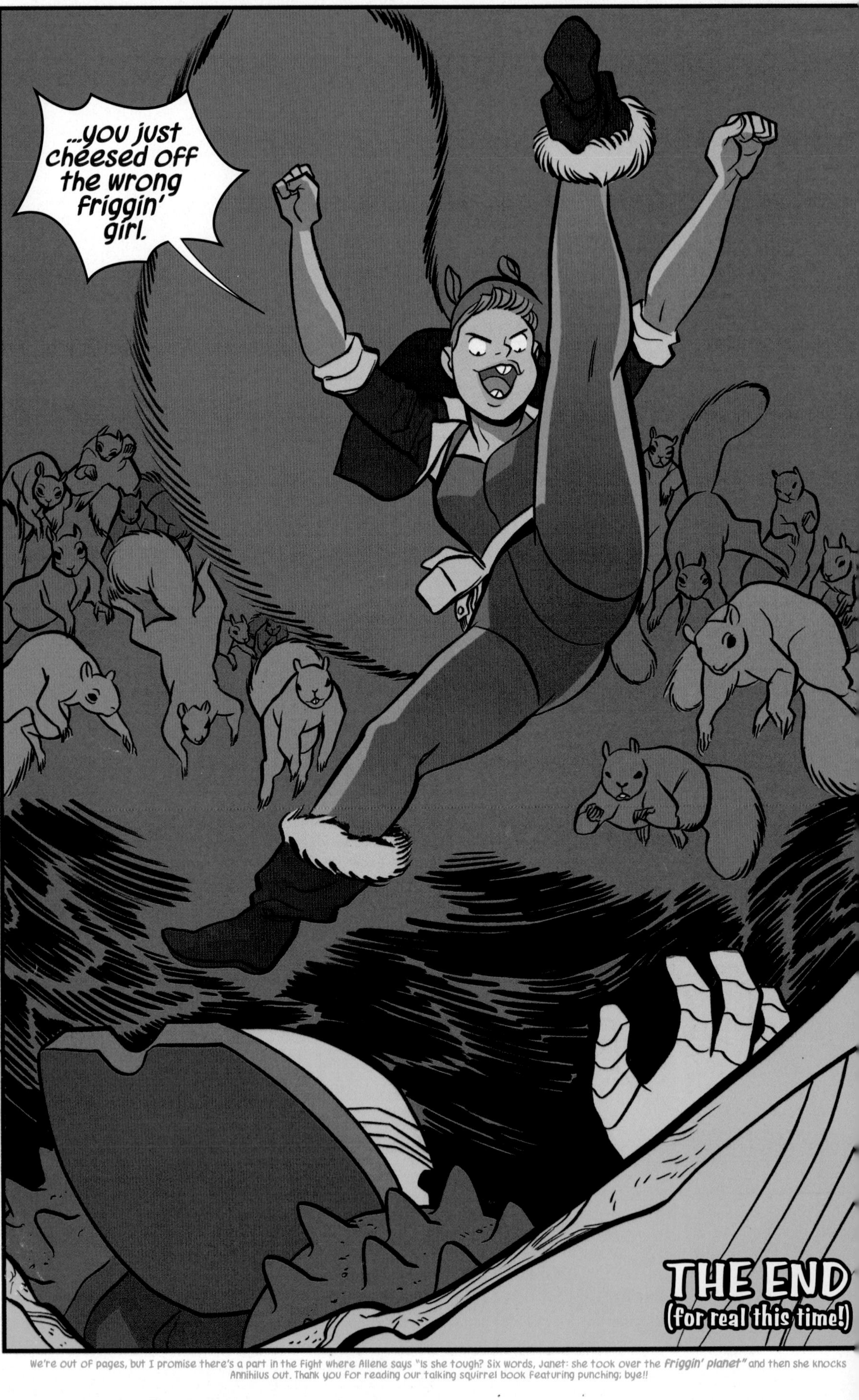
...you just cheesed off the wrong friggin' girl.
THE END
(for real this time!)

We're out of pages, but I promise there's a part in the fight where Allene says "Is she tough? Six words, Janet: she took over the ***friggin' planet"*** and then she knocks Annihilus out. Thank you for reading our talking squirrel book featuring punching; bye!!

TEAM SQUIRREL GIRL!

RYAN NORTH lives in Toronto, where he writes *Dinosaur Comics* (you can read those for free at qwantz.com!), wrote the Eisner and Harvey Award-winning *Adventure Time* comics (those ones cost money!), and now writes the Eisner-nominated *The Unbeatable Squirrel Girl* for Marvel (again: they want your $$$). You've just read his latest book, but his book BEFORE this one, *Romeo and/or Juliet*, allows YOU to play through and make the decisions for Shakespeare's heroes, which is absolutely a great idea and won't at all cause them to get into trouble three choices in. He once messed up walking his dog so badly that it made the news. ryannorth.ca.

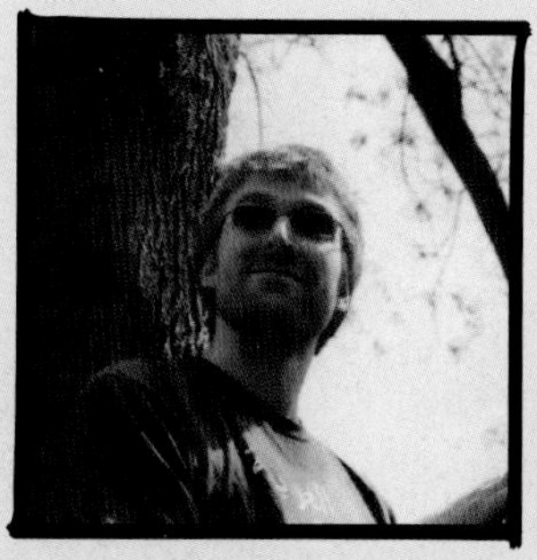

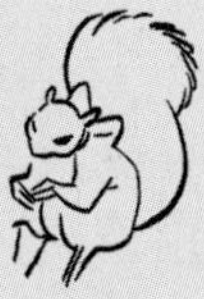

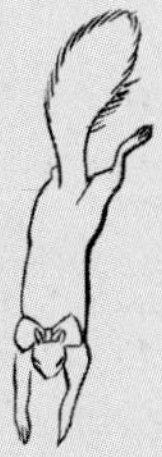

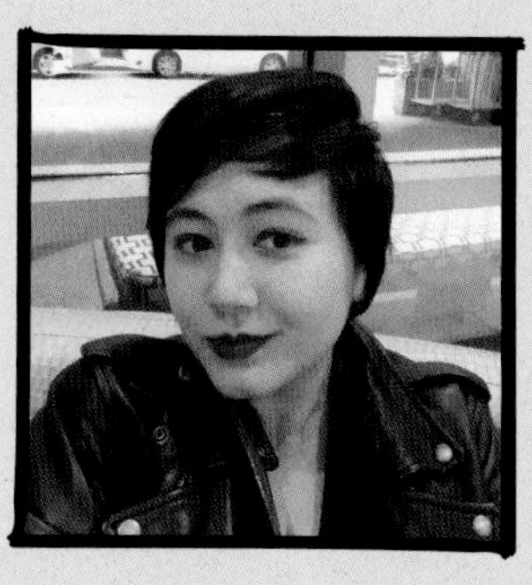

ERICA HENDERSON studied film at the Rhode Island School of Design, but decided that was boring and chose to work on video games and comic books instead. (Although lately it's all comic books!) Erica has done work for Archie, Boom, DC, IDW, Monkeybrain, Tesladyne, Thrillbent and — most importantly — Marvel, on *The Unbeatable Squirrel Girl*! These days Erica can be found at a local coffee shop sketching out comic pages, or at least drinking too much coffee.

RICO RENZI is a color artist and designer from Washington, D.C. His work has appeared in WIRED and Fast Company magazines, and various publications from DC, Marvel, Fantagraphics, Image, Dark Horse, Scholastic, Boom Studios, Oni Press and IDW. He currently colors *Spider-Gwen*, *The Unbeatable Squirrel Girl*, and a bunch of covers every month in Charlotte, North Carolina, where he resides with his wife and daughter.

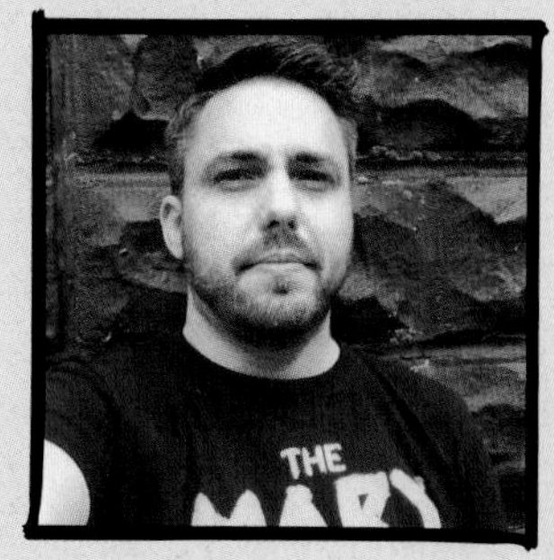

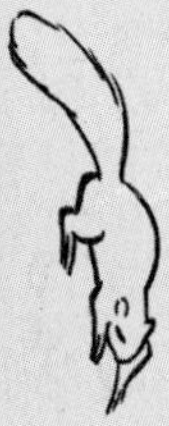

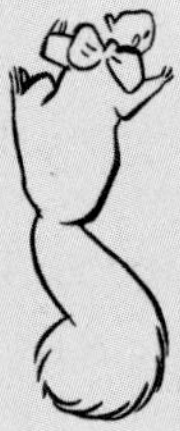

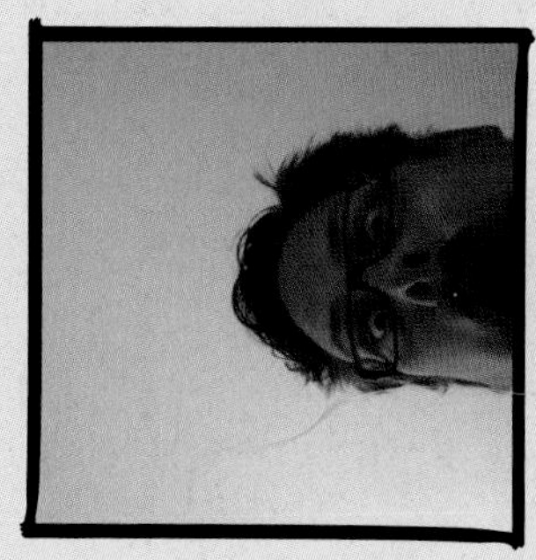

Cartoonist and illustrator **TOM FOWLER** has worked for just about everyone, including Disney, WOTC, Hasbro, MAD, Simon & Schuster, Valiant, DC Comics and Marvel. He is best known for his work on the feature strip "Monroe" for *MAD Magazine*, his critically acclaimed series *Mysterius the Unfathomable* with writer Jeff Parker, *Quantum & Woody* and most recently writing (and occasionally drawing) the *Rick and Morty* comic series. For Marvel, he has drawn the Spider-Man spinoff series *Venom* and the original graphic novel *Hulk: Season One*.

Letterer **TRAVIS LANHAM** has worked on books such as *Wonder Woman*, *Infinity Man and the Forever People*, *All-Star-Superman* and *Gotham City Sirens* for DC Comics; *Spider-Woman*, *Nightcrawler*, *Scarlet Spiders*, *Ant-Man*, *Silk* and *Spider-Verse* for Marvel; *Northlanders* for Vertigo; and Clive Barker's *Hellraiser* for BOOM! Studios. A Colorado transplant and graduate of the Savannah College of Art and Design, Lanham is also creator of the webcomic *Carl & Zip's Adventures Through Time*.

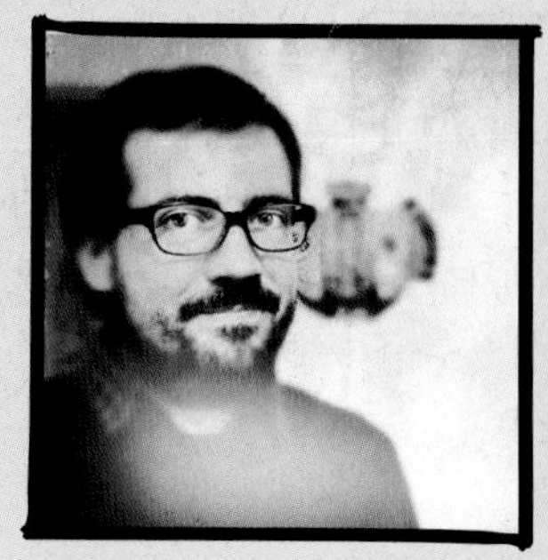

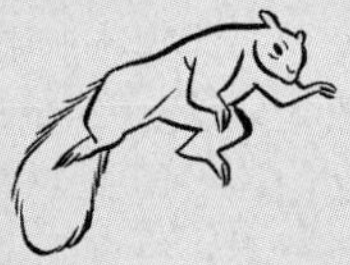

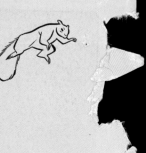

FREE DIGITAL COPY!

TO REDEEM YOUR CODE FOR A FREE DIGITAL COPY:

1. GO TO MARVEL.COM/REDEEM. OFFER EXPIRES ON 10/5/18.
2. FOLLOW THE ON-SCREEN INSTRUCTIONS TO REDEEM YOUR DIGITAL COPY.
3. LAUNCH THE MARVEL COMICS APP TO READ YOUR COMIC NOW.
4. YOUR DIGITAL COPY WILL BE FOUND UNDER THE "MY COMICS" TAB.
5. READ AND ENJOY.

YOUR FREE DIGITAL COPY WILL BE AVAILABLE ON:
MARVEL COMICS APP FOR APPLE IOS® DEVICES
MARVEL COMICS APP FOR ANDROID™ DEVICES

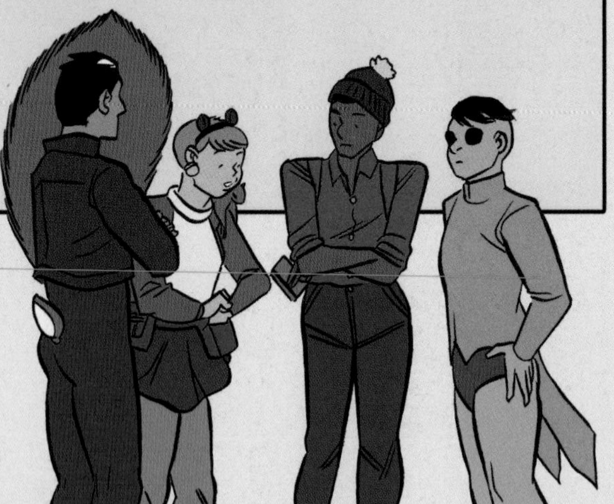

MARVEL
FREE DIGITAL COPY OFFER
PEEL HERE TO REVEAL CODE

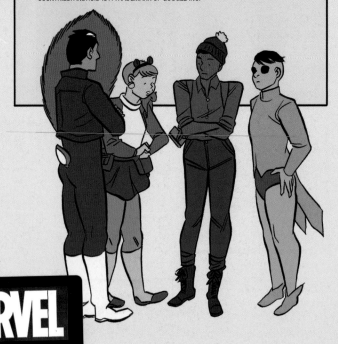